NEW PERSPECTIVES

Microsoft® Office 365™ & Word 2016

NEW PERSPECTIVES

Microsoft® Office 365™ & Word 2016

INTRODUCTORY

Ann Shaffer
Katherine T. Pinard

CENGAGE
Learning·

Australia • Brazil • Mexico • Singapore • United Kingdom • United States

New Perspectives Microsoft® Office 365™ & Word 2016, Introductory
Ann Shaffer, Katherine T. Pinard

SVP, GM Skills & Global Product Management: Dawn Gerrain

Product Director: Kathleen McMahon

Senior Product Team Manager: Lauren Murphy

Product Team Manager: Andrea Topping

Associate Product Managers: William Guiliani, Melissa Stehler

Senior Director, Development: Marah Bellegarde

Product Development Manager: Leigh Hefferon

Senior Content Developer: Kathy Finnegan

Developmental Editor: Mary Pat Shaffer

Product Assistant: Erica Chapman

Marketing Director: Michele McTighe

Marketing Manager: Stephanie Albracht

Senior Production Director: Wendy Troeger

Production Director: Patty Stephan

Senior Content Project Manager: Jennifer Goguen McGrail

Designer: Diana Graham

Composition: GEX Publishing Services

Cover image(s): BEPictured/Shutterstock.com

For product information and technology assistance, contact us at
Cengage Learning Customer & Sales Support, 1-800-354-9706

For permission to use material from this text or product, submit all requests online at **www.cengage.com/permissions**.
Further permissions questions can be e-mailed to
permissionrequest@cengage.com

Mac users: If you're working through this product using a Mac, some of the steps may vary. Additional information for Mac users is included with the Data Files for this product.

Some of the product names and company names used in this book have been used for identification purposes only and may be trademarks or registered trademarks of their respective manufacturers and sellers.

Windows® is a registered trademark of Microsoft Corporation. © 2012 Microsoft. Microsoft and the Office logo are either registered trademarks or trademarks of Microsoft Corporation in the United States and/or other countries. Cengage Learning is an independent entity from Microsoft Corporation and not affiliated with Microsoft in any manner.

Disclaimer: Any fictional data related to persons or companies or URLs used throughout this text is intended for instructional purposes only. At the time this text was published, any such data was fictional and not belonging to any real persons or companies.

Disclaimer: The material in this text was written using Microsoft Office 365 ProPlus and Microsoft Word 2016 running on Microsoft Windows 10 Professional and was Quality Assurance tested before the publication date. As Microsoft continually updates the Microsoft Office suite and the Windows 10 operating system, your software experience may vary slightly from what is presented in the printed text.

Library of Congress Control Number: 2015960053
ISBN: 978-1-305-88095-5

Cengage Learning
20 Channel Center Street
Boston, MA 02210
USA

Cengage Learning is a leading provider of customized learning solutions with employees residing in nearly 40 different countries and sales in more than 125 countries around the world. Find your local representative at **www.cengage.com.**

Cengage Learning products are represented in Canada by Nelson Education, Ltd.

To learn more about Cengage Learning, visit **www.cengage.com**

Purchase any of our products at your local college store or at our preferred online store **www.cengagebrain.com**

Printed in the United States of America
Print Number: 02   Print Year: 2017

BRIEF CONTENTS

TABLE OF CONTENTS

WORD MODULES

Productivity Apps for School and Work

Corinne Hoisington

Lochlan keeps track of his class notes, football plays, and internship meetings with OneNote.

Zoe is using the annotation features of Microsoft Edge to take and save web notes for her research paper.

Nori is creating a Sway site to highlight this year's activities for the Student Government Association.

Hunter is adding interactive videos and screen recordings to his PowerPoint resume.

© Rawpixel/Shutterstock.com

Being computer literate no longer means mastery of only Word, Excel, PowerPoint, Outlook, and Access. To become technology power users, Hunter, Nori, Zoe, and Lochlan are exploring Microsoft OneNote, Sway, Mix, and Edge in Office 2016 and Windows 10.

In this Module

Learn to use productivity apps!
Links to companion **Sways**, featuring **videos** with hands-on instructions, are located on www.cengagebrain.com.

Introduction to OneNote 2016

notebook | section tab | To Do tag | screen clipping | note | template | Microsoft OneNote Mobile app | sync | drawing canvas | inked handwriting | Ink to Text

As you glance around any classroom, you invariably see paper notebooks and notepads on each desk. Because deciphering and sharing handwritten notes can be a challenge, Microsoft OneNote 2016 replaces physical notebooks, binders, and paper notes with a searchable, digital notebook. OneNote captures your ideas and schoolwork on any device so you can stay organized, share notes, and work with others on projects. Whether you are a student taking class notes as shown in Figure 1 or an employee taking notes in company meetings, OneNote is the one place to keep notes for all of your projects.

Figure 1: OneNote 2016 notebook

Each **notebook** is divided into sections, also called **section tabs**, by subject or topic.

Use **To Do tags**, icons that help you keep track of your assignments and other tasks.

Type on a page to add a **note**, a small window that contains text or other types of information.

Personalize a page with a **template**, or stationery.

Write or draw directly on the page using drawing tools.

Pages can include pictures such as **screen clippings**, images from any part of a computer screen.

Attach files and enter equations so you have everything you need in one place.

Creating a OneNote Notebook

OneNote is divided into sections similar to those in a spiral-bound notebook. Each OneNote notebook contains sections, pages, and other notebooks. You can use OneNote for school, business, and personal projects. Store information for each type of project in different notebooks to keep your tasks separate, or use any other organization that suits you. OneNote is flexible enough to adapt to the way you want to work.

When you create a notebook, it contains a blank page with a plain white background by default, though you can use templates, or stationery, to apply designs in categories such as Academic, Business, Decorative, and Planners. Start typing or use the buttons on the Insert tab to insert notes, which are small resizable windows that can contain text, equations, tables, on-screen writing, images, audio and video recordings, to-do lists, file attachments, and file printouts. Add as many notes as you need to each page.

Syncing a Notebook to the Cloud

OneNote saves your notes every time you make a change in a notebook. To make sure you can access your notebooks with a laptop, tablet, or smartphone wherever you are, OneNote uses cloud-based storage, such as OneDrive or SharePoint. **Microsoft OneNote Mobile app**, a lightweight version of OneNote 2016 shown in Figure 2, is available for free in the Windows Store, Google Play for Android devices, and the AppStore for iOS devices.

If you have a Microsoft account, OneNote saves your notes on OneDrive automatically for all your mobile devices and computers, which is called **syncing**. For example, you can use OneNote to take notes on your laptop during class, and then open OneNote on your phone to study later. To use a notebook stored on your computer with your OneNote Mobile app, move the notebook to OneDrive. You can quickly share notebook content with other people using OneDrive.

Figure 2: Microsoft OneNote Mobile app

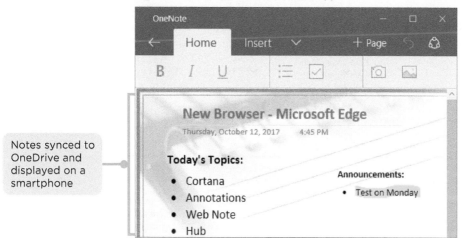

Notes synced to OneDrive and displayed on a smartphone

Taking Notes

Use OneNote pages to organize your notes by class and topic or lecture. Beyond simple typed notes, OneNote stores drawings, converts handwriting to searchable text and mathematical sketches to equations, and records audio and video.

OneNote includes drawing tools that let you sketch freehand drawings such as biological cell diagrams and financial supply-and-demand charts. As shown in Figure 3, the Draw tab on the ribbon provides these drawing tools along with shapes so you can insert diagrams and other illustrations to represent your ideas. When you draw on a page, OneNote creates a **drawing canvas**, which is a container for shapes and lines.

On the Job Now

OneNote is ideal for taking notes during meetings, whether you are recording minutes, documenting a discussion, sketching product diagrams, or listing follow-up items. Use a meeting template to add pages with content appropriate for meetings.

Figure 3: Tools on the Draw tab

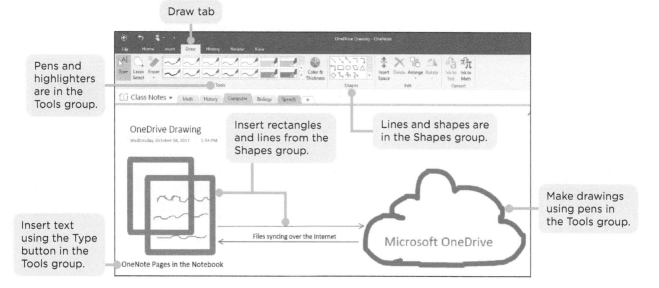

Draw tab

Pens and highlighters are in the Tools group.

Insert rectangles and lines from the Shapes group.

Lines and shapes are in the Shapes group.

Make drawings using pens in the Tools group.

Insert text using the Type button in the Tools group.

Converting Handwriting to Text

When you use a pen tool to write on a notebook page, the text you enter is called **inked handwriting**. OneNote can convert inked handwriting to typed text when you use the **Ink to Text** button in the Convert group on the Draw tab, as shown in Figure 4. After OneNote converts the handwriting to text, you can use the Search box to find terms in the converted text or any other note in your notebooks.

Figure 4: Converting handwriting to text

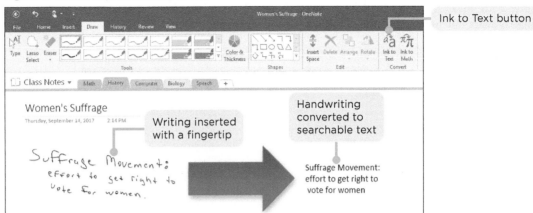

Ink to Text button

Women's Suffrage
Thursday, September 14, 2017   2:14 PM

Suffrage Movements: effort to get right to vote for women.

Writing inserted with a fingertip

Handwriting converted to searchable text

Suffrage Movement: effort to get right to vote for women

On the Job Now

Use OneNote as a place to brainstorm ongoing work projects. If a notebook contains sensitive material, you can password-protect some or all of the notebook so that only certain people can open it.

Recording a Lecture

If your computer or mobile device has a microphone or camera, OneNote can record the audio or video from a lecture or business meeting as shown in Figure 5. When you record a lecture (with your instructor's permission), you can follow along, take regular notes at your own pace, and review the video recording later. You can control the start, pause, and stop motions of the recording when you play back the recording of your notes.

Figure 5: Video inserted in a notebook

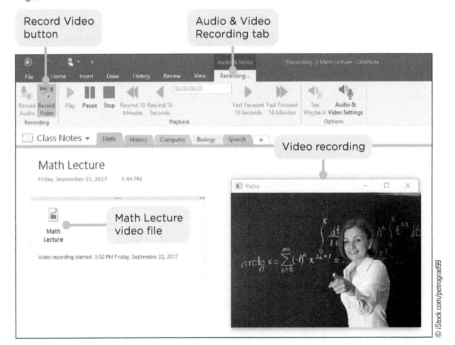

Record Video button

Audio & Video Recording tab

Video recording

Math Lecture
Friday, September 22, 2017   2:44 PM

Math Lecture

Math Lecture video file

Video recording started: 3:00 PM Friday, September 22, 2017

© iStock.com/petrograd99

Try This Now

Learn to use OneNote!
Links to companion **Sways**, featuring **videos** with hands-on instructions, are located on www.cengagebrain.com.

1: Taking Notes for a Week

As a student, you can get organized by using OneNote to take detailed notes in your classes. Perform the following tasks:

a. Create a new OneNote notebook on your Microsoft OneDrive account (the default location for new notebooks). Name the notebook with your first name followed by "Notes," as in **Caleb Notes**.

b. Create four section tabs, each with a different class name.

c. Take detailed notes in those classes for one week. Be sure to include notes, drawings, and other types of content.

d. Sync your notes with your OneDrive. Submit your assignment in the format specified by your instructor.

2: Using OneNote to Organize a Research Paper

You have a research paper due on the topic of three habits of successful students. Use OneNote to organize your research. Perform the following tasks:

a. Create a new OneNote notebook on your Microsoft OneDrive account. Name the notebook **Success Research**.

b. Create three section tabs with the following names:

- **Take Detailed Notes**
- **Be Respectful in Class**
- **Come to Class Prepared**

c. On the web, research the topics and find three sources for each section. Copy a sentence from each source and paste the sentence into the appropriate section. When you paste the sentence, OneNote inserts it in a note with a link to the source.

d. Sync your notes with your OneDrive. Submit your assignment in the format specified by your instructor.

3: Planning Your Career

Note: This activity requires a webcam or built-in video camera on any type of device.

Consider an occupation that interests you. Using OneNote, examine the responsibilities, education requirements, potential salary, and employment outlook of a specific career. Perform the following tasks:

a. Create a new OneNote notebook on your Microsoft OneDrive account. Name the notebook with your first name followed by a career title, such as **Kara - App Developer**.

b. Create four section tabs with the names **Responsibilities, Education Requirements, Median Salary**, and **Employment Outlook**.

c. Research the responsibilities of your career path. Using OneNote, record a short video (approximately 30 seconds) of yourself explaining the responsibilities of your career path. Place the video in the Responsibilities section.

d. On the web, research the educational requirements for your career path and find two appropriate sources. Copy a paragraph from each source and paste them into the appropriate section. When you paste a paragraph, OneNote inserts it in a note with a link to the source.

e. Research the median salary for a single year for this career. Create a mathematical equation in the Median Salary section that multiplies the amount of the median salary times 20 years to calculate how much you will possibly earn.

f. For the Employment Outlook section, research the outlook for your career path. Take at least four notes about what you find when researching the topic.

g. Sync your notes with your OneDrive. Submit your assignment in the format specified by your instructor.

Introduction to Sway

Sway site | responsive design | Storyline | card | Creative Commons license | animation emphasis effects | Docs.com

Expressing your ideas in a presentation typically means creating PowerPoint slides or a Word document. Microsoft Sway gives you another way to engage an audience. Sway is a free Microsoft tool available at Sway.com or as an app in Office 365. Using Sway, you can combine text, images, videos, and social media in a website called a **Sway site** that you can share and display on any device. To get started, you create a digital story on a web-based canvas without borders, slides, cells, or page breaks. A Sway site organizes the text, images, and video into a **responsive design**, which means your content adapts perfectly to any screen size as shown in **Figure 6**. You store a Sway site in the cloud on OneDrive using a free Microsoft account.

Figure 6: Sway site with responsive design

You can display a Sway presentation in a web browser.

Sway uses responsive design to make sure pages fit perfectly on any device.

© iStock.com/marinello, © iStock.com/marekuliasz

Creating a Sway Presentation

You can use Sway to build a digital flyer, a club newsletter, a vacation blog, an informational site, a digital art portfolio, or a new product rollout. After you select your topic and sign into Sway with your Microsoft account, a **Storyline** opens, providing tools and a work area for composing your digital story. See **Figure 7**. Each story can include text, images, and videos. You create a Sway by adding text and media content into a Storyline section, or **card**. To add pictures, videos, or documents, select a card in the left pane and then select the Insert Content button. The first card in a Sway presentation contains a title and background image.

Figure 7: Creating a Sway site

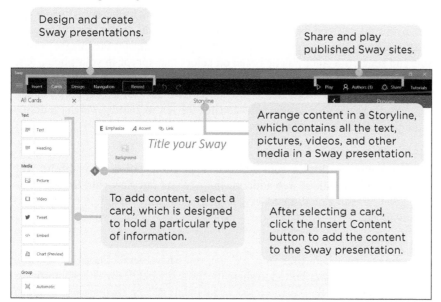

Design and create Sway presentations.

Share and play published Sway sites.

Arrange content in a Storyline, which contains all the text, pictures, videos, and other media in a Sway presentation.

To add content, select a card, which is designed to hold a particular type of information.

After selecting a card, click the Insert Content button to add the content to the Sway presentation.

Adding Content to Build a Story

As you work, Sway searches the Internet to help you find relevant images, videos, tweets, and other content from online sources such as Bing, YouTube, Twitter, and Facebook. You can drag content from the search results right into the Storyline. In addition, you can upload your own images and videos directly in the presentation. For example, if you are creating a Sway presentation about the market for commercial drones, Sway suggests content to incorporate into the presentation by displaying it in the left pane as search results. The search results include drone images tagged with a **Creative Commons license** at online sources as shown in **Figure 8**. A Creative Commons license is a public copyright license that allows the free distribution of an otherwise copyrighted work. In addition, you can specify the source of the media. For example, you can add your own Facebook or OneNote pictures and videos in Sway without leaving the app.

On the Job Now

If you have a Microsoft Word document containing an outline of your business content, drag the outline into Sway to create a card for each topic.

Figure 8: Images in Sway search results

Select the source of media objects

Information about Creative Commons licenses

Storyline title

The Market for Commercial Drones

Drag an image to the picture placeholder box

Suggested images in the search results

Designing a Sway

Sway professionally designs your Storyline content by resizing background images and fonts to fit your display, and by floating text, animating media, embedding video, and removing images as a page scrolls out of view. Sway also evaluates the images in your Storyline and suggests a color palette based on colors that appear in your photos. Use the Design button to display tools including color palettes, font choices, **animation emphasis effects**, and style templates to provide a personality for a Sway presentation. Instead of creating your own design, you can click the Remix button, which randomly selects unique designs for your Sway site.

Publishing a Sway

Use the Play button to display your finished Sway presentation as a website. The Address bar includes a unique web address where others can view your Sway site. As the author, you can edit a published Sway site by clicking the Edit button (pencil icon) on the Sway toolbar.

Sharing a Sway

When you are ready to share your Sway website, you have several options as shown in Figure 9. Use the Share slider button to share the Sway site publically or keep it private. If you add the Sway site to the Microsoft **Docs.com** public gallery, anyone worldwide can use Bing, Google, or other search engines to find, view, and share your Sway site. You can also share your Sway site using Facebook, Twitter, Google+, Yammer, and other social media sites. Link your presentation to any webpage or email the link to your audience. Sway can also generate a code for embedding the link within another webpage.

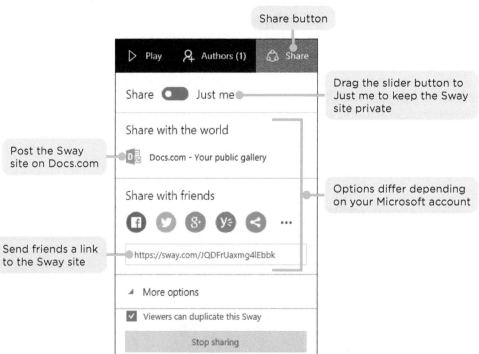

Figure 9: Sharing a Sway site

Try This Now

Learn to use Sway!
Links to companion **Sways**, featuring **videos** with hands-on instructions, are located on www.cengagebrain.com.

1: Creating a Sway Resume

Sway is a digital storytelling app. Create a Sway resume to share the skills, job experiences, and achievements you have that match the requirements of a future job interest. Perform the following tasks:

a. Create a new presentation in Sway to use as a digital resume. Title the Sway Storyline with your full name and then select a background image.
b. Create three separate sections titled **Academic Background, Work Experience**, and **Skills**, and insert text, a picture, and a paragraph or bulleted points in each section. Be sure to include your own picture.
c. Add a fourth section that includes a video about your school that you find online.
d. Customize the design of your presentation.
e. Submit your assignment link in the format specified by your instructor.

2: Creating an Online Sway Newsletter

Newsletters are designed to capture the attention of their target audience. Using Sway, create a newsletter for a club, organization, or your favorite music group. Perform the following tasks:

a. Create a new presentation in Sway to use as a digital newsletter for a club, organization, or your favorite music group. Provide a title for the Sway Storyline and select an appropriate background image.
b. Select three separate sections with appropriate titles, such as Upcoming Events. In each section, insert text, a picture, and a paragraph or bulleted points.
c. Add a fourth section that includes a video about your selected topic.
d. Customize the design of your presentation.
e. Submit your assignment link in the format specified by your instructor.

3: Creating and Sharing a Technology Presentation

To place a Sway presentation in the hands of your entire audience, you can share a link to the Sway presentation. Create a Sway presentation on a new technology and share it with your class. Perform the following tasks:

a. Create a new presentation in Sway about a cutting-edge technology topic. Provide a title for the Sway Storyline and select a background image.
b. Create four separate sections about your topic, and include text, a picture, and a paragraph in each section.
c. Add a fifth section that includes a video about your topic.
d. Customize the design of your presentation.
e. Share the link to your Sway with your classmates and submit your assignment link in the format specified by your instructor.

Introduction to Office Mix

add-in | clip | slide recording | Slide Notes | screen recording | free-response quiz

Bottom Line

- Office Mix is a free PowerPoint add-in from Microsoft that adds features to PowerPoint.
- The Mix tab on the PowerPoint ribbon provides tools for creating screen recordings, videos, interactive quizzes, and live webpages.

To enliven business meetings and lectures, Microsoft adds a new dimension to presentations with a powerful toolset called Office Mix, a free add-in for PowerPoint. (An **add-in** is software that works with an installed app to extend its features.) Using Office Mix, you can record yourself on video, capture still and moving images on your desktop, and insert interactive elements such as quizzes and live webpages directly into PowerPoint slides. When you post the finished presentation to OneDrive, Office Mix provides a link you can share with friends and colleagues. Anyone with an Internet connection and a web browser can watch a published Office Mix presentation, such as the one in Figure 10, on a computer or mobile device.

Figure 10: Office Mix presentation

Adding Office Mix to PowerPoint

To get started, you create an Office Mix account at the website mix.office.com using an email address or a Facebook or Google account. Next, you download and install the Office Mix add-in (see Figure 11). Office Mix appears as a new tab named Mix on the PowerPoint ribbon in versions of Office 2013 and Office 2016 running on personal computers (PCs).

Learn to use Office Mix!

Links to companion **Sways**, featuring **videos** with hands-on instructions, are located on www.cengagebrain.com.

Figure 11: Getting started with Office Mix

Capturing Video Clips

A **clip** is a short segment of audio, such as music, or video. After finishing the content on a PowerPoint slide, you can use Office Mix to add a video clip to animate or illustrate the content. Office Mix creates video clips in two ways: by recording live action on a webcam and by capturing screen images and movements. If your computer has a webcam, you can record yourself and annotate the slide to create a **slide recording** as shown in Figure 12.

On the Job Now

Companies are using Office Mix to train employees about new products, to explain benefit packages to new workers, and to educate interns about office procedures.

Figure 12: Making a slide recording

Record your voice; also record video if your computer has a camera.

Use the Slide Notes button to display notes for your narration.

For best results, look directly at your webcam while recording video.

Use inking tools to write and draw on the slide as you record.

Choose a video and audio device to record images and sound.

When you are making a slide recording, you can record your spoken narration at the same time. The **Slide Notes** feature works like a teleprompter to help you focus on your presentation content instead of memorizing your narration. Use the Inking tools to make annotations or add highlighting using different pen types and colors. After finishing a recording, edit the video in PowerPoint to trim the length or set playback options.

The second way to create a video is to capture on-screen images and actions with or without a voiceover. This method is ideal if you want to show how to use your favorite website or demonstrate an app such as OneNote. To share your screen with an audience, select the part of the screen you want to show in the video. Office Mix captures everything that happens in that area to create a **screen recording**, as shown in Figure 13. Office Mix inserts the screen recording as a video in the slide.

On the Job Now

To make your video recordings accessible to people with hearing impairments, use the Office Mix closed-captioning tools. You can also use closed captions to supplement audio that is difficult to understand and to provide an aid for those learning to read.

Figure 13: Making a screen recording

Record the action on the screen within the red dashed outline.

Record audio while capturing your on-screen actions.

Select Area button

Inserting Quizzes, Live Webpages, and Apps

To enhance and assess audience understanding, make your slides interactive by adding quizzes, live webpages, and apps. Quizzes give immediate feedback to the user as shown in Figure 14. Office Mix supports several quiz formats, including a **free-response quiz** similar to a short answer quiz, and true/false, multiple-choice, and multiple-response formats.

Figure 14: Creating an interactive quiz

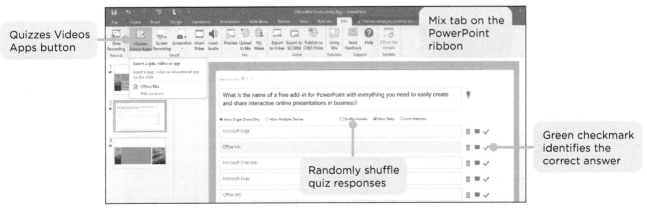

Sharing an Office Mix Presentation

When you complete your work with Office Mix, upload the presentation to your personal Office Mix dashboard as shown in Figure 15. Users of PCs, Macs, iOS devices, and Android devices can access and play Office Mix presentations. The Office Mix dashboard displays built-in analytics that include the quiz results and how much time viewers spent on each slide. You can play completed Office Mix presentations online or download them as movies.

Figure 15: Sharing an Office Mix presentation

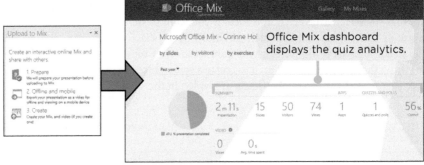

Try This Now

Learn to use Office Mix!
Links to companion **Sways**, featuring **videos** with hands-on instructions, are located on www.cengagebrain.com.

1: Creating an Office Mix Tutorial for OneNote

Note: This activity requires a microphone on your computer.

Office Mix makes it easy to record screens and their contents. Create PowerPoint slides with an Office Mix screen recording to show OneNote 2016 features. Perform the following tasks:

   a. Create a PowerPoint presentation with the Ion Boardroom template. Create an opening slide with the title **My Favorite OneNote Features** and enter your name in the subtitle.
   b. Create three additional slides, each titled with a new feature of OneNote. Open OneNote and use the Mix tab in PowerPoint to capture three separate screen recordings that teach your favorite features.
   c. Add a fifth slide that quizzes the user with a multiple-choice question about OneNote and includes four responses. Be sure to insert a checkmark indicating the correct response.
   d. Upload the completed presentation to your Office Mix dashboard and share the link with your instructor.
   e. Submit your assignment link in the format specified by your instructor.

2: Teaching Augmented Reality with Office Mix

Note: This activity requires a webcam or built-in video camera on your computer.

A local elementary school has asked you to teach augmented reality to its students using Office Mix. Perform the following tasks:

   a. Research augmented reality using your favorite online search tools.
   b. Create a PowerPoint presentation with the Frame template. Create an opening slide with the title **Augmented Reality** and enter your name in the subtitle.
   c. Create a slide with four bullets summarizing your research of augmented reality. Create a 20-second slide recording of yourself providing a quick overview of augmented reality.
   d. Create another slide with a 30-second screen recording of a video about augmented reality from a site such as YouTube or another video-sharing site.
   e. Add a final slide that quizzes the user with a true/false question about augmented reality. Be sure to insert a checkmark indicating the correct response.
   f. Upload the completed presentation to your Office Mix dashboard and share the link with your instructor.
   g. Submit your assignment link in the format specified by your instructor.

3: Marketing a Travel Destination with Office Mix

Note: This activity requires a webcam or built-in video camera on your computer.

To convince your audience to travel to a particular city, create a slide presentation marketing any city in the world using a slide recording, screen recording, and a quiz. Perform the following tasks:

   a. Create a PowerPoint presentation with any template. Create an opening slide with the title of the city you are marketing as a travel destination and your name in the subtitle.
   b. Create a slide with four bullets about the featured city. Create a 30-second slide recording of yourself explaining why this city is the perfect vacation destination.
   c. Create another slide with a 20-second screen recording of a travel video about the city from a site such as YouTube or another video-sharing site.
   d. Add a final slide that quizzes the user with a multiple-choice question about the featured city with five responses. Be sure to include a checkmark indicating the correct response.
   e. Upload the completed presentation to your Office Mix dashboard and share your link with your instructor.
   f. Submit your assignment link in the format specified by your instructor.

Introduction to Microsoft Edge

Reading view | Hub | Cortana | Web Note | Inking | sandbox

Bottom Line
- Microsoft Edge is the name of the new web browser built into Windows 10.
- Microsoft Edge allows you to search the web faster, take web notes, read webpages without distractions, and get instant assistance from Cortana.

Microsoft Edge is the default web browser developed for the Windows 10 operating system as a replacement for Internet Explorer. Unlike its predecessor, Edge lets you write on webpages, read webpages without advertisements and other distractions, and search for information using a virtual personal assistant. The Edge interface is clean and basic, as shown in Figure 16, meaning you can pay more attention to the webpage content.

Figure 16: Microsoft Edge tools

Forward button

New tab button

Web address in the Address bar

Add to favorites or reading list button

Reading view button

Back button

More button

Refresh (F5) button

Hub (Favorites, reading list, history, and downloads) button

Share Web Note button

Make a Web Note button

Learn to use Edge!
Links to companion **Sways**, featuring **videos** with hands-on instructions, are located on www.cengagebrain.com.

Browsing the Web with Microsoft Edge
One of the fastest browsers available, Edge allows you to type search text directly in the Address bar. As you view the resulting webpage, you can switch to **Reading view**, which is available for most news and research sites, to eliminate distracting advertisements. For example, if you are catching up on technology news online, the webpage might be difficult to read due to a busy layout cluttered with ads. Switch to Reading view to refresh the page and remove the original page formatting, ads, and menu sidebars to read the article distraction-free.

Consider the **Hub** in Microsoft Edge as providing one-stop access to all the things you collect on the web, such as your favorite websites, reading list, surfing history, and downloaded files.

On the Job Now

Businesses started adopting Internet Explorer more than 20 years ago simply to view webpages. Today, Microsoft Edge has a different purpose: to promote interaction with the web and share its contents with colleagues.

Locating Information with Cortana
Cortana, the Windows 10 virtual assistant, plays an important role in Microsoft Edge. After you turn on Cortana, it appears as an animated circle in the Address bar when you might need assistance, as shown in the restaurant website in Figure 17. When you click the Cortana icon, a pane slides in from the right of the browser window to display detailed information about the restaurant, including maps and reviews. Cortana can also assist you in defining words, finding the weather, suggesting coupons for shopping, updating stock market information, and calculating math.

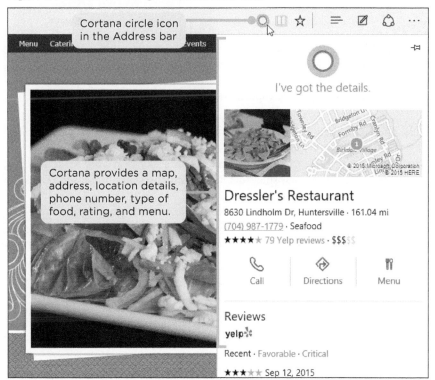

Annotating Webpages

One of the most impressive Microsoft Edge features are the **Web Note** tools, which you use to write on a webpage or to highlight text. When you click the Make a Web Note button, an **Inking** toolbar appears, as shown in **Figure 18**, that provides writing and drawing tools. These tools include an eraser, a pen, and a highlighter with different colors. You can also insert a typed note and copy a screen image (called a screen clipping). You can draw with a pointing device, fingertip, or stylus using different pen colors. Whether you add notes to a recipe, annotate sources for a research paper, or select a product while shopping online, the Web Note tools can enhance your productivity. After you complete your notes, click the Save button to save the annotations to OneNote, your Favorites list, or your Reading list. You can share the inked page with others using the Share Web Note button.

On the Job Now

To enhance security, Microsoft Edge runs in a partial sandbox, an arrangement that prevents attackers from gaining control of your computer. Browsing within the **sandbox** protects computer resources and information from hackers.

Figure 18: Web Note tools in Microsoft Edge

Try This Now

Learn to use Edge!

Links to companion **Sways**, featuring **videos** with hands-on instructions, are located on www.cengagebrain.com.

1: Using Cortana in Microsoft Edge

Note: This activity requires using Microsoft Edge on a Windows 10 computer.

Cortana can assist you in finding information on a webpage in Microsoft Edge. Perform the following tasks:

a. Create a Word document using the Word Screen Clipping tool to capture the following screenshots.

- Screenshot A—Using Microsoft Edge, open a webpage with a technology news article. Right-click a term in the article and ask Cortana to define it.
- Screenshot B—Using Microsoft Edge, open the website of a fancy restaurant in a city near you. Make sure the Cortana circle icon is displayed in the Address bar. (If it's not displayed, find a different restaurant website.) Click the Cortana circle icon to display a pane with information about the restaurant.
- Screenshot C—Using Microsoft Edge, type **10 USD to Euros** in the Address bar without pressing the Enter key. Cortana converts the U.S. dollars to Euros.
- Screenshot D—Using Microsoft Edge, type **Apple stock** in the Address bar without pressing the Enter key. Cortana displays the current stock quote.

b. Submit your assignment in the format specified by your instructor.

2: Viewing Online News with Reading View

Note: This activity requires using Microsoft Edge on a Windows 10 computer.

Reading view in Microsoft Edge can make a webpage less cluttered with ads and other distractions. Perform the following tasks:

a. Create a Word document using the Word Screen Clipping tool to capture the following screenshots.

- Screenshot A—Using Microsoft Edge, open the website **mashable.com**. Open a technology article. Click the Reading view button to display an ad-free page that uses only basic text formatting.
- Screenshot B—Using Microsoft Edge, open the website **bbc.com**. Open any news article. Click the Reading view button to display an ad-free page that uses only basic text formatting.
- Screenshot C—Make three types of annotations (Pen, Highlighter, and Add a typed note) on the BBC article page displayed in Reading view.

b. Submit your assignment in the format specified by your instructor.

3: Inking with Microsoft Edge

Note: This activity requires using Microsoft Edge on a Windows 10 computer.

Microsoft Edge provides many annotation options to record your ideas. Perform the following tasks:

a. Open the website **wolframalpha.com** in the Microsoft Edge browser. Wolfram Alpha is a well-respected academic search engine. Type **US$100 1965 dollars in 2015** in the Wolfram Alpha search text box and press the Enter key.

b. Click the Make a Web Note button to display the Web Note tools. Using the Pen tool, draw a circle around the result on the webpage. Save the page to OneNote.

c. In the Wolfram Alpha search text box, type the name of the city closest to where you live and press the Enter key. Using the Highlighter tool, highlight at least three interesting results. Add a note and then type a sentence about what you learned about this city. Save the page to OneNote. Share your OneNote notebook with your instructor.

d. Submit your assignment link in the format specified by your instructor.

WORD

Creating and Editing a Document

Writing a Business Letter and Formatting a Flyer

OBJECTIVES

Session 1.1
- Create and save a document
- Enter text and correct errors as you type
- Use AutoComplete and AutoCorrect
- Select text and move the insertion point
- Undo and redo actions
- Adjust paragraph spacing, line spacing, and margins
- Preview and print a document
- Create an envelope

Session 1.2
- Open an existing document
- Use the Spelling and Grammar task panes
- Change page orientation, font, font color, and font size
- Apply text effects and align text
- Copy formatting with the Format Painter
- Insert a paragraph border and shading
- Delete, insert, and edit a photo
- Use Word Help

Case | *Villa Rio Records*

Villa Rio Records, in Wilmington, Delaware, specializes in vinyl records, which have been making a comeback in the past few years. To replenish the store's stock, the purchasing manager, Leo Barinov, frequently appraises and bids on record collections from around the state. Leo has asked you to create a cover letter to accompany an appraisal that he needs to send to a potential seller and an envelope for sending an appraisal to another potential seller. He also wants your help creating a flyer reminding store customers that Villa Rio Records buys old vinyl records.

You will create the letter and flyer using **Microsoft Office Word 2016** (or simply **Word**), a word-processing program. You'll start by opening Word and saving a new document. Then you'll type the text of the cover letter and print it. In the process of entering the text, you'll learn several ways to correct typing errors and how to adjust paragraph and line spacing. When you create the envelope, you'll learn how to save it as part of a document for later use. As you work on the flyer, you will learn how to open an existing document, change the way text is laid out on the page, format text, and insert and resize a photo. Finally, you'll learn how to use Word's Help system.

STARTING DATA FILES

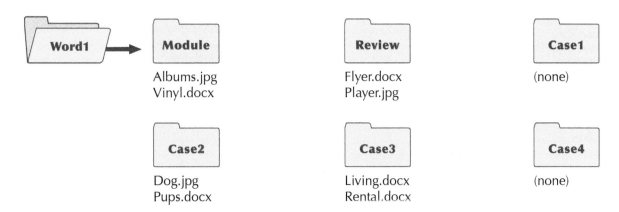

Word1 → **Module**
Albums.jpg
Vinyl.docx

Review
Flyer.docx
Player.jpg

Case1
(none)

Case2
Dog.jpg
Pups.docx

Case3
Living.docx
Rental.docx

Case4
(none)

Session 1.1 Visual Overview:

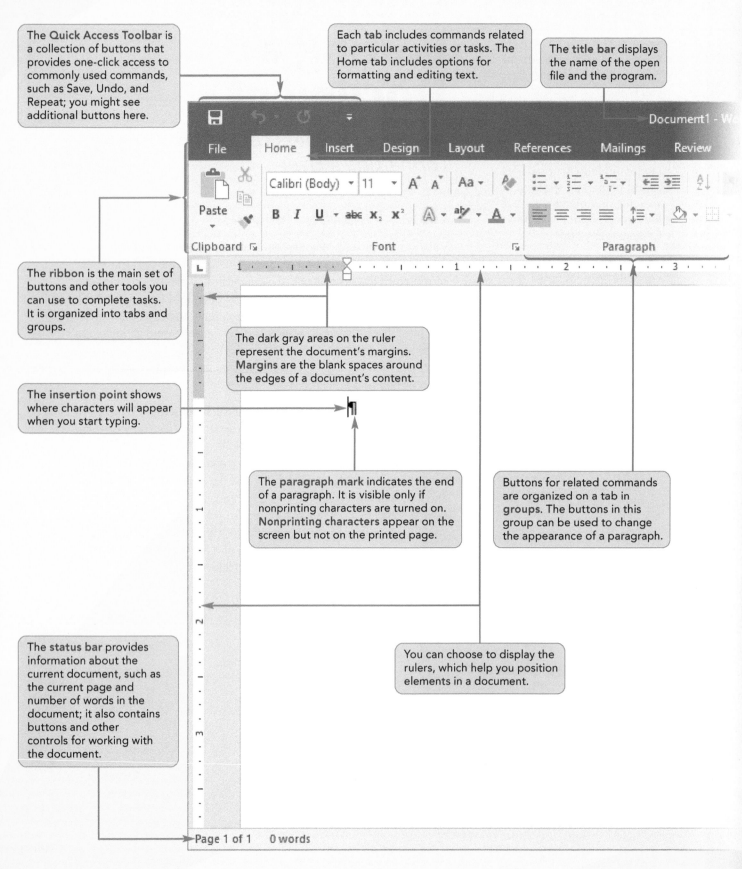

The **Quick Access Toolbar** is a collection of buttons that provides one-click access to commonly used commands, such as Save, Undo, and Repeat; you might see additional buttons here.

Each tab includes commands related to particular activities or tasks. The Home tab includes options for formatting and editing text.

The **title bar** displays the name of the open file and the program.

The **ribbon** is the main set of buttons and other tools you can use to complete tasks. It is organized into tabs and groups.

The dark gray areas on the ruler represent the document's margins. **Margins** are the blank spaces around the edges of a document's content.

The **insertion point** shows where characters will appear when you start typing.

The **paragraph mark** indicates the end of a paragraph. It is visible only if nonprinting characters are turned on. **Nonprinting characters** appear on the screen but not on the printed page.

Buttons for related commands are organized on a tab in **groups.** The buttons in this group can be used to change the appearance of a paragraph.

The **status bar** provides information about the current document, such as the current page and number of words in the document; it also contains buttons and other controls for working with the document.

You can choose to display the **rulers,** which help you position elements in a document.

The Word Window

The Show/Hide button is selected, meaning that nonprinting characters are displayed in the document.

You can click the Ribbon Display Options button to display a menu with options for how the ribbon looks. If the ribbon is hidden, click Show Tabs and Commands in this menu to redisplay it.

You use the Minimize button to reduce the Word window to an icon in the taskbar, which you can click later to display the Word window again.

You use the Restore Down button to reduce the Word window to a smaller size; the Restore Down button is then replaced with the Maximize button, which you can click to restore the Word window to its full size.

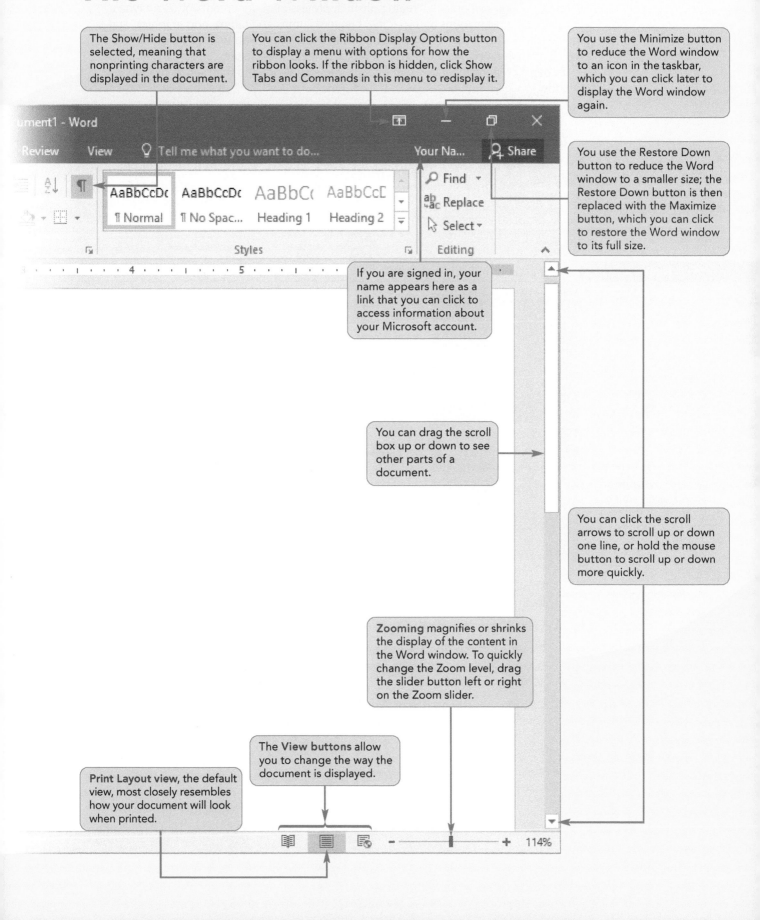

If you are signed in, your name appears here as a link that you can click to access information about your Microsoft account.

You can drag the scroll box up or down to see other parts of a document.

You can click the scroll arrows to scroll up or down one line, or hold the mouse button to scroll up or down more quickly.

Zooming magnifies or shrinks the display of the content in the Word window. To quickly change the Zoom level, drag the slider button left or right on the Zoom slider.

The View buttons allow you to change the way the document is displayed.

Print Layout view, the default view, most closely resembles how your document will look when printed.

Starting Word

With Word, you can quickly create polished, professional documents. You can type a document, adjust margins and spacing, create columns and tables, add graphics, and then easily make revisions and corrections. In this session, you will create one of the most common types of documents—a block-style business letter.

To begin creating the letter, you first need to start Word and then set up the Word window.

To start Microsoft Word:

▶ **1.** On the Windows taskbar, click the **Start** button ⊞. The Start menu opens.

▶ **2.** Click **All apps** on the Start menu, scroll the list, and then click **Word 2016**. Word starts and displays the Recent screen in Backstage view. **Backstage view** provides access to various screens with commands that allow you to manage files and Word options. See Figure 1-1.

| Figure 1-1 | Recent screen in Backstage view |

a list of recently opened documents might appear here

click to open a new, blank document

your list of available templates may differ

Trouble? If you don't see Word 2016 on the Windows Start menu, ask your instructor or technical support person for help.

▶ **3.** Click **Blank document**. The Word window opens, with the ribbon displayed.

Trouble? If you don't see the ribbon, click the Ribbon Display Options button 🔲, as shown in the Session 1.1 Visual Overview, and then click Show Tabs and Commands.

Don't be concerned if your Word window doesn't match the Session 1.1 Visual Overview exactly. You'll have a chance to adjust its appearance shortly.

Working in Touch Mode

You can interact with the Word screen using a mouse, or, if you have a touchscreen, you can work in Touch Mode, using a finger instead of the mouse pointer. In **Touch Mode**, extra space around the buttons on the ribbon makes it easier to tap the specific button you need. The figures in this text show the screen with Mouse Mode on, but it's helpful to learn how to switch back and forth between Touch Mode and Mouse Mode.

Note: The following steps assume that you are using a mouse. If you are instead using a touch device, please read these steps but don't complete them so that you remain working in Touch Mode.

To switch between Touch and Mouse Mode:

▶ **1.** On the Quick Access Toolbar, click the **Customize Quick Access Toolbar** button ▼ to open the menu. The Touch/Mouse Mode command near the bottom of the menu does not have a checkmark next to it, indicating that it is currently not selected.

> **Trouble?** If the Touch/Mouse Mode command has a checkmark next to it, press the Esc key to close the menu, and then skip to Step 3.

▶ **2.** On the menu, click **Touch/Mouse Mode**. The menu closes, and the Touch/Mouse Mode button 👆▼ appears on the Quick Access Toolbar.

▶ **3.** On the Quick Access Toolbar, click the **Touch/Mouse Mode** button 👆▼. A menu opens with two options—Mouse and Touch. The icon next to Mouse is shaded blue to indicate it is selected.

> **Trouble?** If the icon next to Touch is shaded blue, press the Esc key to close the menu and skip to Step 5.

▶ **4.** On the menu, click **Touch**. The menu closes, and the ribbon increases in height so that there is more space around each button on the ribbon. See Figure 1-2.

| Figure 1-2 | Word window in Touch Mode |

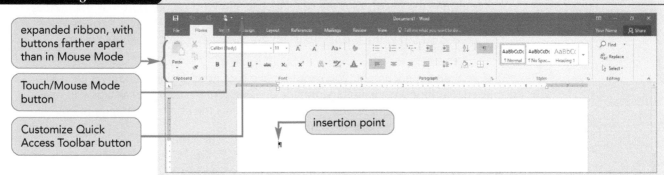

expanded ribbon, with buttons farther apart than in Mouse Mode

Touch/Mouse Mode button

Customize Quick Access Toolbar button

insertion point

> **Trouble?** If you are working with a touchscreen and want to use Touch Mode, skip Steps 5 and 6.

▶ **5.** On the Quick Access Toolbar, click the **Touch/Mouse Mode** button 👆▼, and then click **Mouse**. The ribbon changes back to its Mouse Mode appearance, as shown in the Session 1.1 Visual Overview.

▶ **6.** On the Quick Access Toolbar, click the **Customize Quick Access Toolbar** button ▼, and then click **Touch/Mouse Mode** to deselect it. The Touch/Mouse Mode button is removed from the Quick Access Toolbar.

Setting Up the Word Window

Before you start using Word, you should make sure you can locate and identify the different elements of the Word window, as shown in the Session 1.1 Visual Overview. In the following steps, you'll make sure your screen matches the Visual Overview.

To set up your Word window to match the figures in this book:

▶ **1.** If the Word window does not fill the entire screen, click the **Maximize** button ▣ in the upper-right corner of the Word window.

The insertion point on your computer should be positioned about an inch from the top of the document, as shown in Figure 1-2, with the top margin visible.

Trouble? If the insertion point appears at the top of the document, with no white space above it, position the mouse pointer between the top of the document and the horizontal ruler, until it changes to ⬍, double-click, and then scroll up to top of the document.

▶ **2.** On the ribbon, click the **View** tab. The ribbon changes to show options for changing the appearance of the Word window.

▶ **3.** In the Show group, click the **Ruler** check box to insert a checkmark, if necessary. If the rulers were not displayed, they are displayed now.

Next, you'll change the Zoom level to a setting that ensures that your Word window will match the figures in this book. To increase or decrease the screen's magnification, you could drag the slider button on the Zoom slider in the lower-right corner of the Word window. But to choose a specific Zoom level, it's easier to use the Zoom dialog box.

▶ **4.** In the Zoom group, click the **Zoom** button to open the Zoom dialog box. Double-click the current value in the **Percent** box to select it, type **120**, and then click the **OK** button to close the Zoom dialog box.

▶ **5.** On the status bar, click the **Print Layout** button 🗒 to select it, if necessary. As shown in the Session 1.1 Visual Overview, the Print Layout button is the middle of the three View buttons located on the right side of the status bar. The Print Layout button in the Views group on the View tab is also now selected.

Before typing a document, you should make sure nonprinting characters are displayed. Nonprinting characters provide a visual representation of details you might otherwise miss. For example, the (¶) character marks the end of a paragraph, and the (•) character marks the space between words.

To verify that nonprinting characters are displayed:

▶ **1.** On the ribbon, click the **Home** tab.

▶ **2.** In the blank Word document, look for the paragraph mark (¶) in the first line of the document, just to the right of the blinking insertion point.

Trouble? If you don't see the paragraph mark, click the Show/Hide ¶ button ¶ in the Paragraph group.

In the Paragraph group, the Show/Hide ¶ button should be highlighted in gray, indicating that it is selected, and the paragraph mark (¶) should appear in the first line of the document, just to the right of the insertion point.

Saving a Document

Before you begin working on a document, you should save it with a new name. When you use the Save button on the Quick Access Toolbar to save a document for the first time, Word displays the Save As screen in Backstage view. In the Save As screen, you can select the location where you want to store your document. After that, when you click the Save button, Word saves your document to the same location you specified earlier and with the same name.

To save the document:

▶ **1.** On the Quick Access Toolbar, click the **Save** button 🖫. Word switches to the Save As screen in Backstage view, as shown in Figure 1-3.

| Figure 1-3 | Save As screen in Backstage view |

navigation bar

click to return to the document window

Save As selected in the navigation bar

click to open the Save As dialog box

Document1 - Word

Your Name

Save As

OneDrive - Personal
your_name@example.com

This PC

Add a Place

Browse

Your Name's OneDrive

you might see additional folders here; if you want to save a document in a folder that is listed here, click the folder to open the Save As dialog box with that folder selected

Because a document is now open, more commands are available in Backstage view than when you started Word. The **navigation bar** on the left contains commands for working with the open document and for changing settings that control how Word works.

▶ **2.** Click the **Browse** button. The Save As dialog box opens.

Trouble? If your instructor wants you to save your files to your OneDrive account, click OneDrive - Personal, and then log in to your account.

▶ **3.** Navigate to the location specified by your instructor. The default filename, "Doc1," appears in the File name box. You will change that to something more descriptive. See Figure 1-4.

Figure 1-4	Save As dialog box

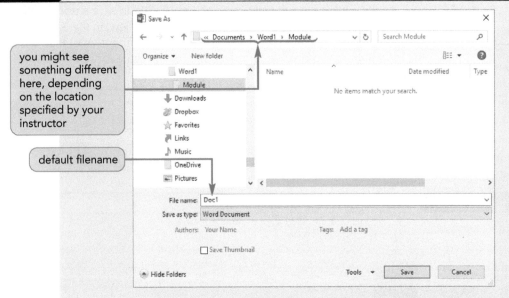

you might see something different here, depending on the location specified by your instructor

default filename

▶ **4.** Click the **File name** box, and then type **Brooks Letter**. The text you type replaces the selected text in the File name box.

▶ **5.** Click the **Save** button. The file is saved, the dialog box and Backstage view close, and the document window appears again, with the new filename in the title bar.

Now that you have saved the document, you can begin typing the letter. Leo has asked you to type a block-style letter to accompany an appraisal that will be sent to Jayla Brooks. Figure 1-5 shows the block-style letter you will create in this module.

Figure 1-5   **Completed block-style letter**

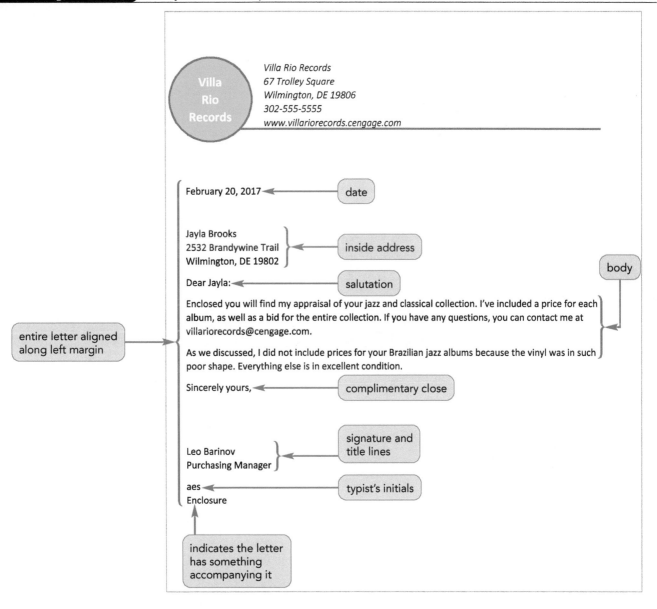

Villa Rio Records

Villa Rio Records
67 Trolley Square
Wilmington, DE 19806
302-555-5555
www.villariorecords.cengage.com

February 20, 2017 ← date

Jayla Brooks
2532 Brandywine Trail ← inside address
Wilmington, DE 19802

Dear Jayla: ← salutation

Enclosed you will find my appraisal of your jazz and classical collection. I've included a price for each album, as well as a bid for the entire collection. If you have any questions, you can contact me at villariorecords@cengage.com.

As we discussed, I did not include prices for your Brazilian jazz albums because the vinyl was in such poor shape. Everything else is in excellent condition.

body

Sincerely yours, ← complimentary close

Leo Barinov
Purchasing Manager ← signature and title lines

aes ← typist's initials
Enclosure

entire letter aligned along left margin

indicates the letter has something accompanying it

Written Communication: Creating a Business Letter

PROSKILLS

Several styles are considered acceptable for business letters. The main differences among the styles have to do with how parts of the letter are indented from the left margin. In the block style, which you will use in this module, each line of text starts at the left margin. In other words, nothing is indented. Another style is to indent the first line of each paragraph. The choice of style is largely a matter of personal preference, or it can be determined by the standards used in a particular business or organization. To further enhance your skills in writing business correspondence, you should consult an authoritative book on business writing that provides guidelines for creating a variety of business documents, such as *Business Communication: Process & Product*, by Mary Ellen Guffey.

Entering Text

The letters you type in a Word document appear at the current location of the blinking insertion point.

Inserting a Date with AutoComplete

The first item in a block-style business letter is the date. Leo plans to send the letter to Jayla on February 20, so you need to insert that date into the document. To do so, you can take advantage of **AutoComplete**, a Word feature that automatically inserts dates and other regularly used items for you. In this case, you can type the first few characters of the month and let Word insert the rest.

To insert the date:

▶ **1.** Type **Febr** (the first four letters of "February"). A ScreenTip appears above the letters, as shown in Figure 1-6, suggesting "February" as the complete word.

| Figure 1-6 | AutoComplete suggestion |

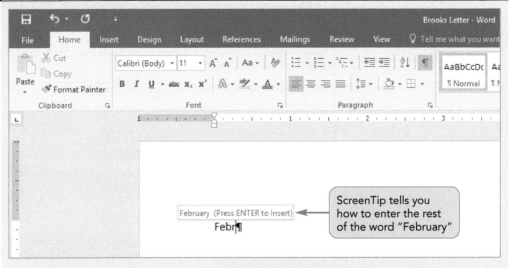

A **ScreenTip** is a box with descriptive text about an object or button you are pointing to.

If you wanted to type something other than "February," you could continue typing to complete the word. In this case, you want to accept the AutoComplete suggestion.

▶ **2.** Press the **Enter** key. The rest of the word "February" is inserted in the document. Note that AutoComplete works for long month names like February but not shorter ones like May, because "Ma" could be the beginning of many words besides "May."

▶ **3.** Press the **spacebar**, type **20, 2017** and then press the **Enter** key twice, leaving a blank paragraph between the date and the line where you will begin typing the inside address, which contains the recipient's name and address. Notice the nonprinting character (•) after the word "February" and before the number "20," which indicates a space. Word inserts this nonprinting character every time you press the spacebar.

Trouble? If February happens to be the current month, you will see a second AutoComplete suggestion displaying the current date after you press the spacebar. To ignore that AutoComplete suggestion, continue typing the rest of the date, as instructed in Step 3.

Continuing to Type the Block-Style Letter

In a block-style business letter, the inside address appears below the date, with one blank paragraph in between. Some style guides recommend including even more space between the date and the inside address. But in the short letter you are typing, more space would make the document look out of balance.

To insert the inside address:

1. Type the following information, pressing the **Enter** key after each item:

   Jayla Brooks

   2532 Brandywine Trail

   Wilmington, DE 19802

   Remember to press the Enter key after you type the ZIP code. Your screen should look like Figure 1-7. Don't be concerned if the lines of the inside address seem too far apart. You'll use the default spacing for now, and then adjust it after you finish typing the letter.

Figure 1-7	Letter with inside address

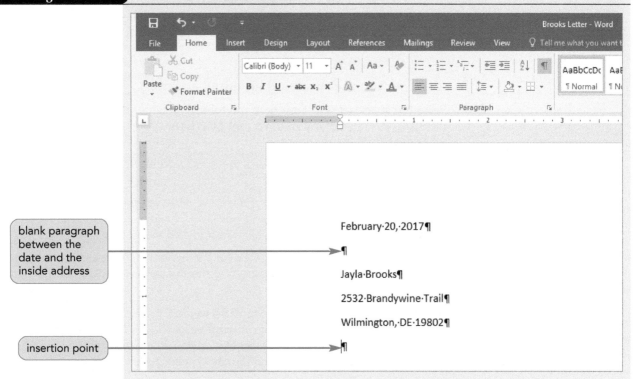

blank paragraph between the date and the inside address

insertion point

Trouble? If you make a mistake while typing, press the Backspace key to delete the incorrect character, and then type the correct character.

Now you can move on to the salutation and the body of the letter. As you type the body of the letter, notice that Word automatically moves the insertion point to a new line when the current line is full.

To type the salutation and the body of the letter:

▶ **1.** Type **Dear Jayla:** and then press the **Enter** key to start a new paragraph for the body of the letter.

▶ **2.** Type the following sentence, including the period: **Enclosed you will find my appraisal of your jazz and classical collection.**

▶ **3.** Press the **spacebar**. Note that you should only include one space between sentences.

▶ **4.** Type the following sentence, including the period: **I've included a price for each album, as well as a bid for the complete collection.**

▶ **5.** On the Quick Access Toolbar, click the **Save** button 🖫. Word saves the document as Brooks Letter to the same location you specified earlier.

TIP

The obsolete practice of pressing the spacebar twice at the end of a sentence dates back to the age of typewriters, when the extra space made it easier to see where one sentence ended and another began.

The next sentence you need to type includes Leo's email address.

Typing a Hyperlink

When you type an email address and then press the spacebar or the Enter key, Word converts it to a hyperlink, with blue font and an underline. A **hyperlink** is text or a graphic you can click to jump to another file or to somewhere else in the same file. The two most common types of hyperlinks are: 1) an email hyperlink, which you can click to open an email message to the recipient specified by the hyperlink; and 2) a web hyperlink, which opens a webpage in a browser. Hyperlinks are useful in documents that you plan to distribute via email. In printed documents, where blue font and underlines can be distracting, you'll usually want to convert a hyperlink back to regular text.

To add a sentence containing an email address:

▶ **1.** Press the spacebar, and then type the following sentence, including the period: **If you have any questions, you can contact me at villariorecords@cengage.com.**

▶ **2.** Press the **Enter** key. Word converts the email address to a hyperlink, with blue font and an underline.

▶ **3.** Position the mouse pointer over the hyperlink. A ScreenTip appears, indicating that you could press and hold the Ctrl key and then click the link to follow it—that is, to open an email message addressed to Villa Rio Records.

▶ **4.** With the mouse pointer positioned over the hyperlink, right-click—that is, press the right mouse button. A shortcut menu opens with commands related to working with hyperlinks.

You can right-click many items in the Word window to display a shortcut menu with commands related to the item you right-clicked. The Mini toolbar also appears when you right-click or select text, giving you easy access to the buttons and settings most often used when formatting text. See Figure 1-8.

Figure 1-8 ▶ **Shortcut menu**

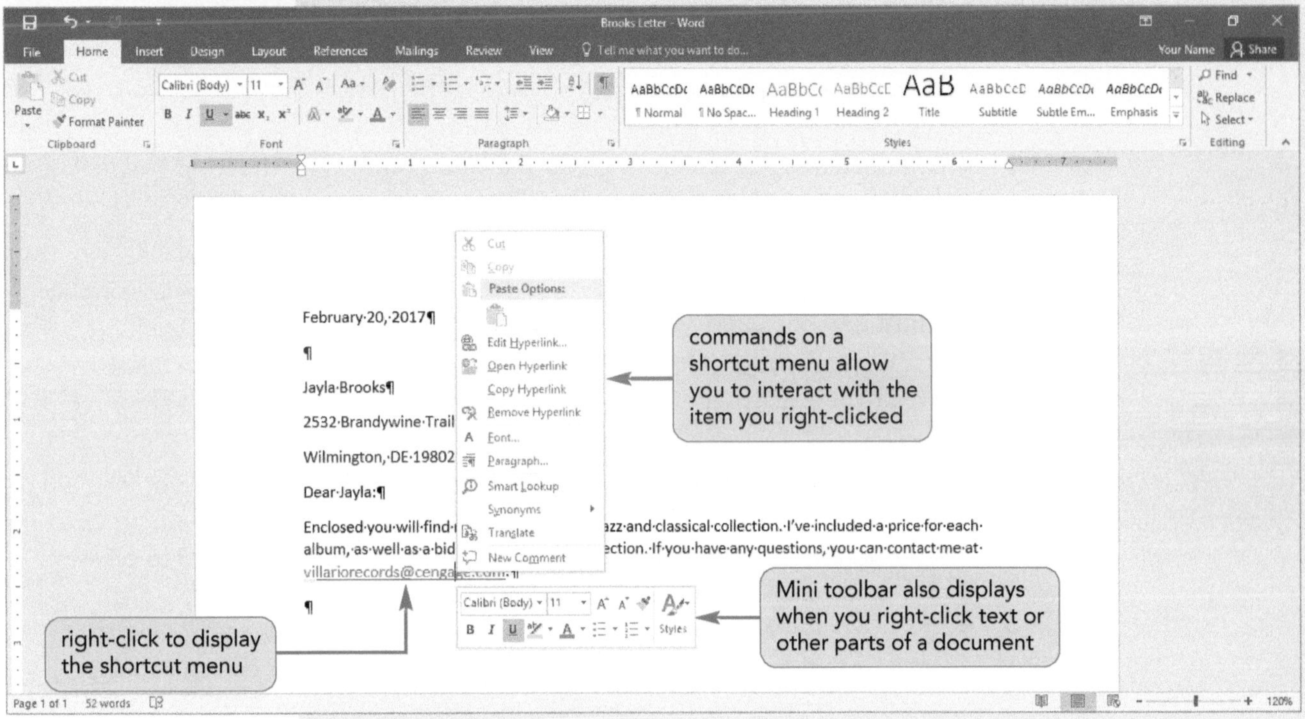

commands on a shortcut menu allow you to interact with the item you right-clicked

right-click to display the shortcut menu

Mini toolbar also displays when you right-click text or other parts of a document

▶ **5.** Click **Remove Hyperlink** in the shortcut menu. The shortcut menu and the Mini toolbar are no longer visible. The email address is now formatted in black, like the rest of the document text.

▶ **6.** On the Quick Access Toolbar, click the **Save** button 🔲.

Using the Undo and Redo Buttons

To undo (or reverse) the last thing you did in a document, click the Undo button on the Quick Access Toolbar. To restore your original change, click the Redo button, which reverses the action of the Undo button (or redoes the undo). To undo more than your last action, you can continue to click the Undo button, or you can click the Undo button arrow on the Quick Access Toolbar to open a list of your most recent actions. When you click an action in the list, Word undoes every action in the list up to and including the action you clicked.

Leo asks you to change the word "complete" to "entire" in the second-to-last sentence you typed. You'll make the change now. If Leo decides he doesn't like it after all, you can always undo it. To delete a character, space, or blank paragraph to the right of the insertion point, you use the Delete key; or to delete an entire word, you can press the Ctrl+Delete keys. To delete a character, space, or blank paragraph to the left of the insertion point, you use the Backspace key; or to delete an entire word, you can press the Ctrl+Backspace keys.

To change the word "complete":

▶ **1.** Press the ↑ key once and then press the → key as necessary to move the insertion point to the left of the "c" in the word "complete."

▶ **2.** Press and hold the **Ctrl** key, and then press the **Delete** key to delete the word "complete."

▶ **3.** Type **entire** as a replacement, and then press the **spacebar**.

After reviewing the sentence, Leo decides he prefers the original wording, so you'll undo the change.

▶ **4.** On the Quick Access Toolbar, click the **Undo** button 🔄. The word "entire" is removed from the sentence.

▶ **5.** Click the **Undo** button 🔄 again to restore the word "complete."

Leo decides that he does want to use "entire" after all. Instead of retyping it, you'll redo the undo.

▶ **6.** On the Quick Access Toolbar, click the **Redo** button 🔁 twice. The word "entire" replaces "complete" in the document, so that the phrase reads "…for the entire collection."

▶ **7.** Press and hold the **Ctrl** key, and then press the **End** key to move the insertion point to the blank paragraph at the end of the document.

Trouble? If you are working on a small keyboard, you might need to press and hold a key labeled "Function" or "FN" before pressing the End key.

▶ **8.** On the Quick Access Toolbar, click the **Save** button 💾. Word saves your letter with the same name and to the same location you specified earlier.

In the previous steps, you used the arrow keys and a key combination to move the insertion point to specific locations in the document. For your reference, Figure 1-9 summarizes the most common keystrokes for moving the insertion point in a document.

Figure 1-9 **Keystrokes for moving the insertion point**

To Move the Insertion Point	Press
Left or right one character at a time	← or →
Up or down one line at a time	↑ or ↓
Left or right one word at a time	Ctrl+← or Ctrl+→
Up or down one paragraph at a time	Ctrl+↑ or Ctrl+↓
To the beginning or to the end of the current line	Home or End
To the beginning or to the end of the document	Ctrl+Home or Ctrl+End
To the previous screen or to the next screen	Page Up or Page Down
To the top or to the bottom of the document window	Alt+Ctrl+Page Up or Alt+Ctrl+Page Down

Correcting Errors as You Type

As you have seen, you can use the Backspace or Delete keys to remove an error, and then type a correction. In many cases, however, Word's AutoCorrect feature will do the work for you. Among other things, **AutoCorrect** automatically corrects common typing errors, such as typing "adn" instead of "and." For example, you might have noticed AutoCorrect at work if you forgot to capitalize the first letter in a sentence as you typed the letter. After you type this kind of error, AutoCorrect automatically corrects it when you press the spacebar, the Tab key, or the Enter key.

Word draws your attention to other potential errors by marking them with wavy underlines. If you type a word that doesn't match the correct spelling in Word's dictionary, or if a word is not in the dictionary at all, a wavy red line appears beneath it. A wavy red underline also appears if you mistakenly type the same word twice in a row. Misused words (for example, "you're" instead of "your") are underlined with a wavy blue line, as are problems with possessives, punctuation, and plurals.

You'll see how this works as you continue typing the letter and make some intentional typing errors.

To learn more about correcting errors as you type:

1. Type the following sentence, including the errors shown here: **as we discussed, I did not include priices for you're Brazilian jazz albums because teh vynil was in such poor shape. Everything else else is in excellent condition.**

As you type, AutoCorrect changes the lowercase "a" at the beginning of the sentence to uppercase. It also changes "priices" to "prices and "teh" to "the." Also, the incorrectly used word "you're" is marked with a wavy blue underline. The spelling error "vynil" and the second "else" are marked with wavy red underlines. See Figure 1-10.

| Figure 1-10 | Errors marked in the document |

To correct an error marked with a wavy underline, you can right-click the error and then click a replacement in the shortcut menu. If you don't see the correct word in the shortcut menu, click anywhere in the document to close the menu, and then type the correction yourself. You can also bypass the shortcut menu entirely and simply delete the error and type a correction.

To correct the spelling and grammar errors:

▶ **1.** Right-click **you're** to display the shortcut menu shown in Figure 1-11.

Figure 1-11	Shortcut menu with suggested spelling

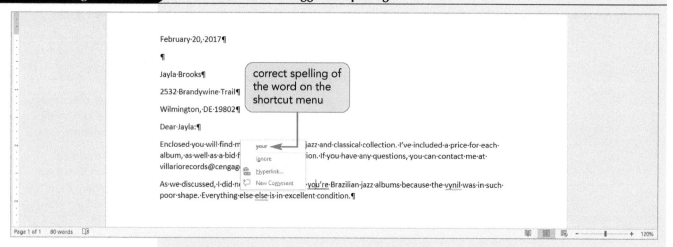

February·20,·2017¶

¶

Jayla·Brooks¶

2532·Brandywine·Trail¶

Wilmington,·DE·19802¶

Dear·Jayla:¶

Enclosed·you·will·find·m [your] jazz·and·classical·collection.·I've·included·a·price·for·each·
album,·as·well·as·a·bid·f Ignore ion.·If·you·have·any·questions,·you·can·contact·me·at·
villariorecords@cengag Hyperlink...

As·we·discussed,·I·did·n New Comment ·you're·Brazilian·jazz·albums·because·the·vynil·was·in·such·
poor·shape.·Everything·else·else·is·in·excellent·condition.¶

correct spelling of
the word on the
shortcut menu

Page 1 of 1   80 words   120%

Trouble? If you see a shortcut menu other than the one shown in Figure 1-11, you didn't right-click exactly on the word "you're." Press the Esc key to close the menu, and then repeat Step 1.

▶ **2.** On the shortcut menu, click **your**. The correct word is inserted into the sentence, and the shortcut menu closes.

▶ **3.** Use a shortcut menu to replace the spelling error "vynil" with the correct word "vinyl."

You could use a shortcut menu to remove the second instance of "else," but in the next step you'll try a different method—selecting the word and deleting it.

TIP

To deselect highlighted text, click anywhere in the document.

▶ **4.** Double-click anywhere in the underlined word **else**. The word and the space following it are highlighted in gray, indicating that they are selected. The Mini toolbar is also visible, but you can ignore it.

Trouble? If the entire paragraph is selected, you triple-clicked the word by mistake. Click anywhere in the document to deselect it, and then repeat Step 4.

▶ **5.** Press the **Delete** key. The second instance of "else" and the space following it are deleted from the sentence.

▶ **6.** On the Quick Access Toolbar, click the **Save** button 🖫.

You can see how quick and easy it is to correct common typing errors with AutoCorrect and the wavy underlines, especially in a short document that you are typing yourself. If you are working on a longer document or a document typed by someone else, you'll also want to have Word check the entire document for errors. You'll learn how to do this in Session 1.2.

Next, you'll finish typing the letter.

To finish typing the letter:

▶ **1.** Press the **Ctrl+End** keys. The insertion point moves to the end of the document.

▶ **2.** Press the **Enter** key, and then type **Sincerely yours,** (including the comma).

▶ **3.** Press the **Enter** key three times to leave space for the signature.

▶ **4.** Type **Leo Barinov** and then press the **Enter** key. Because Leo's last name is not in Word's dictionary, a wavy red line appears below it. You can ignore this for now.

TIP

You need to include your initials in a letter only if you are typing it for someone else.

▶ **5.** Type your first, middle, and last initials in lowercase, and then press the **Enter** key. AutoCorrect wrongly assumes your first initial is the first letter of a new sentence and changes it to uppercase. If your initials do not form a word, a red wavy underline appears beneath them. You can ignore this for now.

▶ **6.** On the Quick Access Toolbar, click the **Undo** button ↺. Word reverses the change, replacing the uppercase initial with a lowercase one.

▶ **7.** Type **Enclosure**. At this point, your screen should look similar to Figure 1-12.

Figure 1-12	Letter to Jayla Brooks

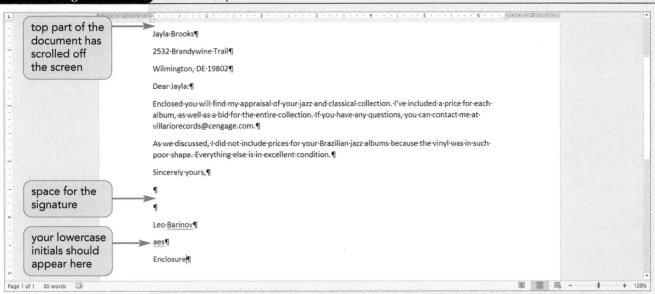

top part of the document has scrolled off the screen

Jayla·Brooks¶

2532·Brandywine·Trail¶

Wilmington,·DE·19802¶

Dear·Jayla:¶

Enclosed·you·will·find·my·appraisal·of·your·jazz·and·classical·collection.·I've·included·a·price·for·each· album,·as·well·as·a·bid·for·the·entire·collection.·If·you·have·any·questions,·you·can·contact·me·at· villariorecords@cengage.com.¶

As·we·discussed,·I·did·not·include·prices·for·your·Brazilian·jazz·albums·because·the·vinyl·was·in·such· poor·shape.·Everything·else·is·in·excellent·condition.¶

Sincerely·yours,¶

space for the signature

¶

¶

Leo·Barinov¶

your lowercase initials should appear here

aes¶

Enclosure¶

Page 1 of 1   85 words   120%

Notice that as you continue to add lines to the letter, the top part of the letter scrolls off the screen. For example, in Figure 1-12, you can no longer see the date.

▶ **8.** Save the document.

Now that you have finished typing the letter, you need to proofread it.

Proofreading a Document

After you finish typing a document, you need to proofread it carefully from start to finish. Part of proofreading a document in Word is removing all wavy underlines, either by correcting the text or by telling Word to ignore the underlined text because it isn't really an error. For example, Leo's last name is marked as an error, when in fact it is spelled correctly. You need to tell Word to ignore "Barinov" wherever it occurs in the letter. You need to do the same for your initials.

To proofread and correct the remaining marked errors in the letter:

▶ **1.** Right-click **Barinov**. A shortcut menu opens.

▶ **2.** On the shortcut menu, click **Ignore All** to indicate that Word should ignore the word "Barinov" each time it occurs in this document. (The Ignore All option can be particularly helpful in a longer document.) The wavy red underline disappears from below Leo's last name.

▶ **3.** If you see a wavy red underline below your initials, right-click your initials. On the shortcut menu, click **Ignore All** to remove the red wavy underline.

▶ **4.** Read the entire letter to proofread it for typing errors. Correct any errors using the techniques you have just learned.

▶ **5.** Save the document.

The text of the letter is finished. Now you need to think about its appearance—that is, you need to think about the document's **formatting**. First, you need to adjust the spacing in the inside address.

Adjusting Paragraph and Line Spacing

When typing a letter, you might need to adjust two types of spacing—paragraph spacing and line spacing. **Paragraph spacing** is the space that appears directly above and below a paragraph. In Word, any text that ends with a paragraph mark symbol (¶) is a paragraph. So, a **paragraph** can be a group of words that is many lines long, a single word, or even a blank line, in which case you see a paragraph mark alone on a single line. Paragraph spacing is measured in points; a **point** is 1/72 of an inch. The default setting for paragraph spacing in Word is 0 points before each paragraph and 8 points after each paragraph. When laying out a complicated document, resist the temptation to simply press the Enter key to insert extra space between paragraphs. Changing the paragraph spacing gives you much more control over the final result.

Line spacing is the space between lines of text within a paragraph. Word offers a number of preset line spacing options. The 1.0 setting, which is often called **single-spacing**, allows the least amount of space between lines. All other line spacing options are measured as multiples of 1.0 spacing. For example, 2.0 spacing (sometimes called **double-spacing**) allows for twice the space of single-spacing. The default line spacing setting is 1.08, which allows a little more space between lines than 1.0 spacing.

Now consider the line and paragraph spacing in the Brooks letter. The three lines of the inside address are too far apart. That's because each line of the inside address is actually a separate paragraph. Word inserted the default 8 points of paragraph spacing after each of these separate paragraphs. See Figure 1-13.

Figure 1-13   Line and paragraph spacing in the letter to Jayla Brooks

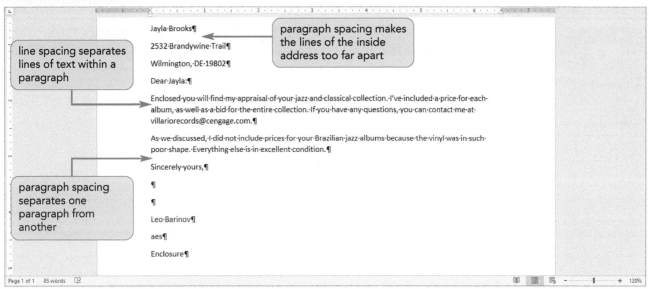

To follow the conventions of a block-style business letter, the three paragraphs that make up the inside address should have the same spacing as the lines of text within a single paragraph—that is, they need to be closer together. You can accomplish this by removing the 8 points of paragraph spacing after the first two paragraphs in the inside address. To conform to the block-style business letter format, you also need to close up the spacing between your initials and the word "Enclosure" at the end of the letter.

To adjust paragraph and line spacing in Word, you use the Line and Paragraph Spacing button in the Paragraph group on the Home tab. Clicking this button displays a menu of preset line spacing options (1.0, 1.15, 2.0, and so on). The menu also includes two paragraph spacing options that allow you to add 12 points before a paragraph or remove the default 8 points of space after a paragraph.

Next you'll adjust the paragraph spacing in the inside address and after your initials. In the process, you'll also learn some techniques for selecting text in a document.

To adjust the paragraph spacing in the inside address and after your initials:

1. Move the pointer to the white space just to the left of "Jayla Brooks" until it changes to a right-facing arrow ⌐.

2. Click the mouse button. The entire name, including the paragraph symbol after it, is selected.

   Trouble? If the Mini toolbar obscures your view of Jayla's name, move the mouse pointer away from the address to close the Mini toolbar.

3. Press and hold the mouse button, drag the pointer ⌐ down to select the next paragraph of the inside address as well, and then release the mouse button.

   The name and street address are selected as well as the paragraph marks at the end of each paragraph. You did not select the paragraph containing the city, state, and ZIP code because you do not need to change its paragraph spacing. See Figure 1-14.

TIP

The white space in the left margin is sometimes referred to as the selection bar because you click it to select text.

Figure 1-14 **Inside address selected**

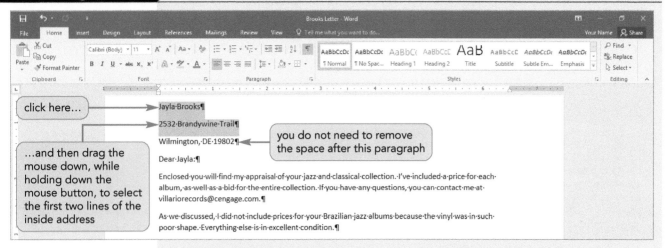

4. Make sure the Home tab is selected on the ribbon.

5. In the Paragraph group on the Home tab, click the **Line and Paragraph Spacing** button. A menu of line spacing options appears, with two paragraph spacing options at the bottom. See Figure 1-15.

Figure 1-15 **Line and paragraph spacing options**

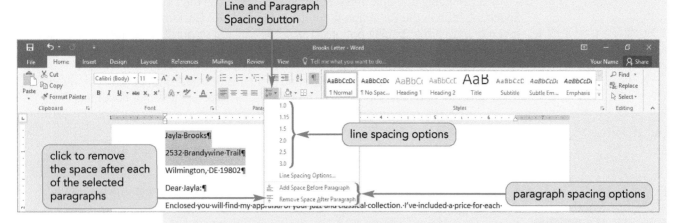

At the moment, you are interested only in the paragraph spacing options. Your goal is to remove the default 8 points of space after the first two paragraphs in the inside address.

6. Click **Remove Space After Paragraph**. The menu closes, and the paragraphs are now closer together.

7. Double-click your initials to select them and the paragraph symbol after them.

8. In the Paragraph group, click the **Line and Paragraph Spacing** button, click **Remove Space After Paragraph**, and then click anywhere in the document to deselect your initials.

Another way to compress lines of text is to press the Shift+Enter keys at the end of a line. This inserts a **manual line break**, also called a **soft return**, which moves the insertion point to a new line without starting a new paragraph. You will use this technique now as you add Leo's title below his name in the signature line.

To use a manual line break to move the insertion point to a new line without starting a new paragraph:

▶ **1.** Click to the right of the "v" in "Barinov."

▶ **2.** Press the **Shift+Enter** keys. Word inserts a small arrow symbol ↵ , indicating a manual line break, and the insertion point moves to the line below Leo's name.

▶ **3.** Type **Purchasing Manager**. Leo's title now appears directly below his name with no intervening paragraph spacing, just like the lines of the inside address.

▶ **4.** Save the document.

INSIGHT

Understanding Spacing Between Paragraphs

When discussing the correct format for letters, many business style guides talk about single-spacing and double-spacing between paragraphs. In these style guides, to single-space between paragraphs means to press the Enter key once after each paragraph. Likewise, to double-space between paragraphs means to press the Enter key twice after each paragraph. With the default paragraph spacing in Word 2016, however, you need to press the Enter key only once after a paragraph. The space Word adds after a paragraph is not quite the equivalent of double-spacing, but it is enough to make it easy to see where one paragraph ends and another begins. Keep this in mind if you're accustomed to pressing the Enter key twice; otherwise, you could end up with more space than you want between paragraphs.

As you corrected line and paragraph spacing in the previous set of steps, you used the mouse to select text. Word provides multiple ways to select, or highlight, text as you work. Figure 1-16 summarizes these methods and explains when to use them most effectively.

| Figure 1-16 | Methods for selecting text |

To Select	Mouse	Keyboard	Mouse and Keyboard
A word	Double-click the word	Move the insertion point to the beginning of the word, press and hold Ctrl+Shift, and then press →	
A line	Click in the white space to the left of the line	Move the insertion point to the beginning of the line, press and hold Shift, and then press ↓	
A sentence	Click at the beginning of the sentence, then drag the pointer until the sentence is selected		Press and hold Ctrl, then click any location within the sentence
Multiple lines	Click and drag in the white space to the left of the lines	Move the insertion point to the beginning of the first line, press and hold Shift, and then press ↓ until all the lines are selected	
A paragraph	Double-click in the white space to the left of the paragraph, or triple-click at any location within the paragraph	Move the insertion point to the beginning of the paragraph, press and hold Ctrl+Shift, and then press ↓	
Multiple paragraphs	Click in the white space to the left of the first paragraph you want to select, and then drag to select the remaining paragraphs	Move the insertion point to the beginning of the first paragraph, press and hold Ctrl+Shift, and then press ↓ until all the paragraphs are selected	
An entire document	Triple-click in the white space to the left of the document text	Press Ctrl+A	Press and hold Ctrl, and click in the white space to the left of the document text
A block of text	Click at the beginning of the block, then drag the pointer until the entire block is selected		Click at the beginning of the block, press and hold Shift, and then click at the end of the block
Nonadjacent blocks of text			Press and hold Ctrl, then drag the mouse pointer to select multiple blocks of nonadjacent text

Adjusting the Margins

Another important aspect of document formatting is the amount of margin space between the document text and the edge of the page. You can check the document's margins by changing the Zoom level to display the entire page.

To change the Zoom level to display the entire page:

1. On the ribbon, click the **View** tab.

2. In the Zoom group, click the **One Page** button. The entire document is now visible in the Word window. See Figure 1-17.

Figure 1-17   Document zoomed to show entire page

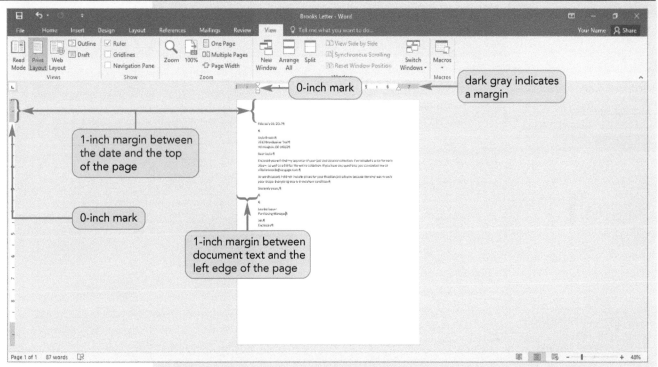

On the rulers, the margins appear dark gray. By default, Word documents include 1-inch margins on all sides of the document. By looking at the vertical ruler, you can see that the date in the letter, the first line in the document, is located 1 inch from the top of the page. Likewise, the horizontal ruler indicates the document text begins 1 inch from the left edge of the page.

Reading the measurements on the rulers can be tricky at first. On the horizontal ruler, the 0-inch mark is like the origin on a number line. You measure from the 0-inch mark to the left or to the right. On the vertical ruler, you measure up or down from the 0-inch mark.

Leo plans to print the letter on Villa Rio Records letterhead, which includes a graphic and the company's address. To allow more blank space for the letterhead, and to move the text down so that it doesn't look so crowded at the top of the page, you need to increase the top margin. The settings for changing the page margins are located on the Layout tab on the ribbon.

To change the page margins:

1. On the ribbon, click the **Layout** tab. The Layout tab displays options for adjusting the layout of your document.

2. In the Page Setup group, click the **Margins** button. The Margins gallery opens, as shown in Figure 1-18.

Figure 1-18 | **Margins gallery**

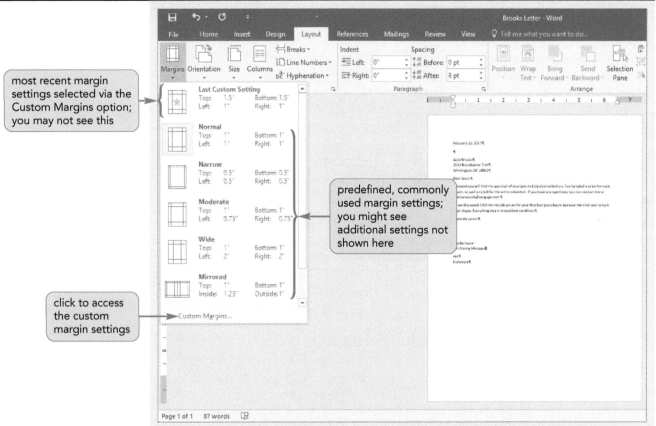

most recent margin settings selected via the Custom Margins option; you may not see this

predefined, commonly used margin settings; you might see additional settings not shown here

click to access the custom margin settings

In the Margins gallery, you can choose from a number of predefined margin options, or you can click the Custom Margins command to select your own settings. After you create custom margin settings, the most recent set appears as an option at the top of the menu. For the Brooks Letter document, you will create custom margins.

3. Click **Custom Margins**. The Page Setup dialog box opens with the Margins tab displayed. The default margin settings are displayed in the boxes at the top of the Margins tab. The top margin of 1" is already selected, ready for you to type a new margin setting.

4. In the Top box in the Margins section, type **2.5**. You do not need to type an inch mark ("). See Figure 1-19.

Figure 1-19	Creating custom margins in the Page Setup dialog box

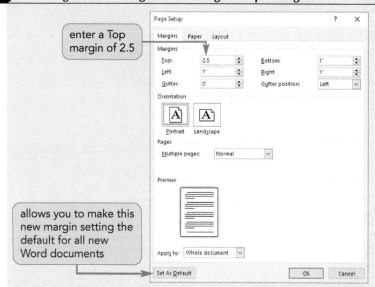

enter a Top margin of 2.5

allows you to make this new margin setting the default for all new Word documents

▶ **5.** Click the **OK** button. The text of the letter is now lower on the page. The page looks less crowded, with room for the company's letterhead.

▶ **6.** Change the Zoom level back to **120%**, and then save the document.

For most documents, the Word default of 1-inch margins is fine. In some professional settings, however, you might need to use a particular custom margin setting for all your documents. In that case, define the custom margins using the Margins tab in the Page Setup dialog box, and then click the Set As Default button to make your settings the default for all new documents. Keep in mind that most printers can't print to the edge of the page; if you select custom margins that are too narrow for your printer's specifications, Word alerts you to change your margin settings.

Previewing and Printing a Document

To make sure the document is ready to print, and to avoid wasting paper and time, you should first review it in Backstage view to make sure it will look right when printed. Like the One Page zoom setting you used earlier, the Print option in Backstage view displays a full-page preview of the document, allowing you to see how it will fit on the printed page. However, you cannot actually edit this preview. It simply provides one last opportunity to look at the document before printing.

To preview the document:

▶ **1.** Proofread the document one last time, and correct any remaining errors.

▶ **2.** Click the **File** tab to display Backstage view.

▶ **3.** In the navigation bar, click **Print**.

The Print screen displays a full-page version of your document, showing how the letter will fit on the printed page. The Print settings to the left of the preview allow you to control a variety of print options. For example, you can change the number of copies from the default setting of "1." The 1 Page Per Sheet button opens a menu where you can choose to print multiple pages on a single sheet of paper or to scale the printed page to a particular paper size. You can also use the navigation controls at the bottom of the screen to display other pages in a document. See Figure 1-20.

Figure 1-20   **Print settings in Backstage view**

click to close Backstage view and return to the document

click when you are ready to print

in a multipage document, click to display subsequent pages

click to open a menu where you can choose to print multiple pages on a single sheet of paper or to scale the printed page to a particular paper size

specify the number of copies here

preview of the page when printed

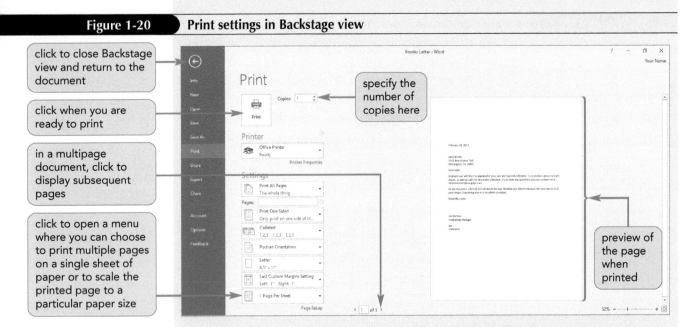

▶ **4.** Review your document and make sure its overall layout matches that of the document in Figure 1-20. If you notice a problem with paragraph breaks or spacing, click the **Back** button ⬅ at the top of the navigation bar to return to the document, make any necessary changes, and then start again at Step 2.

At this point, you can print the document or you can leave Backstage view and return to the document in Print Layout view. In the following steps, you should print the document only if your instructor asks you to. If you will be printing the document, make sure your printer is turned on and contains paper.

To leave Backstage view or to print the document:

▶ **1.** Click the **Back** button at the top of the navigation bar ⬅ to leave Backstage view and return to the document in Print Layout view, or click the **Print** button. Backstage view closes, and the letter prints if you clicked the Print button.

▶ **2.** Click the **File** tab, and then click **Close** in the navigation bar to close the document without closing Word.

Next, Leo asks you to create an envelope he can use to send an appraisal to another potential record seller.

Creating an Envelope

Before you can create the envelope, you need to open a new, blank document. To create a new document, you can start with a blank document—as you did with the letter to Jayla Brooks—or you can start with one that already contains formatting and generic text commonly used in a variety of professional documents, such as a fax cover sheet or a memo. These preformatted files are called **templates**. You could use a template to create a formatted envelope, but first you'll learn how to create one on your own in a new, blank document. You'll have a chance to try out a template in the Case Problems at the end of this module.

To create a new document for the envelope:

1. Click the **File** tab, and then click **New** in the navigation bar. The New screen is similar to the one you saw when you first started Word, with a blank document in the upper-left corner, along with a variety of templates. See Figure 1-21.

Figure 1-21	New options in Backstage view

use this search box to find even more templates online

click to open a document that describes Word's features

click to create a blank document

document templates; your list of available templates may differ

scroll down to see more templates

2. Click **Blank document**. A new document named Document2 opens in the document window, with the Home tab selected on the ribbon.

3. If necessary, change the Zoom level to **120%**, and display nonprinting characters and the rulers.

4. Save the new document as **Gomez Envelope** in the location specified by your instructor.

To create the envelope:

1. On the ribbon, click the **Mailings** tab. The ribbon changes to display the various Mailings options.

2. In the Create group, click the **Envelopes** button. The Envelopes and Labels dialog box opens, with the Envelopes tab displayed. The insertion point appears in the Delivery address box, ready for you to type the recipient's address. Depending on how your computer is set up, and whether you are working on your own computer or a school computer, you might see an address in the Return address box.

3. In the Delivery address box, type the following address, pressing the Enter key to start each new line:

Alexis Gomez

6549 West 16th Street

Wilmington, DE 19806

Because Leo will be using the store's printed envelopes, you don't need to print a return address on this envelope.

4. Click the **Omit** check box to insert a checkmark, if necessary.

At this point, if you had a printer stocked with envelopes, you could click the Print button to print the envelope. To save an envelope for printing later, you need to add it to the document. Your Envelopes and Labels dialog box should match the one in Figure 1-22.

| Figure 1-22 | Envelopes and Labels dialog box |

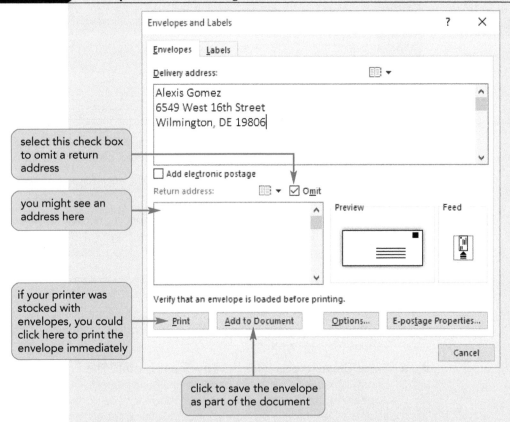

select this check box to omit a return address

you might see an address here

if your printer was stocked with envelopes, you could click here to print the envelope immediately

click to save the envelope as part of the document

5. Click the **Add to Document** button. The dialog box closes, and you return to the document window. The envelope is inserted at the top of your document, with 1.0 line spacing. The double line with the words "Section Break (Next Page)" is related to how the envelope is formatted and will not be visible when you print the envelope. The envelope will print in the standard business envelope format. In this case, you added the envelope to a blank document, but you could also add an envelope to a completed letter, in which case Word adds the envelope as a new page before the letter.

6. Save the document. Leo will print the envelope later, so you can close the document now.

7. Click the **File** tab, and then click **Close** in the navigation bar. The document closes, but Word remains open.

You're finished creating the cover letter and the envelope. In the next session, you will modify a flyer by formatting the text and adding a photo.

INSIGHT

Creating Documents with Templates

Microsoft offers predesigned templates for all kinds of documents, including calendars, reports, and thank-you cards. You can use the scroll bar on the right of the New screen (shown earlier in Figure 1-21) to scroll down to see more templates, or you can use the Search for online templates box in the New screen to search among thousands of other options available at Office.com. When you open a template, you actually open a new document containing the formatting and text stored in the template, leaving the original template untouched. A typical template includes placeholder text that you replace with your own information.

Templates allow you to create stylish, professional-looking documents quickly and easily. To use them effectively, however, you need to be knowledgeable about Word and its many options for manipulating text, graphics, and page layouts. Otherwise, the complicated formatting of some Word templates can be more frustrating than helpful. As you become a more experienced Word user, you'll learn how to create your own templates.

REVIEW

Session 1.1 Quick Check

1. What Word feature automatically inserts dates and other regularly used items for you?

2. In a block-style letter, does the inside address appear above or below the date?

3. Explain how to display nonprinting characters.

4. Explain how to use a hyperlink in a Word document to open a new email message.

5. Define the term "line spacing."

6. Explain how to display a shortcut menu with options for correcting a word with a wavy red underline.

Session 1.2 Visual Overview:

Alignment buttons control the text's alignment—that is, the way it lines up horizontally between the left and right margins. Here, the Center button is selected because the text containing the insertion point is center-aligned.

You can click the Clear All Formatting button to restore selected text to the default font, font size, and color.

Clicking the Format Painter button displays the Format Painter pointer, which you can use to copy formatting from the selected text to other text in the document.

The Font group on the Home tab includes the Font box and the Font size box for setting the text's font and the font size, respectively. A font is a set of characters that uses the same typeface.

This document has a landscape orientation, meaning it is wider than it is tall.

You can insert a photo or another type of picture in a document by using the Pictures button located on the Insert tab of the ribbon. After you insert a photo or another picture, you can format it with a style that adds a border or a shadow or changes its shape.

You click the Shading button arrow to apply a colored background to a selected paragraph.

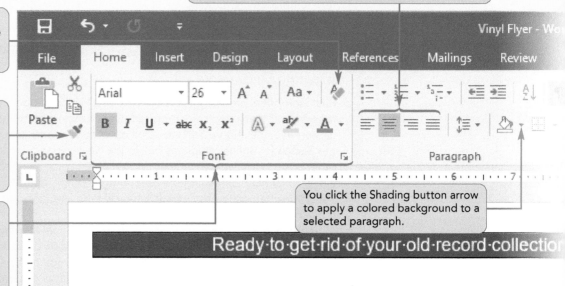

Ready·to·get·rid·of·your·old·record·collection

Villa·Rio·Records·pays·cash·for·used

We'll·come·to·your·home.¶

No·collection·is·too·small·or·too·large!

Contact·Leo·Barinov·at·villariorecords@cengage.co

The boldface and blue font color applied to this text are examples of formatting that you should use sparingly to draw attention to a specific part of a document.

Page 1 of 1   1 of 36 words

Formatting a Document

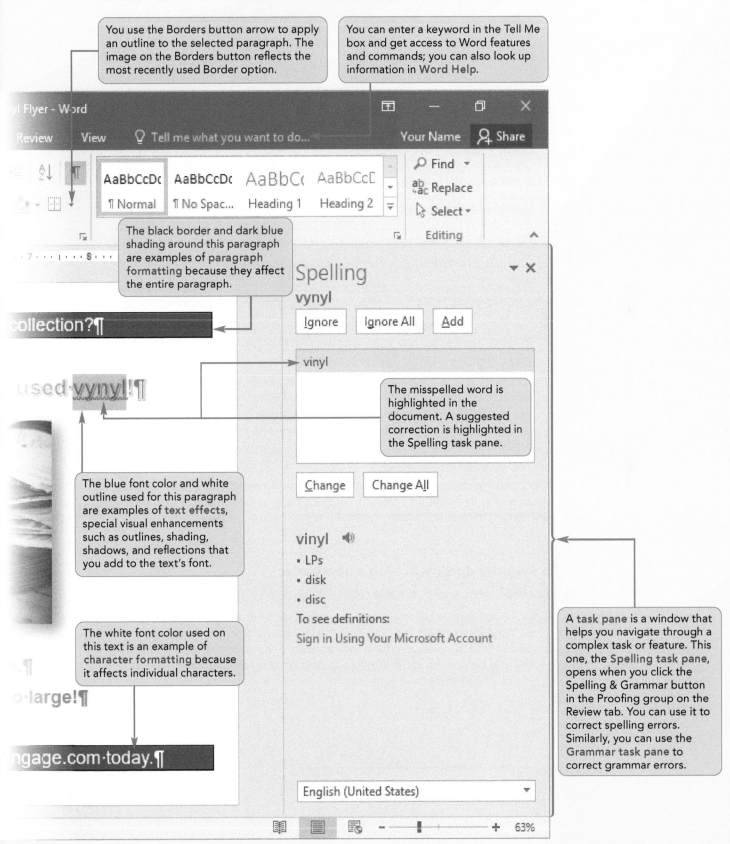

You use the Borders button arrow to apply an outline to the selected paragraph. The image on the Borders button reflects the most recently used Border option.

You can enter a keyword in the Tell Me box and get access to Word features and commands; you can also look up information in Word Help.

The black border and dark blue shading around this paragraph are examples of paragraph formatting because they affect the entire paragraph.

The blue font color and white outline used for this paragraph are examples of text effects, special visual enhancements such as outlines, shading, shadows, and reflections that you add to the text's font.

The white font color used on this text is an example of character formatting because it affects individual characters.

The misspelled word is highlighted in the document. A suggested correction is highlighted in the Spelling task pane.

A task pane is a window that helps you navigate through a complex task or feature. This one, the Spelling task pane, opens when you click the Spelling & Grammar button in the Proofing group on the Review tab. You can use it to correct spelling errors. Similarly, you can use the Grammar task pane to correct grammar errors.

Opening an Existing Document

In this session, you'll complete a flyer reminding customers that Villa Rio Records buys old record collections. Leo has already typed the text of the flyer, inserted a photo into it, and saved it as a Word document. He would like you to check the document for spelling and grammar errors, format the flyer to make it eye-catching and easy to read, and then replace the current photo with a new one. You'll start by opening the document.

To open the flyer document:

▶ **1.** On the ribbon, click the **File** tab to open Backstage view, and then verify that **Open** is selected in the navigation bar. On the left side of the Open screen is a list of places you can go to locate other documents, and on the right is a list of recently opened documents.

   Trouble? If you closed Word at the end of the previous session, start Word now, click Open Other Documents at the bottom of the navigation bar in Backstage view, and then begin with Step 2.

▶ **2.** Click the **Browse** button. The Open dialog box opens.

   Trouble? If your instructor asked you to store your files to your OneDrive account, click OneDrive - Personal, and then log in to your account.

▶ **3.** Navigate to the **Word1 > Module folder** included with your Data Files, click **Vinyl** in the file list, and then click the **Open** button. The document opens with the insertion point blinking in the first line of the document.

   Trouble? If you don't have the starting Data Files, you need to get them before you can proceed. Your instructor will either give you the Data Files or ask you to obtain them from a specified location (such as a network drive). If you have any questions about the Data Files, see your instructor or technical support person for assistance.

Before making changes to Leo's document, you will save it with a new name. Saving the document with a different filename creates a copy of the file and leaves the original file unchanged in case you want to work through the module again.

To save the document with a new name:

▶ **1.** On the ribbon, click the **File** tab.

▶ **2.** In the navigation bar in Backstage view, click **Save As**. Save the document as **Vinyl Flyer** in the location specified by your instructor. Backstage view closes, and the document window appears again with the new filename in the title bar. The original Vinyl document closes, remaining unchanged.

PROSKILLS

Decision Making: Creating Effective Documents

Before you create a new document or revise an existing document, take a moment to think about your audience. Ask yourself these questions:

- Who is your audience?
- What do they know?
- What do they need to know?
- How can the document you are creating change your audience's behavior or opinions?

Every decision you make about your document should be based on your answers to these questions. To take a simple example, if you are creating a flyer to announce an upcoming seminar on college financial aid, your audience would be students and their parents. They probably all know what the term "financial aid" means, so you don't need to explain that in your flyer. Instead, you can focus on telling them what they need to know—the date, time, and location of the seminar. The behavior you want to affect, in this case, is whether or not your audience will show up for the seminar. By making the flyer professional looking and easy to read, you increase the chance that they will.

You might find it more challenging to answer these questions about your audience when creating more complicated documents, such as corporate reports. But the focus remains the same—connecting with the audience. As you are deciding what information to include in your document, remember that the goal of a professional document is to convey the information as effectively as possible to your target audience.

Before revising a document for someone else, it's a good idea to familiarize yourself with its overall structure.

To review the document:

1. Verify that the document is displayed in Print Layout view and that nonprinting characters and the rulers are displayed. For now, you can ignore the wavy underlines that appear in the document.

2. Change the Zoom level to **120%**, if necessary, and then scroll down, if necessary, so that you can read the last line of the document.

   At this point, the document is very simple. By the time you are finished, it will look like the document shown in the Session 1.2 Visual Overview, with the spelling and grammar errors corrected. Figure 1-23 summarizes the tasks you will perform.

Figure 1-23 Formatting changes requested by Leo

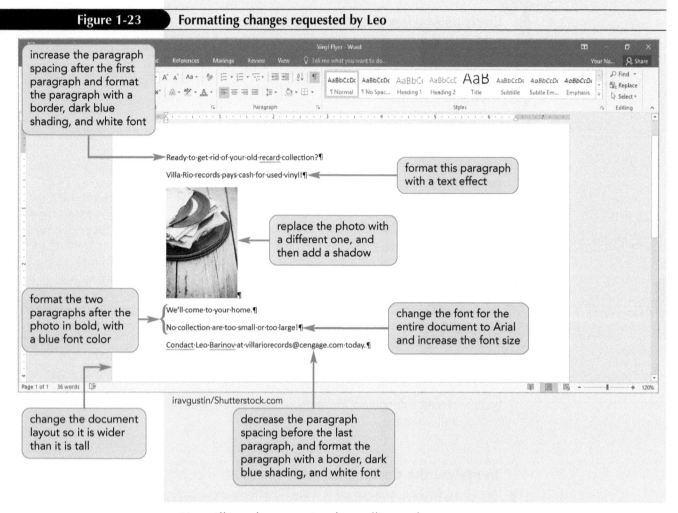

iravgustin/Shutterstock.com

You will start by correcting the spelling and grammar errors.

Using the Spelling and Grammar Task Panes

Word marks possible spelling and grammatical errors with wavy underlines as you type so that you can quickly go back and correct those errors. A more thorough way of checking the spelling in a document is to use the Spelling and Grammar task panes to check a document word by word for a variety of errors. You can customize the spelling and grammar settings to add or ignore certain types of errors.

Leo asks you to use the Spelling and Grammar task panes to check the flyer for mistakes. Before you do, you'll review the various Spelling and Grammar settings.

To review the Spelling and Grammar settings:

▶ 1. On the ribbon, click the **File** tab, and then click **Options** in the navigation bar. The Word Options dialog box opens. You can use this dialog box to change a variety of settings related to how Word looks and works.

2. In the left pane, click **Proofing**.

Note the four selected options in the "When correcting spelling and grammar in Word" section. The first three options tell you that Word will check for misspellings, grammatical errors, and frequently confused words as you type, marking them with wavy underlines as necessary. The fourth option, "Check grammar with spelling," tells you that Word will check both grammar and spelling when you use the Spelling and Grammar task pane. If you want to check only spelling, you could deselect this check box.

3. In the "When correcting spelling and grammar in Word" section, click the **Settings** button. The Grammar Settings dialog box opens. Here you can control the types of grammar errors Word checks for. All of the boxes are selected by default, which is what you want. See Figure 1-24.

| Figure 1-24 | Grammar Settings dialog box |

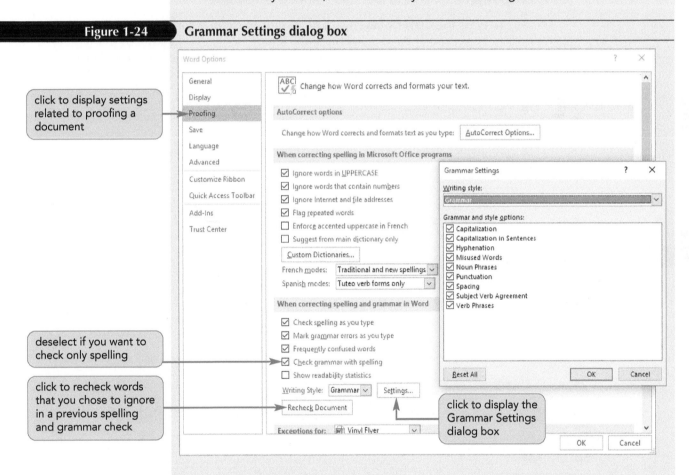

click to display settings related to proofing a document

deselect if you want to check only spelling

click to recheck words that you chose to ignore in a previous spelling and grammar check

click to display the Grammar Settings dialog box

4. Click the **Cancel** button to close the Grammar Settings dialog box and return to the Word Options dialog box.

Note that the results of the Spelling and Grammar checker are sometimes hard to predict. For example, in some documents Word will mark a misused word or duplicate punctuation as errors and then fail to mark the same items as errors in another document. Also, if you choose to ignore a misspelling in a document, and then, without closing Word, type the same misspelled word in another document, Word will probably not mark it as an error. These issues can be especially problematic when working on a document typed by someone else. So to ensure that you get the best possible results, it's a good idea to click the Recheck Document button before you use the Spelling and Grammar checker.

5. Click the **Recheck Document** button, and then click **Yes** in the warning dialog box.

6. In the Word Options dialog box, click the **OK** button to close the dialog box. You return to the Vinyl Flyer document.

Now you are ready to check the document's spelling and grammar. All errors marked with red underlines are considered spelling errors, while all errors marked with blue underlines are considered grammatical errors.

To check the Vinyl Flyer document for spelling and grammatical errors:

1. Press the **Ctrl+Home** keys, if necessary, to move the insertion point to the beginning of the document, to the left of the "R" in "Ready." By placing the insertion point at the beginning of the document, you ensure that Word will check the entire document from start to finish, without having to go back and check an earlier part.

2. On the ribbon, click the **Review** tab. The ribbon changes to display reviewing options.

3. In the Proofing group, click the **Spelling & Grammar** button.

The Spelling task pane opens on the right side of the Word window, with the word "recard" listed as a possible spelling error. The same word is highlighted in gray in the document. In the task pane's list of possible corrections, the correctly spelled word "record" is highlighted in light blue. See Figure 1-25.

Figure 1-25	Spelling task pane

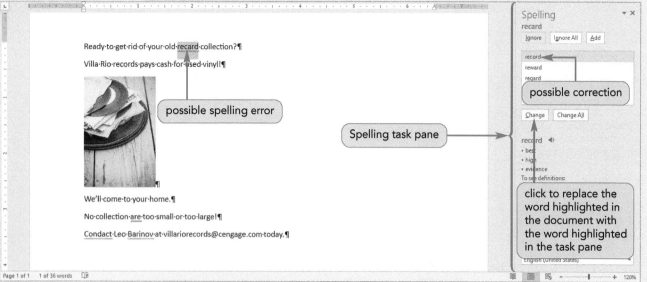

iravgustin/Shutterstock.com

4. In the task pane, click the **Change** button. The misspelled word "recard" is replaced with "record."

Next, Word highlights the second to last sentence, indicating another possible error. The Spelling task pane changes to the Grammar task pane, and the information at the bottom of the task pane explains that the error is related to subject-verb agreement.

5. Verify that "is" is selected in the Grammar task pane, and then click the **Change** button. The first word of the last sentence is now highlighted in the document, and the Grammar task pane changes to the Spelling task pane. You could correct this misspelling by using the options in the Spelling task pane, but this time you'll try typing directly in the document.

6. In the document, click to the right of the "d" in "Condact," press the **Backspace** key, type **t**, and then click the **Resume** button in the Spelling task pane. Leo's last name is now highlighted in the document. Although the Spelling task pane doesn't recognize "Barinov" as a word, it is spelled correctly, so you can ignore it.

7. Click the **Ignore** button in the Spelling task pane. The task pane closes, and a dialog box opens, indicating that the spelling and grammar check is complete.

8. Click the **OK** button to close the dialog box.

PROSKILLS

Written Communication: Proofreading Your Document

Although the Spelling and Grammar task panes are useful tools, they won't always catch every error in a document, and they sometimes flag "errors" that are actually correct. This means there is no substitute for careful proofreading. Always take the time to read through your document to check for errors the Spelling and Grammar task panes might have missed. Keep in mind that the Spelling and Grammar task panes cannot pinpoint inaccurate phrases or poorly chosen words. You'll have to find those yourself. To produce a professional document, you must read it carefully several times. It's a good idea to ask one or two other people to read your documents as well; they might catch something you missed.

You still need to proofread the Vinyl Flyer document. You'll do that next.

To proofread the Vinyl Flyer document:

1. Review the document text for any remaining errors. In the second paragraph, change the lowercase "r" in "records" to an uppercase "R."

2. In the last line of text, replace "Leo Barinov" with your first and last names, and then save the document. Including your name in the document will make it easier for you to find your copy later if you print it on a shared printer.

Now you're ready to begin formatting the document. You will start by turning the page so it is wider than it is tall. In other words, you will change the document's **orientation**.

Changing Page Orientation

Portrait orientation, with the page taller than it is wide, is the default page orientation for Word documents because it is the orientation most commonly used for letters, reports, and other formal documents. However, Leo wants you to format the flyer in **landscape orientation**—that is, with the page turned so it is wider than it is tall—to better accommodate the photo. You can accomplish this task by using the Orientation button located on the Layout tab on the ribbon. After you change the page orientation, you will select narrower margins so you can maximize the amount of color on the page.

To change the page orientation:

▸ **1.** Change the document Zoom level to **One Page** so that you can see the entire document.

▸ **2.** On the ribbon, click the **Layout** tab. The ribbon changes to display options for formatting the overall layout of text and images in the document.

▸ **3.** In the Page Setup group, click the **Orientation** button, and then click **Landscape** on the menu. The document changes to landscape orientation.

▸ **4.** In the Page Setup group, click the **Margins** button, and then click the **Narrow** option on the menu. The margins shrink from 1 inch to .5 inch on all four sides. See Figure 1-26.

| Figure 1-26 | Document in landscape orientation with narrow margins |

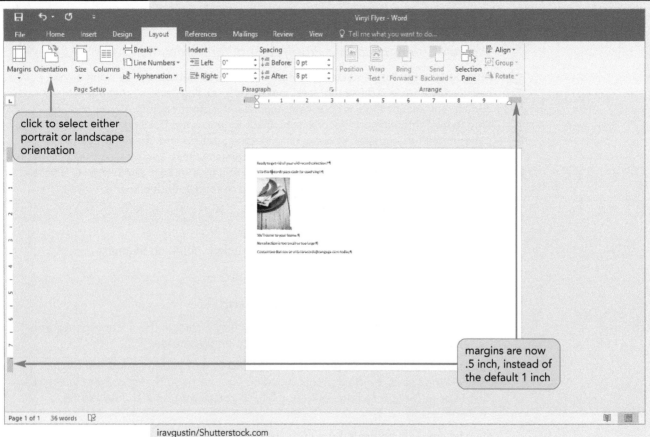

click to select either portrait or landscape orientation

margins are now .5 inch, instead of the default 1 inch

iravgustin/Shutterstock.com

Changing the Font and Font Size

Leo typed the document in the default font size, 11 point, and the default font, Calibri, but he would like to switch to the Arial font instead. Also, he wants to increase the size of all five paragraphs of text. To apply these changes, you start by selecting the text you want to format. Then you select the options you want in the Font group on the Home tab.

To change the font and font size:

▶ **1.** On the ribbon, click the **Home** tab.

▶ **2.** Change the document Zoom level to **120%**.

▶ **3.** To verify that the insertion point is located at the beginning of the document, press the **Ctrl+Home** keys.

▶ **4.** Press and hold the **Shift** key, and then click to the right of the second paragraph marker, at the end of the second paragraph of text. The first two paragraphs of text are selected, as shown in Figure 1-27.

| **Figure 1-27** | Selected text, with default font displayed in Font box |

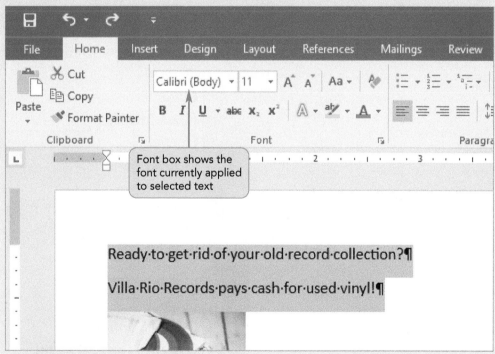

iravgustin/Shutterstock.com

The Font box in the Font group displays the name of the font applied to the selected text, which in this case is Calibri. The word "Body" next to the font name indicates that the Calibri font is intended for formatting body text. **Body text** is ordinary text, as opposed to titles or headings.

▶ **5.** In the Font group on the Home tab, click the **Font** arrow. A list of available fonts appears, with Calibri Light and Calibri at the top of the list. Calibri is highlighted in gray, indicating that this font is currently applied to the selected text. The word "Headings" next to the font name "Calibri Light" indicates that Calibri Light is intended for formatting headings.

Below Calibri Light and Calibri, you might see a list of fonts that have been used recently on your computer, followed by a complete alphabetical list of all available fonts. (You won't see the list of recently used fonts if you just installed Word.) You need to scroll the list to see all the available fonts. Each name in the list is formatted with the relevant font. For example, the name "Arial" appears in the Arial font. See Figure 1-28.

Figure 1-28   **Font list**

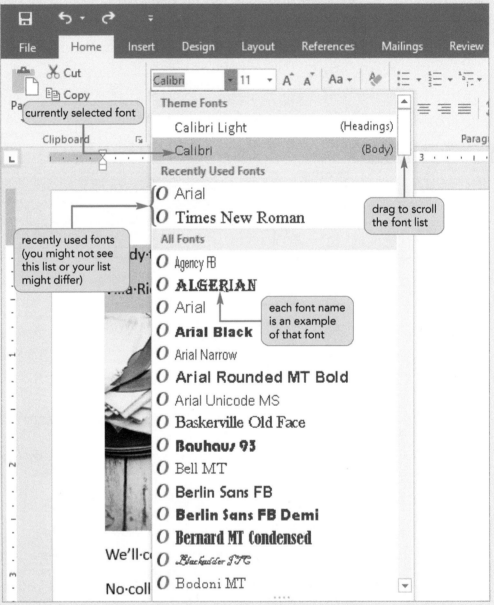

iravgustin/Shutterstock.com

▶ **6.** Without clicking, move the pointer over a dramatic-looking font in the font list, such as Algerian or Arial Black, and then move the pointer over another font.

The selected text in the document changes to show a Live Preview of the font the pointer is resting on. **Live Preview** shows the results that would occur in your document if you clicked the option you are pointing to.

> **7.** When you are finished reviewing the Font list, click **Arial**. The Font menu closes, and the selected text is formatted in Arial.
>
>   Next, you will make the text more eye-catching by increasing the font size. The Font Size box currently displays the number "11," indicating that the selected text is formatted in 11-point font.
>
> **8.** Verify that the first two paragraphs are still selected, and then click the **Font Size** arrow in the Font group to display a menu of font sizes. As with the Font menu, you can move the pointer over options in the Font Size menu to see a Live Preview of that option.
>
> **9.** On the Font Size menu, click **22**. The selected text increases significantly in size, and the Font Size menu closes.
>
> **10.** Select the three paragraphs of text below the photo, format them in the Arial font, and then increase the paragraph's font size to 22 points.
>
> **11.** Click a blank area of the document to deselect the text, and then save the document.

TIP

To restore selected text to its default appearance, click the Clear All Formatting button in the Font group on the Home tab.

Leo examines the flyer and decides he would like to apply more character formatting, which affects the appearance of individual characters, in the middle three paragraphs. After that, you can turn your attention to paragraph formatting, which affects the appearance of the entire paragraph.

Applying Text Effects, Font Colors, and Font Styles

To really make text stand out, you can use text effects. You access these options by clicking the Text Effects and Typography button in the Font group on the Home tab. Keep in mind that text effects can be very dramatic. For formal, professional documents, you probably need to use only **bold** or *italic* to make a word or paragraph stand out.

Leo suggests applying text effects to the second paragraph.

To apply text effects to the second paragraph:

> **1.** Scroll up, if necessary, to display the beginning of the document, and then click in the selection bar to the left of the second paragraph. The entire second paragraph is selected.
>
> **2.** In the Font group on the Home tab, click the **Text Effects and Typography** button A·.
>
>   A gallery of text effects appears. Options that allow you to fine-tune a particular text effect, perhaps by changing the color or adding an even more pronounced shadow, are listed below the gallery. A **gallery** is a menu or grid that shows a visual representation of the options available when you click a button.
>
> **3.** In the middle of the bottom row of the gallery, place the pointer over the blue letter "A." This displays a ScreenTip with the text effect's full name: Fill - Blue, Accent 1, Outline - Background 1, Hard Shadow - Accent 1. A Live Preview of the effect appears in the document. See Figure 1-29.

| Figure 1-29 | Live Preview of a text effect |

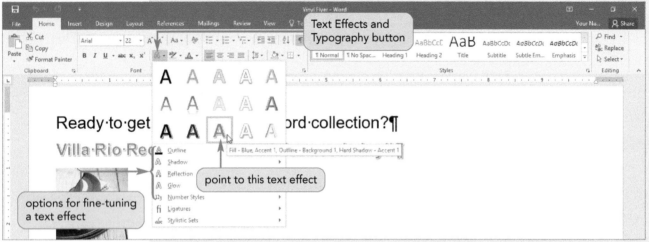

iravgustin/Shutterstock.com

4. In the bottom row of the gallery, click the blue letter "A." The text effect is applied to the selected paragraph and the Text Effects gallery closes. The second paragraph is formatted in blue, as shown in the Session 1.2 Visual Overview. On the ribbon, the Bold button in the Font group is now highlighted because bold formatting is part of this text effect.

Next, to make the text stand out a bit more, you'll increase the font size. This time, instead of using the Font Size button, you'll use a different method.

5. In the Font group, click the **Increase Font Size button** $A^{\cdot}$. The font size increases from 22 points to 24 points.

6. Click the **Increase Font Size button** $A^{\cdot}$ again. The font size increases to 26 points. If you need to decrease the font size of selected text, you can use the Decrease Font Size button.

Leo asks you to emphasize the third and fourth paragraphs by adding bold and a blue font color.

To apply a font color and bold:

1. Select the third and fourth paragraphs of text, which contain the text "We'll come to your home. No collection is too small or too large!"

2. In the Font group on the Home tab, click the **Font Color button arrow** $\underline{A}^{\cdot}$. A gallery of font colors appears. Black is the default font color and appears at the top of the Font Color gallery, with the word "Automatic" next to it.

The options in the Theme Colors section of the menu are complementary colors that work well when used together in a document. The options in the Standard Colors section are more limited. For more advanced color options, you could use the More Colors or Gradient options. Leo prefers a simple blue.

Trouble? If the third and fourth paragraphs turned red, you clicked the Font Color button $\underline{A}$ instead of the arrow next to it. On the Quick Access Toolbar, click the Undo button $\circlearrowleft$, and then repeat Step 2.

3. In the Theme Colors section, place the mouse pointer over the square that's second from the right in the top row. A ScreenTip with the color's name, "Blue, Accent 5," appears. A Live Preview of the color appears in the document, where the text you selected in Step 1 now appears formatted in blue. See Figure 1-30.

| Figure 1-30 | Font Color gallery showing a Live Preview |

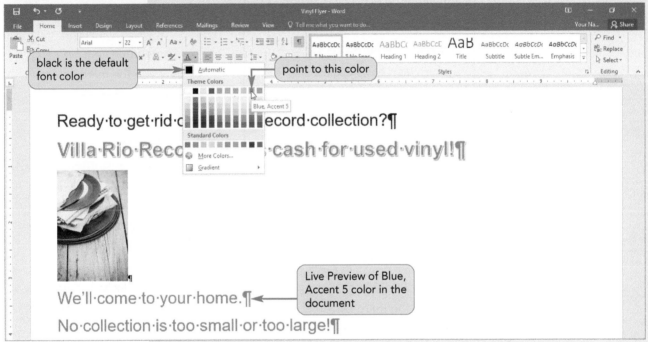

iravgustin/Shutterstock.com

4. Click the **Blue, Accent 5** square. The Font color gallery closes, and the selected text is formatted in blue. On the Font Color button, the bar below the letter "A" is now blue, indicating that if you select text and click the Font Color button, the text will automatically change to blue.

5. In the Font group, click the **Bold** button **B**. The selected text is now formatted in bold, with thicker, darker lettering.

TIP

You can use other buttons in the Font group on the Home tab to apply other character attributes, such as underline, italic, or superscript.

Next, you will complete some paragraph formatting, starting with paragraph alignment.

Aligning Text

Alignment refers to how text and graphics line up between the page margins. By default, Word aligns text along the left margin, with the text along the right margin **ragged**, or uneven. This is called **left alignment**. With **right alignment**, the text is aligned along the right margin and is ragged along the left margin. With **center alignment**, text is centered between the left and right margins and is ragged along both the left and right margins. With **justified alignment**, full lines of text are spaced between both the left and the right margins, and no text is ragged. Text in newspaper columns is often justified. See Figure 1-31.

Figure 1-31   **Varieties of text alignment**

left alignment

The term "alignment" refers to the way a paragraph lines up between the margins. The term "alignment" refers to the way a paragraph lines up between the margins.

right alignment

The term "alignment" refers to the way a paragraph lines up between the margins. The term "alignment" refers to the way a paragraph lines up between the margins.

center alignment

The term "alignment" refers to the way a paragraph lines up between the margins.

justified alignment

The term "alignment" refers to the way a paragraph lines up between the margins. The term "alignment" refers to the way a paragraph lines up between the margins.

The Paragraph group on the Home tab includes a button for each of the four major types of alignment described in Figure 1-31: the Align Left button, the Center button, the Align Right button, and the Justify button. To align a single paragraph, click anywhere in that paragraph, and then click the appropriate alignment button. To align multiple paragraphs, select the paragraphs first, and then click an alignment button.

You need to center all the text in the flyer now. You can center the photo at the same time.

To center-align the text:

1. Make sure the Home tab is still selected, and press the **Ctrl+A** keys to select the entire document.

2. In the Paragraph group, click the **Center** button ≡, and then click a blank area of the document to deselect the selected paragraphs. The text and photo are now centered on the page, similar to the centered text shown earlier in the Session 1.2 Visual Overview.

3. Save the document.

Use the Ctrl+A keys to select the entire document, instead of dragging the mouse pointer. It's easy to miss part of the document when you drag the mouse pointer.

Adding a Paragraph Border and Shading

A **paragraph border** is an outline that appears around one or more paragraphs in a document. You can choose to apply only a partial border—for example, a bottom border that appears as an underline under the last line of text in the paragraph—or an entire box around a paragraph. You can select different colors and line weights for the border as well, making it more or less prominent as needed. You apply paragraph borders using the Borders button in the Paragraph group on the Home tab. **Shading** is background color that you can apply to one or more paragraphs and can be used in conjunction with a border for a more defined effect. You apply shading using the Shading button in the Paragraph group on the Home tab.

Now you will apply a border and shading to the first paragraph, as shown earlier in the Session 1.2 Visual Overview. Then you will use the Format Painter to copy this formatting to the last paragraph in the document.

To add shading and a paragraph border:

1. Select the first paragraph. Be sure to select the paragraph mark at the end of the paragraph.

2. On the Home tab, in the Paragraph group, click the **Borders button arrow** . A gallery of border options appears, as shown in Figure 1-32. To apply a complete outline around the selected text, you use the Outside Borders option.

Figure 1-32	Border gallery

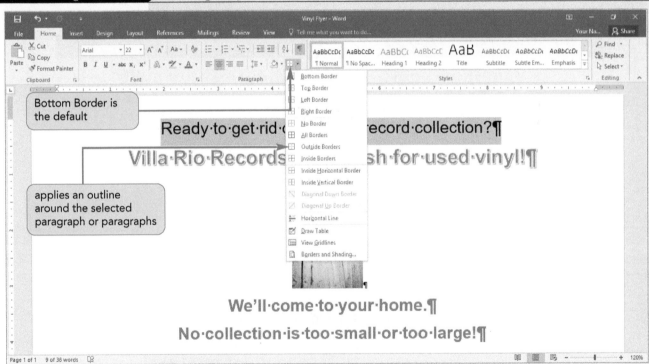

iravgustin/Shutterstock.com

Trouble? If the gallery does not open and instead the paragraph becomes underlined with a single underline, you clicked the Borders button ⊞ instead of the arrow next to it. On the Quick Access Toolbar, click the Undo button ↺, and then repeat Step 2.

3. In the Border gallery, click **Outside Borders**. The menu closes and a black border appears around the selected paragraph, spanning the width of the page. In the Paragraph group, the Borders button ⊞ changes to show the Outside Borders option.

Trouble? If the border around the first paragraph doesn't extend all the way to the left and right margins and instead encloses only the text, you didn't select the paragraph mark as directed in Step 1. Click the Undo button ↺ repeatedly to remove the border, and begin again with Step 1.

4. In the Paragraph group, click the **Shading button arrow** 🖌▾. A gallery of shading options opens, divided into Theme Colors and Standard Colors. You will use a shade of dark blue in the fifth column from the left.

5. In the bottom row in the Theme Colors section, move the pointer over the square in the fifth column from the left to display a ScreenTip that reads "Blue, Accent 1, Darker 50%." A Live Preview of the color appears in the document. See Figure 1-33.

Figure 1-33   **Shading gallery with a Live Preview displayed**

iravgustin/Shutterstock.com

6. Click the **Blue, Accent 1, Darker 50%** square to apply the shading to the selected text.

On a dark background like the one you just applied, a white font creates a striking effect. Leo asks you to change the font color for this paragraph to white.

7. Make sure the Home tab is still selected.

8. In the Font group, click the **Font Color button arrow** A▾ to open the Font Color gallery, and then click the **white** square in the top row of the Theme Colors. The Font Color gallery closes, and the paragraph is now formatted with white font.

9. Click a blank area of the document to deselect the text, review the change, and then save the document. See Figure 1-34.

Figure 1-34 ▶ **Paragraph formatted with dark blue shading, a black border, and white font**

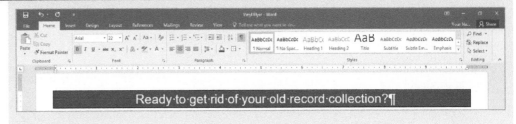

Ready·to·get·rid·of·your·old·record·collection?¶

To add balance to the flyer, Leo suggests formatting the last paragraph in the document with the same shading, border, and font color as the first paragraph. You'll do that next.

Copying Formatting with the Format Painter

You could select the last paragraph and then apply the border, shading, and font color one step at a time. But it's easier to copy all the formatting from the first paragraph to the last paragraph using the Format Painter button in the Clipboard group on the Home tab.

REFERENCE

Using the Format Painter

- Select the text whose formatting you want to copy.
- On the Home tab, in the Clipboard group, click the Format Painter button; or to copy formatting to multiple sections of nonadjacent text, double-click the Format Painter button.
- The mouse pointer changes to the Format Painter pointer, the I-beam pointer with a paintbrush.
- Click the words you want to format, or drag to select and format entire paragraphs.
- When you are finished formatting the text, click the Format Painter button again to turn off the Format Painter.

You'll use the Format Painter now.

To use the Format Painter:

▶ 1. Change the document Zoom level to One Page so you can easily see both the first and last paragraphs.

▶ 2. Select the first paragraph, which is formatted with the dark blue shading, the border, and the white font color.

▶ 3. On the ribbon, click the **Home** tab.

▶ 4. In the Clipboard group, click the **Format Painter** button to activate, or turn on, the Format Painter.

▶ 5. Move the pointer over the document. The pointer changes to the Format Painter pointer 📋I when you move the mouse pointer near an item that can be formatted. See Figure 1-35.

Figure 1-35 **Format Painter**

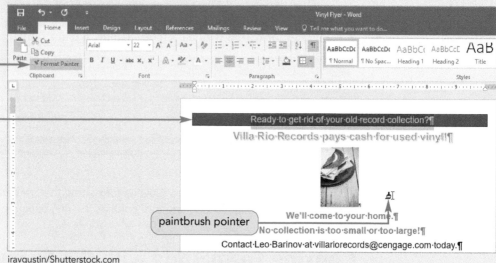

Format Painter is turned on

Format Painter copies the formatting of the selected paragraph

paintbrush pointer

iravgustin/Shutterstock.com

6. Click and drag the Format Painter pointer 📌 to select the last paragraph in the document. The paragraph is now formatted with dark blue shading, a black border, and white font. The mouse pointer returns to its original I-beam shape.

   Trouble? If the text in the newly formatted paragraph wrapped to a second line, replace your full name with your first name, or, if necessary, use only your initials so the paragraph is only one line long.

7. Click anywhere in the document to deselect the text, review the change, and then save the document.

You're almost finished working on the document's paragraph formatting. Your last step is to increase the paragraph spacing below the first paragraph and above the last paragraph. This will give the shaded text even more weight on the page. To complete this task, you will use the settings on the Layout tab, which offer more options than the Line and Paragraph Spacing button on the Home tab.

To increase the paragraph spacing below the first paragraph and above the last paragraph:

1. Click anywhere in the first paragraph, and then click the **Layout** tab. On this tab, the Paragraph group contains settings that control paragraph spacing. Currently, the paragraph spacing for the first paragraph is set to the default 0 points before the paragraph and 8 points after.

2. In the Paragraph group, click the **After** box to select the current setting, type **42**, and then press the **Enter** key. The added space causes the second paragraph to move down 42 points.

3. Click anywhere in the last paragraph.

4. On the Layout tab, in the Paragraph group, click the **Before** box to select the current setting, type **42**, and then press the **Enter** key. The added space causes the last paragraph to move down 42 points.

INSIGHT

Formatting Professional Documents

In more formal documents, use color and special effects sparingly. The goal of letters, reports, and many other types of documents is to convey important information, not to dazzle the reader with fancy fonts and colors. Such elements only serve to distract the reader from your main point. In formal documents, it's a good idea to limit the number of colors to two and to stick with left alignment for text. In a document like the flyer you're currently working on, you have a little more leeway because the goal of the document is to attract attention. However, you still want it to look professional.

Finally, Leo wants you to replace the photo with one that will look better in the document's new landscape orientation. You'll replace the photo, and then you'll resize it so that the flyer fills the entire page.

Working with Pictures

A **picture** is a photo or another type of image that you insert into a document. To work with a picture, you first need to select it. Once a picture is selected, a contextual tab—the Picture Tools Format tab—appears on the ribbon, with options for editing the picture and adding effects such as a border, a shadow, a reflection, or a new shape. A **contextual tab** appears on the ribbon only when an object is selected. It contains commands related to the selected object so that you can manipulate, edit, and format the selected object. You can also use the mouse to resize or move a selected picture. To insert a new picture, you use the Pictures button in the Illustrations group on the Insert tab.

To delete the current photo and insert a new one:

▶ **1.** Click the photo to select it.

The circles, called **handles**, around the edge of the photo indicate the photo is selected. The Layout Options button, to the right of the photo, gives you access to options that control how the document text flows around the photo. You don't need to worry about these options now. Finally, note that the Picture Tools Format tab appeared on the ribbon when you selected the photo. See Figure 1-36.

Figure 1-36   Selected photo

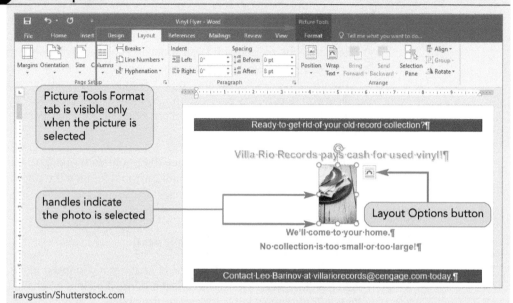

Picture Tools Format tab is visible only when the picture is selected

handles indicate the photo is selected

Layout Options button

Ready·to·get·rid·of·your·old·record·collection?¶

Villa·Rio·Records·pays·cash·for·used·vinyl!¶

We'll·come·to·your·home.¶
No·collection·is·too·small·or·too·large!¶

Contact·Leo·Barinov·at·villariorecords@cengage.com·today.¶

iravgustin/Shutterstock.com

2. Press the **Delete** key. The photo is deleted from the document. The insertion point blinks next to the paragraph symbol. You will insert the new photo in that paragraph.

3. On the ribbon, click the **Insert** tab. The ribbon changes to display the Insert options.

4. In the Illustrations group, click the **Pictures** button. The Insert Picture dialog box opens.

5. Navigate to the **Word1 > Module folder** included with your Data Files, and then click **Albums** to select the file. The name of the selected file appears in the File name box.

6. Click the **Insert** button to close the Insert Picture dialog box and insert the photo. A different album image, with the albums in the upper-right corner, appears in the document, below the second paragraph. The photo is selected, as indicated by the handles on its border. The newly inserted photo is so large that it appears on a second page.

Now you need to shrink the photo to fit the available space on the first page. You could do so by clicking one of the picture's corner handles, holding down the mouse button, and then dragging the handle to resize the picture. But using the Shape Height and Shape Width boxes on the Picture Tools Format tab gives you more precise results.

To resize the photo:

1. Make sure the Picture Tools Format tab is still selected on the ribbon.

2. In the Size group on the far right edge of the ribbon, locate the Shape Height box, which tells you that the height of the selected picture is currently 6.67". The Shape Width box tells you that the width of the picture is 10". As you'll see in the next step, when you change one of these measurements, the other changes accordingly, keeping the overall shape of the picture the same. See Figure 1-37.

Figure 1-37   **Shape Height and Shape Width boxes**

Shape Height box shows the current height

Shape Width box shows the current width

you could also drag a corner handle to resize the picture

click the up arrow to increase the picture's height

iravgustin/Shutterstock.com

3. Click the **down arrow** in the Shape Height box in the Size group. The photo decreases in size slightly. The measurement in the Shape Height box decreases to 6.6", and the measurement in the Shape Width box decreases to 9.9".

4. Click the **down arrow** in the Shape Height box repeatedly until the picture is 3.3" tall and 4.95" wide. As the photo shrinks, it moves back to page 1, along with the text below it. The entire flyer should again appear on one page.

Finally, to make the photo more noticeable, you can add a **picture style**, which is a collection of formatting options, such as a frame, a rounded shape, and a shadow. You can apply a picture style to a selected picture by clicking the style you want in the Picture Styles gallery on the Picture Tools Format tab. In the following steps, you'll start by displaying the gallery.

To add a style to the photo:

1. Make sure the Picture Tools Format tab is still selected on the ribbon.

2. In the Picture Styles group, click the **More** button to the right of the Picture Styles gallery to open the gallery and display more picture styles. Some of the picture styles simply add a border, while others change the picture's shape. Other styles combine these options with effects such as a shadow or a reflection.

3. Place the mouse pointer over various styles to observe the Live Previews in the document, and then place the mouse pointer over the Drop Shadow Rectangle style, which is the middle style in the top row. See Figure 1-38.

Figure 1-38   Previewing a picture style

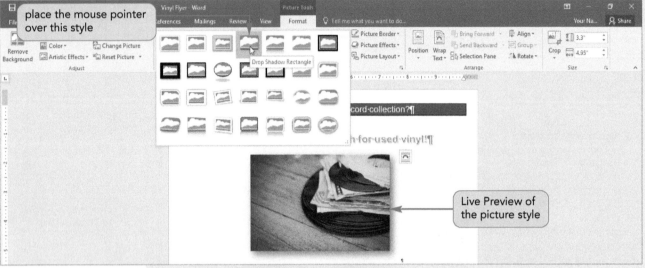

iravgustin/Shutterstock.com

TIP

To return a picture to its original appearance, click the Reset Picture button in the Adjust group on the Picture Tools Format tab.

4. In the gallery, click the **Drop Shadow Rectangle** style to apply it to the photo and close the gallery. The photo is formatted with a shadow on the bottom and right sides, as shown earlier in the Session 1.2 Visual Overview.

5. Click anywhere outside the photo to deselect it, and then save the document.

INSIGHT

Working with Inline Pictures

By default, when you insert a picture in a document, it is treated as an inline object, which means its position changes in the document as you add or delete text. Also, because it is an inline object, you can align the picture just as you would align text, using the alignment buttons in the Paragraph group on the Home tab. Essentially, you can treat an inline picture as just another paragraph.

When you become a more advanced Word user, you'll learn how to wrap text around a picture so that the text flows around the picture—with the picture maintaining its position on the page no matter how much text you add to or delete from the document. The alignment buttons don't work on pictures that have text wrapped around them. Instead, you can drag the picture to the desired position on the page.

The flyer is complete and ready for Leo to print later. Because Leo is considering creating a promotional brochure that would include numerous photographs, he asks you to look up more information about inserting pictures. You can do that using Word's Help system.

Getting Help

To get the most out of Help, your computer must be connected to the Internet so it can access the reference information stored at Office.com. The quickest way to look up information is to use the Tell Me box—which appears with the text "Tell me what you want to do…" within it—on the ribbon. You can also use the Tell Me box to quickly access Word features.

To look up information in Help:

TIP

To search the web for information on a word or phrase in a document, select the text, click the Review tab, and then click the Smart Lookup button in the Insights group.

1. Verify that your computer is connected to the Internet, and then, on the ribbon, click the **Tell Me** box, and type **insert pictures**. A menu of Help topics related to inserting pictures opens. You could click one of the topics in the menu, or you could click the Get Help on "insert pictures" command at the bottom of the menu to open a Word 2016 Help window, where you could continue to search Office.com for more information on inserting pictures. If you prefer to expand your search to the entire web, you could click the Smart Lookup command at the bottom of the menu to open an Insights task pane with links to articles from Wikipedia and other sources. You could also press Enter at this point to open the Insert Pictures dialog box.

2. Click **Get Help on "insert pictures."** After a slight pause, the Word 2016 Help window opens with links to information about inserting pictures. You might see the links shown in Figure 1-39, or you might see other links.

Figure 1-39   **Word Help window**

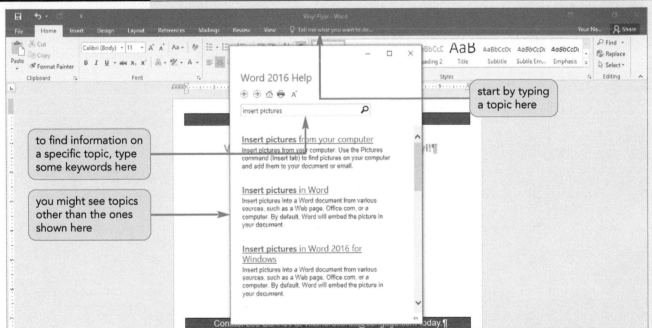

start by typing a topic here

to find information on a specific topic, type some keywords here

you might see topics other than the ones shown here

3. Click the first link, and then read the article to see if it contains any information about inserting pictures that might be useful to Leo. Note that to print information about a topic, you can click the Print button near the top of the Word Help window.

4. When you are finished reading the article, click the **Back** button ⊜ near the top of the Word 2016 Help window to return to the previous list of links.

5. Click the **Home** button 🏠 to go to the home page.

6. Click the **Close** button ✕ in the upper-right corner to close the Word 2016 Help window.

7. Click the **File** tab, and then click **Close** in the navigation bar to close the document without closing Word.

Word Help is a great way to learn about and access Word's many features. Articles and videos on basic skills provide step-by-step guides for completing tasks, while more elaborate, online tutorials walk you through more complicated tasks. Be sure to take some time on your own to explore Word Help so you can find the information and features you want when you need it.

Session 1.2 Quick Check

REVIEW

1. Explain how to accept a spelling correction suggested by the Spelling task pane.
2. What orientation should you choose if you want your document to be wider than it is tall?
3. What is the default font size?
4. What is a gallery?
5. What is the default text alignment?
6. Explain two important facts about a picture inserted as an inline object.

Review Assignments

Data Files needed for the Review Assignments: Flyer.docx, Player.jpg

Leo asks you to write a cover letter to accompany a bid for a collection of reggae albums. After that, he wants you to create an envelope for the letter and to format a flyer reminding customers that Villa Rio Records buys vintage record players in addition to vintage vinyl. Change the Zoom level as necessary while you are working. Complete the following steps:

1. Open a new, blank document and then save the document as **Huang Letter** in the location specified by your instructor.
2. Type the date **February 19, 2017** using AutoComplete for "February."
3. Press the Enter key twice, and then type the following inside address, using the default paragraph spacing and pressing the Enter key once after each line:
   Sabrina Huang
   52 East Dana Parkway
   Wilmington, DE 19802
4. Type **Dear Ms. Huang:** as the salutation, press the Enter key, and then type the following as the body of the letter:
   Enclosed you will find my appraisal of your reggae collection. Please note that you also included some classic rock albums. I've included a separate bid for those titles, as well as a bid for the combined collections.
   I enjoyed our conversation about gospel music of the 1950s. Please let me know if you are looking for more albums from that era. You can see our complete gospel collection online at www.villariorecords.cengage.com.
5. Press the Enter key, type **Sincerely yours,** as the complimentary closing, press the Enter key three times, type **Leo Barinov** as the signature line, insert a manual line break, and type **Purchasing Manager** as his title.
6. Press the Enter key, type your initials, insert a manual line break, and then use the Undo button to make your initials all lowercase, if necessary.
7. Type **Enclosure** and save the document.
8. Scroll to the beginning of the document and proofread your work. Remove any wavy underlines by using a shortcut menu or by typing a correction yourself. Remove the hyperlink formatting from the web address.
9. Remove the paragraph spacing from the first two lines of the inside address.
10. Change the top margin to 2.75 inches. Leave the other margins at their default settings.
11. Save your changes to the letter, preview it, print it if your instructor asks you to, and then close it.
12. Create a new, blank document, and then create an envelope. Use Sabrina Huang's address (from Step 3) as the delivery address. Use your school's name and address for the return address. Add the envelope to the document. If you are asked if you want to save the return address as the new return address, click No.
13. Save the document as **Huang Envelope** in the location specified by your instructor, and then close the document.
14. Open the document **Flyer**, located in the Word1 > Review folder included with your Data Files, and then check your screen to make sure your settings match those in the module.
15. Save the document as **Record Player Flyer** in the location specified by your instructor.
16. Use the Recheck Document button in the Word Options dialog box to reset the Spelling and Grammar checker, and then use the Spelling and Grammar task panes to correct any errors marked with wavy underlines.
17. Proofread the document and correct any other errors. Be sure to change "Today" to "**today**" in the last paragraph.

18. Change the page orientation to Landscape and the margins to Narrow.
19. Format the document text in 22-point Times New Roman font.
20. Center the text and the photo.
21. Format the first paragraph with an outside border, and then add orange shading, using the Orange, Accent 2, Darker 25% color in the Theme Colors section of the Shading gallery. Format the paragraph text in white.
22. Format the last paragraph in the document using the same formatting you applied to the first paragraph.
23. Increase the paragraph spacing after the first paragraph to 42 points. Increase the paragraph spacing before the last paragraph in the document to 42 points.
24. Format the second paragraph with the Fill - Orange, Accent 2, Outline - Accent 2 text effect. Increase the paragraph's font size to 26 points.
25. Format the text in the third and fourth paragraphs (the first two paragraphs below the photo) in orange, using the Orange, Accent 2, Darker 50% font color, and then add bold and italic.
26. Delete the photo and replace it with the **Player.jpg** photo, located in the Word1 > Review folder included with your Data Files.
27. Resize the new photo so that it is 3.8" tall, and then add the Soft Edge Rectangle style in the Pictures Styles gallery.
28. Save your changes to the flyer, preview it, and then close it.
29. Use Word Help to look up the topic **work with pictures**. Read the first article, return to the Help home page, and then close Help.

Case Problem 1

There are no Data Files needed for this Case Problem.

Brightly Water Quality Consultants   You are a program administrator at Brightly Water Quality Consultants, in Springfield, Missouri. Over the past few months, you have collected handwritten journals from local residents documenting their daily water use. Now you need to send the journals to the researcher in charge of compiling the information. Create a cover letter to accompany the journals by completing the following steps. Because your office is currently out of letterhead, you'll start the letter by typing a return address. As you type the letter, remember to include the appropriate number of blank paragraphs between the various parts of the letter. Complete the following steps:

1. Open a new, blank document, and then save the document as **Brightly Letter** in the location specified by your instructor. If necessary, change the Zoom level to 120%.
2. Type the following return address, using the default paragraph spacing and replacing [Your Name] with your first and last names:
   [Your Name]
   Brightly Water Quality Consultants
   39985 Pepperdine Avenue, Suite 52
   Springfield, MO 65806
3. Type **November 6, 2017** as the date, leaving a blank paragraph between the last line of the return address and the date.
4. Type the following inside address, using the default paragraph spacing and leaving the appropriate number of blank paragraphs after the date:
   Dr. Albert Strome
   4643 College Drive
   Columbia, MO 65211
5. Type **Dear Dr. Strome:** as the salutation.

6. To begin the body of the letter, type the following paragraph:

   Enclosed please find the journals our participants have completed. I should have thirty more by the end of next month, but I thought you would like to get started on these now. Please review the enclosed journals, and then call or email me with your answers to these questions:

7. Add the following questions as separate paragraphs, using the default paragraph spacing:

   Did the participants include enough helpful information?

   Should we consider expanding the program to additional communities?

   Can you complete your analysis by early March?

8. Insert a new paragraph before the second question, and then add the following as the new second question in the list: **Is the journal format useful, or would you prefer a simple questionnaire?**

9. Insert a new paragraph after the last question, and then type the complimentary closing **Sincerely,** (including the comma).

10. Leave the appropriate amount of space for your signature, type your full name, insert a manual line break, and then type **Program Administrator**.

11. Type **Enclosure** in the appropriate place.

12. Use the Recheck Document button in the Word Options dialog box to reset the Spelling and Grammar checker, and then use the Spelling and Grammar task panes to correct any errors. Instruct the Spelling task pane to ignore the recipient's name.

13. Italicize the four paragraphs containing the questions.

14. Remove the paragraph spacing from the first three lines of the return address. Do the same for the first two paragraphs of the inside address.

15. Center the four paragraphs containing the return address, format them in 16-point font, and then add the Fill – Gray – 50%, Accent 3, Sharp Bevel text effect.

16. Save the document, preview it, and then close it.

17. Create a new, blank document, and create an envelope. Use Dr. Strome's address (from Step 4) as the delivery address. Use the return address shown in Step 2. Add the envelope to the document. If you are asked if you want to save the return address as the new return address, click No.

18. Save the document as **Strome Envelope** in the location specified by your instructor, and then close the document.

Case Problem 2

Data Files needed for this Case Problem: Dog.jpg, Pups.docx

Pups & Pals Pet Care   You work as the sales and scheduling coordinator at Pups & Pals Pet Care, a dog-walking service in San Antonio, Texas. You need to create a flyer promoting the company's services. Complete the following steps:

1. Open the document **Pups** located in the Word1 > Case2 folder included with your Data Files, and then save the document as **Pups & Pals Flyer** in the location specified by your instructor.

2. In the document, replace "Student Name" with your first and last names.

3. Use the Recheck Document button in the Word Options dialog box to reset the Spelling and Grammar checker, and then use the Spelling and Grammar task panes to correct any errors. Instruct the Spelling task pane to ignore your name if Word marks it with a wavy underline.

4. Change the page margins to Narrow.

5. Complete the flyer as shown in Figure 1-40. Use the photo **Dog.jpg** located in the Word1 > Case2 folder included with your Data Files. Use the default line spacing and paragraph spacing unless otherwise specified in Figure 1-40.

Figure 1-40   Formatted Pups & Pals flyer

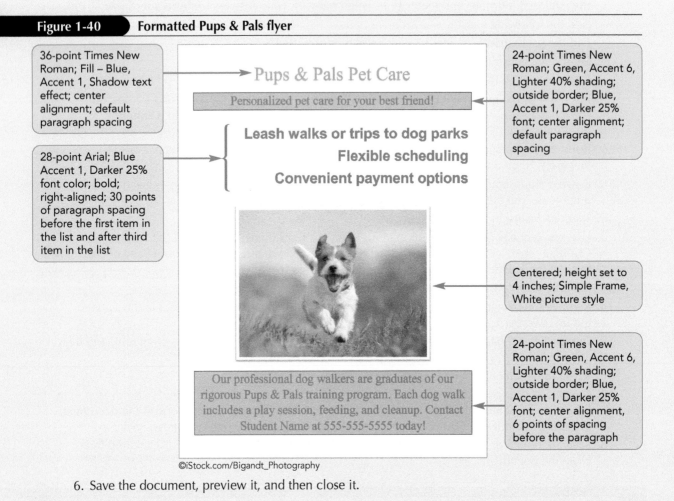

36-point Times New Roman; Fill – Blue, Accent 1, Shadow text effect; center alignment; default paragraph spacing

28-point Arial; Blue Accent 1, Darker 25% font color; bold; right-aligned; 30 points of paragraph spacing before the first item in the list and after third item in the list

24-point Times New Roman; Green, Accent 6, Lighter 40% shading; outside border; Blue, Accent 1, Darker 25% font; center alignment; default paragraph spacing

Centered; height set to 4 inches; Simple Frame, White picture style

24-point Times New Roman; Green, Accent 6, Lighter 40% shading; outside border; Blue, Accent 1, Darker 25% font; center alignment, 6 points of spacing before the paragraph

©iStock.com/Bigandt_Photography

6. Save the document, preview it, and then close it.

Case Problem 3

Data Files needed for this Case Problem: Living.docx, Rental.docx

Salt Lake Synergy Vacation Rentals   You work as the office manager for Salt Lake Synergy Vacation Rentals, a service that rents apartments and houses in Salt Lake City, Utah, to out-of-town visitors. One of the company's rental agents needs to complete a letter to accompany a photo of a rental property. The letter is almost finished, but the agent needs help correcting errors and formatting the text to match the block style. The photo itself is stored in a separate document. The agent mistakenly applied a picture style to the photo that is inappropriate for professional correspondence. She asks you to remove the picture style and then format the page. Complete the following steps:

1. Open the document **Rental** located in the Word1 > Case3 folder included with your Data Files, and then save the document as **Rental Letter** in the location specified by your instructor.

2. Use the Recheck Document button in the Word Options dialog box to reset the Spelling and Grammar checker, and then use the Spelling and Grammar task panes to correct any errors, typing directly in the document as necessary.

⚙ **Troubleshoot** 3. Make any necessary changes to ensure that the letter matches the formatting of a block-style business letter, including the appropriate paragraph spacing. Keep in mind that the letter will include an enclosure. Include your initials where appropriate.

🔧 **Troubleshoot** 4. The letterhead for Salt Lake Synergy Vacation Rentals requires a top margin of 2.5 inches. Determine if the layout of the letter will work with the letterhead, make any necessary changes, and then save the letter.

5. Save the document and preview it.

6. Move the cursor to the beginning of the letter, and then create an envelope. Use the delivery address taken from the letter, but edit the delivery address to remove the salutation, if necessary. Click the Omit check box to deselect it (if necessary), and then, for the return address, type your school's name and address. Add the envelope to the Rental Letter document. If you are asked if you want to save the return address as the new default return address, answer No.

7. Save the document, preview both pages, and then close it.

8. Open the document **Living** located in the Word1 > Case3 folder included with your Data Files, and then save the document as **Living Area Photo** in the location specified by your instructor.

🔧 **Troubleshoot** 9. Reset the picture to its original appearance, before the agent mistakenly added the style with the reflection.

🔧 **Troubleshoot** 10. Modify the page layout and margins and adjust the size of the photo so the photo fills as much of the page as possible without overlapping the page margins.

11. Save the document, preview it, and then close it.

Case Problem 4

CHALLENGE

There are no Data Files needed for this Case Problem.

Palomino Lighting Manufacturers As an assistant facilities manager at Palomino Lighting Manufacturers, you are responsible for alerting the staff when clients plan to visit the factory. In addition to sending out a company-wide email, you also need to post a memo in the break room. Complete the following steps:

⊕ **Explore** 1. Open a new document—but instead of selecting the Blank document option, search for a memo template online. In the list of search results, click the Memo (Simple design) template, and then click the Create button. (Note: If you don't see that template, pick another with a simple style and the word "Memo" at the top. You will need to adapt the steps in this Case Problem to match the design of the template you use.) A memo template opens in the Word window.

2. Save the document as **Visit Memo** in the location specified by your instructor. If you see a dialog box indicating that the document will be upgraded to the newest file format, click the OK button. Note that of the hundreds of templates available online, only a small portion have been created in the most recent version of Word, so you will often see this dialog box when working with templates.

⊕ **Explore** 3. In the document, click the text "[Company name]." The placeholder text appears in a box with gray highlighting. The box containing the highlighted text (with the small rectangle attached) is called a document control. You can enter text in a document control just as you enter text in a dialog box. Type **Palomino Lighting Manufacturers**, and then press the Tab key. The "[Recipient names]" placeholder text now appears in a document control next to the word "To." (Hint: As you work on the memo in the following steps, keep in mind that if you accidentally double-click the word "memo" at the top of the document, you will access the header portion of the document, which is normally closed to editing. In that case, press the Esc key to return to the main document.)

4. Type **All Personnel** and then press the Tab key twice. A document control is now visible to the right of the word "From." Depending on how your computer is set up, you might see your name or another name here, or the document control might be empty. Delete the name, if necessary, and then type your first and last names.

⊕ **Explore** 5. Continue using the Tab key to edit the remaining document controls as indicated below. If you press the Tab key too many times and accidentally skip a document control, you can click the document control to select it.

- In the CC: document control, delete the placeholder text.
- In the Date document control, click the down arrow, and then click the current date in the calendar.
- In the Re: document control, type **Client Visit**.
- In the Comments document control, type **Representatives from Houghton Contractors are scheduled to tour the factory this Tuesday morning. Please greet them warmly, and be prepared to answer any questions they might have.**

6. Use the Recheck Document button in the Word Options dialog box to reset the Spelling and Grammar checker, and then use the Spelling and Grammar task panes to correct any underlined errors. Proofread the document to look for any additional errors.

7. Save the document, preview it, and then close it.

Navigating and Formatting a Document

Editing an Academic Document According to MLA Style

Case | *Quincy Rivers College*

OBJECTIVES

Session 2.1
- Read, reply to, delete, and add comments
- Create bulleted and numbered lists
- Move text using drag and drop
- Cut and paste text
- Copy and paste text
- Navigate through a document using the Navigation pane
- Find and replace text
- Format text with styles
- Apply a theme to a document

Session 2.2
- Review the MLA style for research papers
- Indent paragraphs
- Insert and modify page numbers
- Create citations
- Create and update a bibliography
- Modify a source

Carolina Frey, an architecture student at Quincy Rivers College, is doing a student internship at Wilson and Page Design, an architecture firm in Minneapolis, Minnesota. She has written a handout describing the process of acquiring LEED certification, which serves as proof that a home has been constructed according to strict environmental guidelines specified by the U.S. Green Building Council. She asks you to help her finish the handout. The text needs some reorganization and other editing. The handout also needs formatting so the finished document looks professional and is easy to read.

Carolina is also taking an architecture history class and is writing a research paper on the history of architecture. To complete the paper, she needs to follow a set of very specific formatting and style guidelines for academic documents.

Carolina has asked you to help her edit these two very different documents. In Session 2.1, you will review and respond to some comments in the handout and then revise and format that document. In Session 2.2, you will review the MLA style for research papers and then format Carolina's research paper to match the MLA specifications.

STARTING DATA FILES

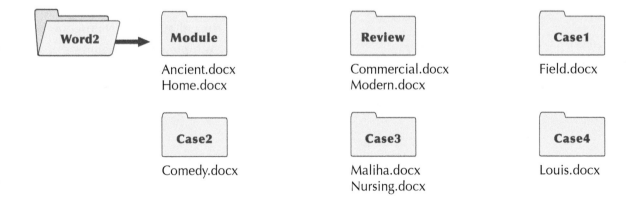

Word2 → **Module**

Ancient.docx
Home.docx

Review

Commercial.docx
Modern.docx

Case1

Field.docx

Case2

Comedy.docx

Case3

Maliha.docx
Nursing.docx

Case4

Louis.docx

Session 2.1 Visual Overview:

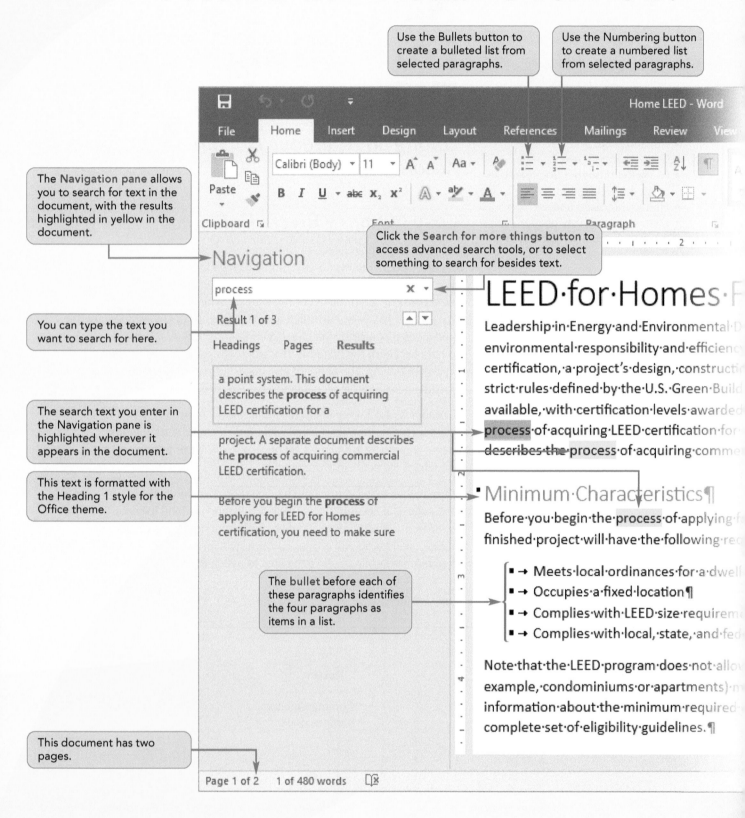

Use the Bullets button to create a bulleted list from selected paragraphs.

Use the Numbering button to create a numbered list from selected paragraphs.

The Navigation pane allows you to search for text in the document, with the results highlighted in yellow in the document.

Click the Search for more things button to access advanced search tools, or to select something to search for besides text.

You can type the text you want to search for here.

The search text you enter in the Navigation pane is highlighted wherever it appears in the document.

This text is formatted with the Heading 1 style for the Office theme.

The bullet before each of these paragraphs identifies the four paragraphs as items in a list.

This document has two pages.

Navigation

process

Result 1 of 3

Headings   Pages   **Results**

a point system. This document describes the **process** of acquiring LEED certification for a

project. A separate document describes the **process** of acquiring commercial LEED certification.

Before you begin the **process** of applying for LEED for Homes certification, you need to make sure

Home LEED - Word

File   Home   Insert   Design   Layout   References   Mailings   Review   View

Calibri (Body)   11   A⁺ A˅   Aa ˅

Paste

B I U ˅ abc x₂ x²   A ˅ ab ˅ A ˅

Clipboard   Font   Paragraph

LEED·for·Homes·F

Leadership·in·Energy·and·Environmental·D
environmental·responsibility·and·efficienc
certification,·a·project's·design,·constructi
strict·rules·defined·by·the·U.S.·Green·Build
available,·with·certification·levels·awarded
process·of·acquiring·LEED·certification·for
describes·the·process·of·acquiring·comme

Minimum·Characteristics¶

Before·you·begin·the·process·of·applying·f
finished·project·will·have·the·following·re

■ → Meets·local·ordinances·for·a·dwel
■ → Occupies·a·fixed·location¶
■ → Complies·with·LEED·size·requirem
■ → Complies·with·local,·state,·and·fed

Note·that·the·LEED·program·does·not·allo
example,·condominiums·or·apartments)·m
information·about·the·minimum·required
complete·set·of·eligibility·guidelines.¶

Working with Lists and Styles

Styles allow you to apply a set of formatting options with one click in the Style gallery.

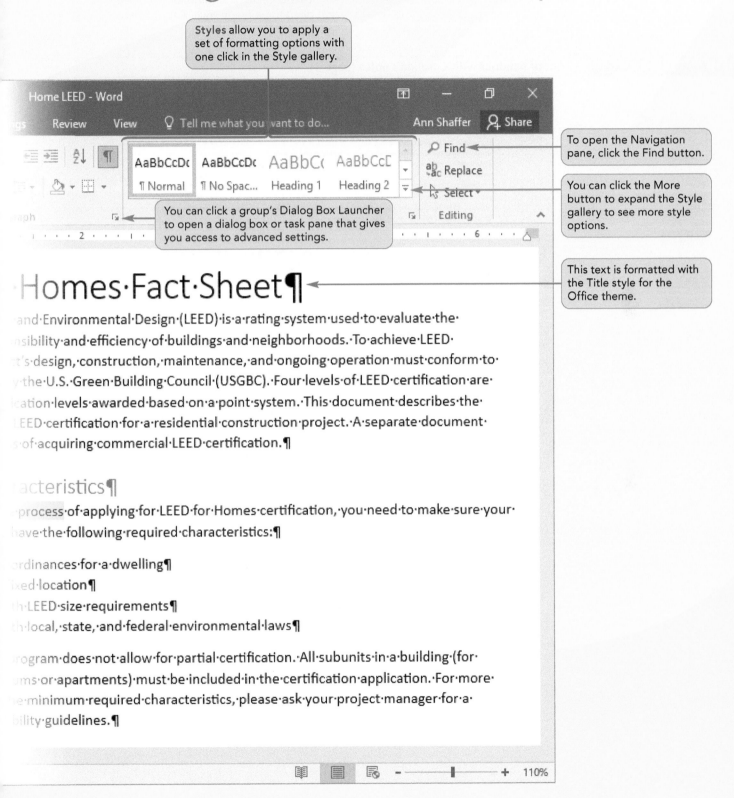

To open the Navigation pane, click the Find button.

You can click the More button to expand the Style gallery to see more style options.

You can click a group's Dialog Box Launcher to open a dialog box or task pane that gives you access to advanced settings.

This text is formatted with the Title style for the Office theme.

Reviewing the Document

Before revising a document for someone else, it's a good idea to familiarize yourself with its overall structure and the revisions that need to be made. Take a moment to review Carolina's notes, which are shown in Figure 2-1.

Figure 2-1   Draft of handout with Carolina's notes (page 1)

format the title with a title style

LEED for Homes Fact Sheet

Leadership in Energy and Environmental Design (LEED) is a rating system used to evaluate the environmental responsibility and efficiency of buildings and neighborhoods. To achieve LEED certification, a project's design, construction, maintenance, and ongoing operation must conform to strict rules defined by the U.S. Green Building Council (USGBC). Four levels of LEED certification are available, with certification levels awarded based on a point system. The staff of *Wilson and Page Architecture* is ready to make your LEED dream a reality. This document describes the process of acquiring LEED certification for a residential construction project. A separate document describes the process of acquiring commercial LEED certification.

replace "leed" with "LEED"

Minimum Characteristics

Before you begin the process of applying for leed for Homes certification, you need to make sure your finished project will have the following required characteristics:

Meets local ordinances for a dwelling

Occupies a fixed location

Complies with LEED size requirements

Complies with local, state, and federal environmental laws

format headings with a heading style

Note that the LEED program does not allow for partial certification. All subunits in a building (for example, condominiums or apartments) must be included in the certification application. For more information about the minimum required characteristics, please ask your project manager for a complete set of eligibility guidelines.

Building Type

Each building is considered a separate project. You can choose from the following registration options for your project or projects:

Single family attached

Single family detached

Multifamily

Batch, for multiple projects that meet the following requirements:

Built by one developer

Located in one country

Pursuing the same LEED certification

format as bulleted lists

indent these three paragraphs within the bulleted list

When registering your project as a multifamily project, you need to choose a multifamily low-rise building or a multifamily mid-rise building.

Rating Systems

| Figure 2-1 | Draft of handout with Carolina's notes (page 2) |

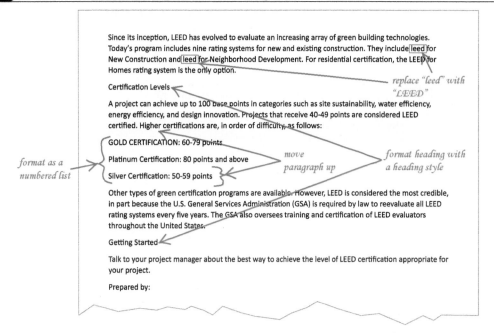

Carolina also included additional guidance in some comments she added to the document file. A **comment** is like an electronic sticky note attached to a word, phrase, or paragraph in a document. Comments appear in the margin, along with the name of the person who added them. Within a single document, you can add new comments, reply to existing comments, and delete comments.

You will open the document now, save it with a new name, and then review Carolina's comments in Word.

To open and rename the document:

▶ **1.** Open the document **Home** located in the Word2 > Module folder included with your Data Files.

▶ **2.** Save the document as **Home LEED** in the location specified by your instructor.

▶ **3.** Verify that the document is displayed in Print Layout view, that the Zoom level is set to **120%**, and that the rulers and nonprinting characters are displayed.

▶ **4.** On the ribbon, click the **Review** tab to display the tools used for working with comments. Comments can be displayed in several different ways, so your first step is to make sure the comments in the Home LEED document are displayed to match the figures in this book—using Simple Markup view.

▶ **5.** In the Tracking group, click the **Display for Review** arrow, and then click **Simple Markup** to select it, if necessary. At this point, you might see comment icons to the right of the document text, or you might see the full text of each comment.

▶ **6.** In the Comments group, click the **Show Comments** button several times to practice displaying and hiding the comments, and then, when you are finished, make sure the Show Comments button is selected so the full text of each comment is displayed.

7. At the bottom of the Word window, drag the horizontal scroll bar all the way to the right, if necessary, so you can read the full text of each comment. See Figure 2-2. Note that the comments on your screen might be a different color than the ones shown in the figure.

Figure 2-2 **Comments displayed in the document**

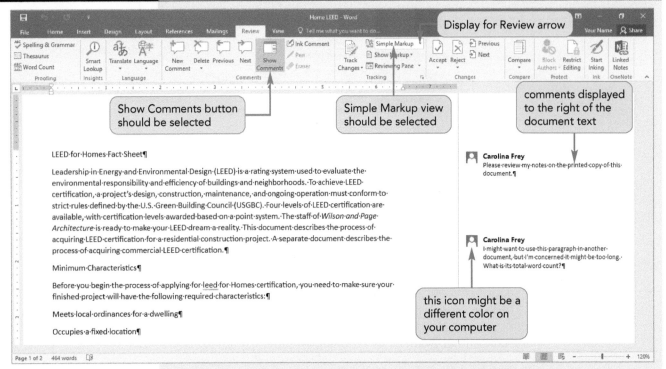

Keep in mind that when working on a small monitor, it can be helpful to switch the document Zoom level to Page Width, in which case Word automatically reduces the width of the document to accommodate the comments on the right.

8. Read the document, including the comments. The handout includes the title "LEED for Homes Fact Sheet" at the top, as well as headings (such as "Minimum Characteristics" and "Building Type") that divide the document into parts. Right now the headings are hard to spot because they don't look different from the surrounding text. Carolina used the default font size, 11-point, and the default font, Calibri (Body), for all the text in the document. Note, too, that the document includes some short paragraphs that would work better as bulleted or numbered lists.

9. Scroll down until you can see the first line on page 2 (which begins "Since its inception…"), and then click anywhere in that sentence. The message "Page 2 of 2" in the status bar, in the lower-left corner of the Word window, tells you that the insertion point is currently located on page 2 of the two-page document. The shaded space between the first and second pages of the document indicates a page break. To hide the top and bottom margins in a document, as well as the space between pages, you can double-click the shaded space between any two pages.

10. Position the mouse pointer over the shaded space between page 1 and page 2 until the pointer changes to ⥯, and then double-click. The shaded space disappears. Instead, the two pages are now separated by a gray, horizontal line.

Trouble? If the Header & Footer Tools Design contextual tab appears on the ribbon, you double-clicked the top or bottom of one of the pages, instead of in the space between them. Click the Close Header and Footer button on the Header & Footer Tools Design tab, and then repeat Step 10.

▶ **11.** Use the ⊞ pointer to double-click the gray horizontal line between pages 1 and 2. The shaded space between the two pages is redisplayed.

Working with Comments

Now that you are familiar with the Home LEED document, you can review and respond to Carolina's comments. The Comment group on the Review tab includes helpful tools for working with comments.

REFERENCE

Working with Comments

- On the ribbon, click the Review tab.
- To display comments in an easy-to-read view, in the Tracking group, click the Display for Review button, and then click Simple Markup.
- To see the text of each comment in Simple Markup view, click the Show Comments button in the Comments group.
- To move the insertion point to the next or previous comment in the document, click the Next button or the Previous button in the Comments group.
- To delete a comment, click anywhere in the comment, and then click the Delete button in the Comments group.
- To delete all the comments in a document, click the Delete button arrow in the Comments group, and then click Delete All Comments in Document.
- To add a new comment, select the document text you want to comment on, click the New Comment button in the Comments group, and then type the comment text.
- To reply to a comment, click the Reply button to the right of the comment, and then type your reply.
- To indicate that a comment or an individual reply to a comment is no longer a concern, right-click the comment or reply, and then click Mark Comment Done in the shortcut menu. To mark a comment and all of the replies attached to it as done, right-click the original comment, and then click Mark Comment Done.

To review and respond to the comments in the document:

▶ **1.** Press the **Ctrl+Home** keys to move the insertion point to the beginning of the document.

▶ **2.** On the Review tab, in the Comments group, click the **Next** button. The first comment now has an outline, indicating that it is selected. See Figure 2-3.

Figure 2-3 Comment attached to document text

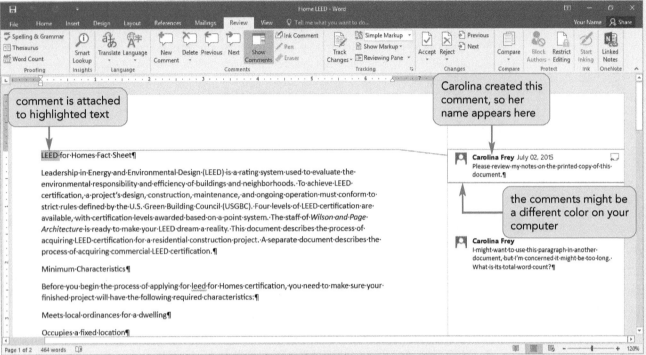

In the document, the text "LEED" is highlighted. A line connects the comment to "LEED," indicating that the comment is attached to that text. Because Carolina created the comment, her name appears at the beginning of the comment, followed by the date on which she created it. The insertion point blinks at the beginning of the comment and is ready for you to edit the comment if you want.

3. Read the comment, and then in the Comments group, click the **Next** button to select the next comment. According to this comment, Carolina wants to know the total word count of the paragraph the comment is attached to. You can get this information by selecting the entire paragraph and locating the word count in the status bar.

4. Triple-click anywhere in the second paragraph of the document (which begins "Leadership in Energy and Environmental Design…") to select the paragraph. In the status bar, the message "105 of 464 words" tells you that 105 of the document's 464 words are currently selected. So the answer to Carolina's question is 105.

5. Point to the second comment to select it again, click the **Reply** button ⬚, and then type **105**. Your reply appears below Carolina's original comment.

Trouble? If you do not see the Reply button in the comment box, drag the horizontal scroll bar at the bottom of the Word window to the right until you can see it.

If you are logged in, the name that appears in your reply comment is the name associated with your Microsoft account. If you are not logged in, the name in the Reply comment is taken from the User name box on the General tab of the Word Options dialog box. You can quickly open the General tab of the Word Options dialog box by clicking the Dialog Box Launcher in the

Tracking group on the Review tab, and then clicking Change User Name. From there, you can change the username and the initials associated with your copy of Word. To override the name associated with your Microsoft account and use the name that appears in the User name box in the Word Options dialog box instead, select the "Always use these values regardless of sign in to Office" check box. However, there is no need to change these settings for this module, and you should never change them on a shared computer at school unless specifically instructed to do so by your instructor.

▶ **6.** In the Comments group, click the **Next** button to move the insertion point to the next comment, which asks you to insert your name after "Prepared by:" at the end of the document.

▶ **7.** Click after the colon in "Prepared by:", press the **spacebar**, and then type your first and last names. To indicate that you have complied with Carolina's request by adding your name, you could right-click the comment, and then click Mark Comment Done. However, in this case, you'll simply delete the comment. Carolina also asks you to delete the first comment in the document.

▶ **8.** Click anywhere in the final comment, and then in the Comments group, click the **Delete** button.

▶ **9.** In the Comments group, click the **Previous** button three times to select the comment at the beginning of the document, and then click the **Delete** button to delete the comment.

As you reviewed the document, you might have noticed that, on page 2, one of the certification levels appears in all uppercase letters. This is probably just a typing mistake. You can correct it and then add a comment that points out the change to Carolina.

To correct the mistake and add a comment:

▶ **1.** Scroll down to page 2, and then, in the fourth paragraph on the page, select the text **GOLD CERTIFICATION**.

▶ **2.** On the ribbon, click the **Home** tab.

▶ **3.** In the Font group, click the **Change Case** button Aa ▾, and then click **Capitalize Each Word**. The text changes to read "Gold Certification."

▶ **4.** Verify that the text is still selected, and then click the **Review** tab on the ribbon.

▶ **5.** In the Comments group, click the **New Comment** button. A new comment appears, with the insertion point ready for you to begin typing.

▶ **6.** In the new comment, type **I assumed you didn't want this all uppercase, so I changed it.** and then save the document.

You can now hide the text of the comments because you are finished working with them.

▶ **7.** In the Comments group, click the **Show Comments** button. A "See comments" icon now appears in the document margin rather than on the right side of the Word screen. The "See comments" icon alerts you to the presence of a comment without taking up all the space required to display the comment text. You can click a comment icon to read a particular comment without displaying the text of all the comments.

▶ **8.** Click the **See comments** icon 💬. The comment icon is highlighted, and the full comment is displayed, as shown in Figure 2-4.

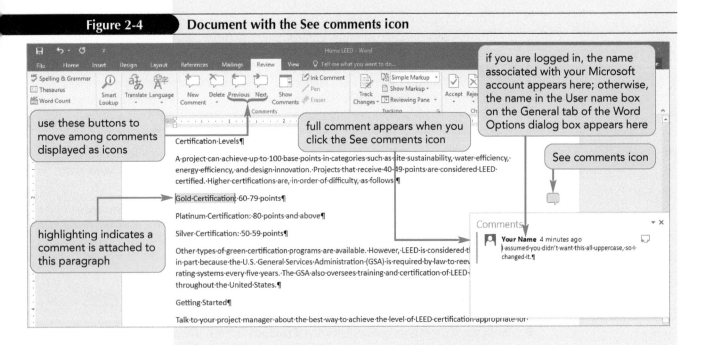

Figure 2-4 ▶ **Document with the See comments icon**

use these buttons to move among comments displayed as icons

full comment appears when you click the See comments icon

if you are logged in, the name associated with your Microsoft account appears here; otherwise, the name in the User name box on the General tab of the Word Options dialog box appears here

See comments icon

highlighting indicates a comment is attached to this paragraph

▶ **9.** Click anywhere outside the comment to close it.

Creating Bulleted and Numbered Lists

A **bulleted list** is a group of related paragraphs with a black circle or other character to the left of each paragraph. For a group of related paragraphs that have a particular order (such as steps in a procedure), you can use consecutive numbers instead of bullets to create a **numbered list**. If you insert a new paragraph, delete a paragraph, or reorder the paragraphs in a numbered list, Word adjusts the numbers to make sure they remain consecutive.

Written Communication: Organizing Information in Lists

Bulleted and numbered lists are both great ways to draw the reader's attention to information. But it's important to know how to use them. Use numbers when your list contains items that are arranged by priority in a specific order. For example, in a document reviewing the procedure for performing CPR, it makes sense to use numbers for the sequential steps. Use bullets when the items in the list are of equal importance or when they can be accomplished in any order. For example, in a resume, you could use bullets for a list of professional certifications.

To add bullets to a series of paragraphs, you use the Bullets button in the Paragraph group on the Home tab. To create a numbered list, you use the Numbering button in the Paragraph group instead. Both the Bullets button and the Numbering button have arrows you can click to open a gallery of bullet or numbering styles.

Carolina asks you to format the list of minimum characteristics on page 1 as a bulleted list. She also asks you to format the list of building types on page 1 as a separate bulleted list. Finally, you need to format the list of certification levels on page 2 as a numbered list, in order of difficulty.

To apply bullets to paragraphs:

▶ **1.** Scroll up until you see the paragraphs containing the list of minimum characteristics (which begins with "Meets local ordinances for a dwelling…"), and then select this paragraph and the three that follow it.

▶ **2.** On the ribbon, click the **Home** tab.

▶ **3.** In the Paragraph group, click the **Bullets** button ⊞. Black circles appear as bullets before each item in the list. Also, the bulleted list is indented and the paragraph spacing between the items is reduced.

After reviewing the default, round bullet in the document, Carolina decides she would prefer square bullets.

▶ **4.** In the Paragraph group, click the **Bullets button arrow** ⊞ ▾. A gallery of bullet styles opens. See Figure 2-5.

| Figure 2-5 | Bullets gallery |

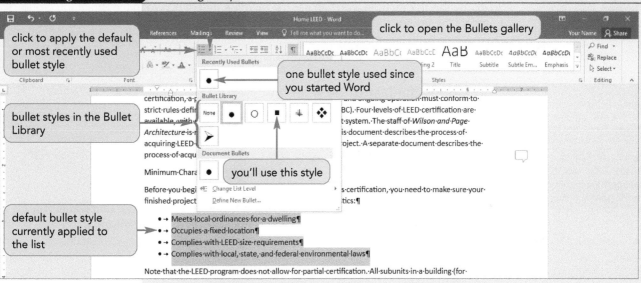

The Recently Used Bullets section appears at the top of the gallery of bullet styles; it displays the bullet styles that have been used since you started Word, which, in this case, is just the round black bullet style that was applied by default when you clicked the Bullets button. The **Bullet Library**, which offers a variety of bullet styles, is shown below the Recently Used Bullets. To create your own bullets from a picture file or from a set of predesigned symbols including diamonds, hearts, or Greek letters, click Define New Bullet, and then click the Symbol button or the Picture button in the Define New Bullet dialog box.

▶ **5.** Move the mouse pointer over the bullet styles in the Bullet Library to see a Live Preview of the bullet styles in the document. Carolina prefers the black square style.

▶ **6.** In the Bullet Library, click the **black square**. The round bullets are replaced with square bullets.

Next, you need to format the list of building types on page 1 with square bullets. When you first start Word, the Bullets button applies the default, round bullets you saw earlier. But after you select a new bullet style, the Bullets button applies the last bullet style you used. So, to add square bullets to the decorating styles list, you just have to select the list and click the Bullets button.

To add bullets to the list of building types:

▶ **1.** Scroll down in the document, and select the paragraphs listing the building types, starting with "Single family attached" and ending with "Pursuing the same LEED certification."

▶ **2.** In the Paragraph group, click the **Bullets** button ▤. The list is now formatted with square black bullets.

The list is finished except for one issue. The "Batch" building type has three subrequirements, but that's not clear because of the way the list is currently formatted. To clarify this information, you can use the Increase Indent button in the Paragraph group to indent the last two bullets. When you do this, Word inserts a different style bullet to make the indented paragraphs visually subordinate to the bulleted paragraphs above.

To indent the last three bullets:

▶ **1.** In the list of building types, select the last three paragraphs.

▶ **2.** In the Paragraph group, click the **Increase Indent** button ▤. The three paragraphs move to the right, and the black square bullets are replaced with open circle bullets.

Next, you will format the list of certification levels on page 2. Carolina wants you to format this information as a numbered list because the levels are listed in order of difficulty.

To apply numbers to the list of certification levels:

▶ **1.** Scroll down to page 2 until you see the "Gold Certification: 60-79 points" paragraph. You added a comment to this paragraph earlier, but that will have no effect on the process of creating the numbered list.

▶ **2.** Select the three paragraphs containing the list of certification levels, starting with "Gold Certification: 60-79 points" and ending with "Silver Certification: 50-59 points."

▶ **3.** In the Paragraph group, click the **Numbering** button ▤. Consecutive numbers appear in front of each item in the list. See Figure 2-6.

Figure 2-6   **Numbered list**

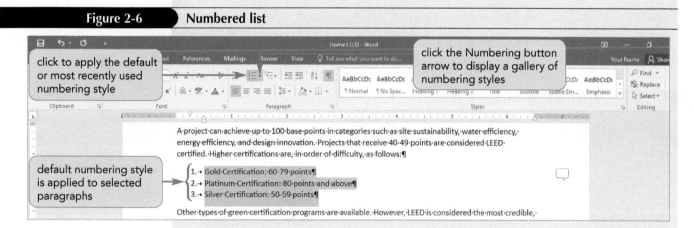

click to apply the default or most recently used numbering style

click the Numbering button arrow to display a gallery of numbering styles

default numbering style is applied to selected paragraphs

A·project·can·achieve·up·to·100·base·points·in·categories·such·as·site·sustainability,·water·efficiency,· energy·efficiency,·and·design·innovation.·Projects·that·receive·40-49·points·are·considered·LEED· certified.·Higher·certifications·are,·in·order·of·difficulty,·as·follows:¶

1.→ Gold·Certification:·60-79·points¶
2.→ Platinum·Certification:·80·points·and·above¶
3.→ Silver·Certification:·50-59·points¶

Other·types·of·green·certification·programs·are·available.·However,·LEED·is·considered·the·most·credible,·

4. Click anywhere in the document to deselect the numbered list, and then save the document.

As with the Bullets button arrow, you can click the Numbering button arrow, and then select from a library of numbering styles. You can also indent paragraphs in a numbered list to create an outline, in which case the indented paragraphs will be preceded by lowercase letters instead of numbers. To apply a different list style to the outline (for example, with Roman numerals and uppercase letters), select the list, click the Multilevel List button in the Paragraph group, and then click a multilevel list style.

Moving Text in a Document

One of the most useful features of a word-processing program is the ability to move text easily. For example, Carolina wants to reorder the information in the numbered list. You could do this by deleting a paragraph and then retyping it at a new location. However, it's easier to select and then move the text. Word provides several ways to move text—drag and drop, cut and paste, and copy and paste.

Dragging and Dropping Text

To move text with **drag and drop**, you select the text you want to move, press and hold the mouse button while you drag the selected text to a new location, and then release the mouse button.

In the numbered list you just created, Carolina wants you to move the paragraph that reads "Silver Certification: 50-59 points" up so it is the first item in the list.

To move text using drag and drop:

1. Select the third paragraph in the numbered list, "Silver Certification: 50-59 points," being sure to include the paragraph marker at the end. The number 3 remains unselected because it's not actually part of the paragraph text.

2. Position the pointer over the selected text. The pointer changes to a left-facing arrow.

3. Press and hold the mouse button, and move the pointer slightly until the drag-and-drop pointer appears. A dark black insertion point appears within the selected text.

▶ **4.** Without releasing the mouse button, drag the pointer to the beginning of the list until the insertion point is positioned to the left of the "G" in "Gold Certification: 60-79 points." Use the insertion point, rather than the mouse pointer, to guide the text to its new location. See Figure 2-7.

| Figure 2-7 | Moving text with the drag-and-drop pointer |

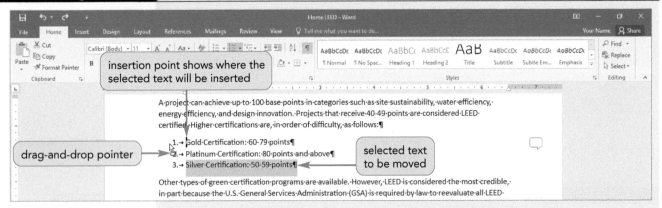

▶ **5.** Release the mouse button, and then click a blank area of the document to deselect the text. The text "Silver Certification: 50-59 points" is now the first item in the list, and the remaining paragraphs have been renumbered as paragraphs 2 and 3. See Figure 2-8.

| Figure 2-8 | Text in new location |

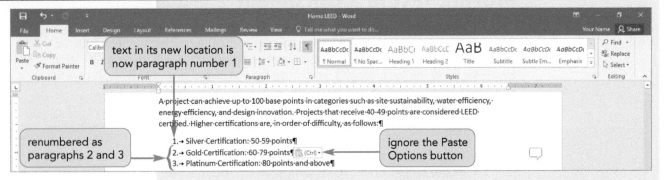

The Paste Options button appears near the newly inserted text, providing access to more advanced options related to pasting text. You don't need to use the Paste Options button right now; it will disappear when you start performing another task.

Trouble? If the selected text moves to the wrong location, click the Undo button 🔄 on the Quick Access Toolbar, and then repeat Steps 2 through 5.

▶ **6.** Save the document.

Dragging and dropping works well when you are moving text a short distance. When you are moving text from one page to another, it's easier to cut, copy, and paste text using the Clipboard.

Cutting or Copying and Pasting Text Using the Clipboard

The **Office Clipboard** is a temporary storage area on your computer that holds objects such as text or graphics until you need them. To **cut** means to remove text or another item from a document and place it on the Clipboard. Once you've cut something, you can paste it somewhere else. To **copy** means to copy a selected item to the Clipboard, leaving the item in its original location. To **paste** means to insert a copy of whatever is on the Clipboard into the document, at the insertion point. When you paste an item from the Clipboard into a document, the item remains on the Clipboard so you can paste it again somewhere else if you want. The buttons for cutting, copying, and pasting are located in the Clipboard group on the Home tab.

By default, Word pastes text in a new location in a document with the same formatting it had in its old location. To select other ways to paste text, you can use the Paste Options button, which appears next to newly pasted text, or the Paste button arrow in the Clipboard group. Both buttons display a menu of paste options. Two particularly useful paste options are Merge Formatting, which combines the formatting of the copied text with the formatting of the text in the new location, and Keep Text Only, which inserts the text using the formatting of the surrounding text in the new location.

When you need to keep track of multiple pieces of cut or copied text, it's helpful to open the **Clipboard task pane**, which displays the contents of the Clipboard. You open the Clipboard task pane by clicking the Dialog Box Launcher in the Clipboard group on the Home tab. When the Clipboard task pane is displayed, the Clipboard can store up to 24 text items. When the Clipboard task pane is not displayed, the Clipboard can hold only the most recently copied item.

Carolina would like to move the third-to-last sentence under the "LEED for Homes Fact Sheet" heading on page 1. You'll use cut and paste to move this sentence to a new location.

To move text using cut and paste:

▶ **1.** Make sure the Home tab is selected on the ribbon.

▶ **2.** Scroll up until you can see the second paragraph in the document, just below the "LEED for Homes Fact Sheet" heading.

▶ **3.** Press and hold the **Ctrl** key, and then click anywhere in the third-to-last sentence of the second paragraph, which reads "The staff of *Wilson and Page Architecture* is ready to make your LEED dream a reality." The entire sentence and the space following it are selected.

▶ **4.** In the Clipboard group, click the **Cut** button. The selected text is removed from the document and copied to the Clipboard.

▶ **5.** Scroll down to page 2, and then click at the beginning of the second-to-last paragraph in the document, just to the left of the "T" in "Talk to your project manager…."

▶ **6.** In the Clipboard group, click the **Paste** button. The sentence and the space following it are displayed in the new location. The Paste Options button appears near the newly inserted sentence.

Trouble? If a menu opens below the Paste button, you clicked the Paste button arrow instead of the Paste button. Press the Esc key to close the menu, and then repeat Step 6, taking care not to click the arrow below the Paste button.

▶ **7.** Save the document.

TIP

You can also press the Ctrl+X keys to cut selected text. Press the Ctrl+V keys to paste the most recently copied item.

Carolina explains that she'll be using some text from the Home LEED document as the basis for another department handout. She asks you to copy that information and paste it into a new document. You can do this using the Clipboard task pane.

To copy text to paste into a new document:

▶ **1.** In the Clipboard group, click the **Dialog Box Launcher**. The Clipboard task pane opens on the left side of the document window, as shown in Figure 2-9.

| Figure 2-9 | Clipboard task pane |

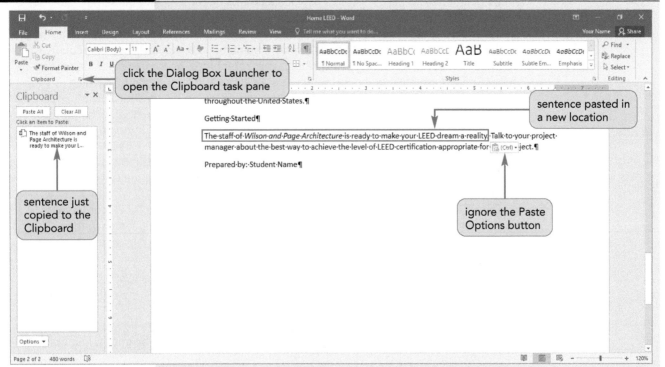

Notice the Clipboard contains the sentence you copied in the last set of steps, although you can see only the first part of the sentence.

▶ **2.** Scroll up, if necessary, and then locate the first sentence on page 2.

▶ **3.** Press and hold the **Ctrl** key, and then click anywhere in the first sentence on page 2, which begins "A project can achieve up to 100…." The sentence and the space following it are selected.

▶ **4.** In the Clipboard group, click the **Copy** button. The first part of the sentence appears at the top of the Clipboard task pane, as shown in Figure 2-10. You can also copy selected text by pressing the Ctrl+C keys.

Figure 2-10   Items in the Clipboard task pane

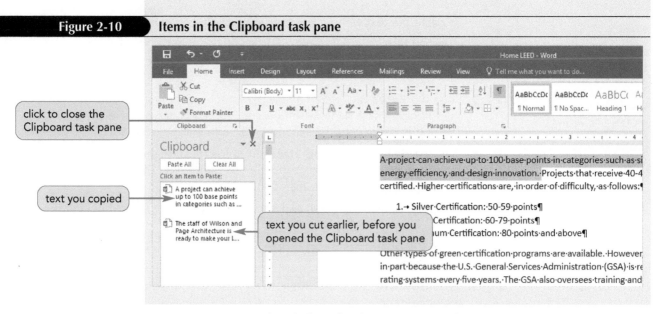

click to close the Clipboard task pane

text you copied

text you cut earlier, before you opened the Clipboard task pane

Now you can use the Clipboard task pane to insert the copied text into a new document.

To insert the copied text into a new document:

▶ **1.** Open a new, blank document. If necessary, open the Clipboard task pane.

▶ **2.** In the Clipboard task pane, click the second item in the list of copied items, which begins "The staff of *Wilson and Page Architecture* is ready...." The text is inserted in the document and the company name, "Wilson and Page Architecture," retains its italic formatting.

Carolina doesn't want to keep the italic formatting in the newly pasted text. You can remove this formatting by using the Paste Options button, which is visible just below the pasted text.

▶ **3.** Click the **Paste Options** button in the document. The Paste Options menu opens, as shown in Figure 2-11.

Figure 2-11   Paste Options menu

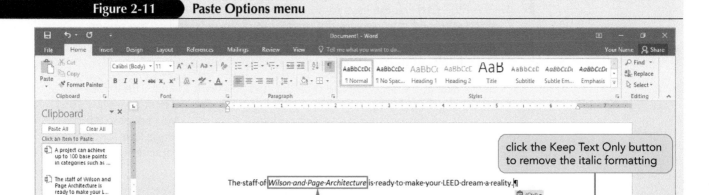

click the Keep Text Only button to remove the italic formatting

text inserted from the Clipboard retains its original formatting

To paste the text without the italic formatting, you can click the Keep Text Only button.

TIP

To select a paste option before pasting an item, click the Paste button arrow in the Clipboard group, and then click the paste option you want.

4. Click the **Keep Text Only** button. Word removes the italic formatting from "Wilson and Page Architecture."

5. Press the **Enter** key to start a new paragraph, and then click the first item in the Clipboard task pane, which begins "A project can achieve up to 100...." The text is inserted as the second paragraph in the document.

6. Save the document as **New Handout** in the location specified by your instructor, and then close it. You return to the Home LEED document, where the Clipboard task pane is still open.

7. In the Clipboard task pane, click the **Clear All** button. The copied items are removed from the Clipboard.

8. In the Clipboard task pane, click the **Close** button. The Clipboard task pane closes.

9. Click anywhere in the document to deselect the paragraph, and then save the document.

Using the Navigation Pane

The Navigation pane simplifies the process of moving through a document page by page. You can also use the Navigation pane to locate a particular word or phrase. You start by typing the text you're searching for—the **search text**—in the Search box at the top of the Navigation pane. As shown in the Session 2.1 Visual Overview, Word highlights every instance of the search text in the document. At the same time, a list of the **search results** appears in the Navigation pane. You can click a search result to go immediately to that location in the document.

To become familiar with the Navigation pane, you'll use it to navigate through the Home LEED document page by page. You'll start by moving the insertion point to the beginning of the document.

To navigate through the document page by page:

1. Press the **Ctrl+Home** keys to move the insertion point to the beginning of the document, making sure the Home tab is still selected on the ribbon.

2. In the Editing group, click the **Find** button. The Navigation pane opens on the left side of the Word window.

   In the box at the top, you can type the text you want to find. The three links below the Search document box—Headings, Pages, and Results—allow you to navigate through the document in different ways. As you become a more experienced Word user, you'll learn how to use the Headings link; for now, you'll ignore it. To move quickly among the pages of a document, you can use the Pages link.

3. In the Navigation pane, click the **Pages** link. The Navigation pane displays thumbnail icons of the document's two pages, as shown in Figure 2-12. You can click a page in the Navigation pane to display that page in the document window.

| Figure 2-12 | Document pages displayed in the Navigation pane |

click to display page thumbnails

Search document box

page 1

page 2

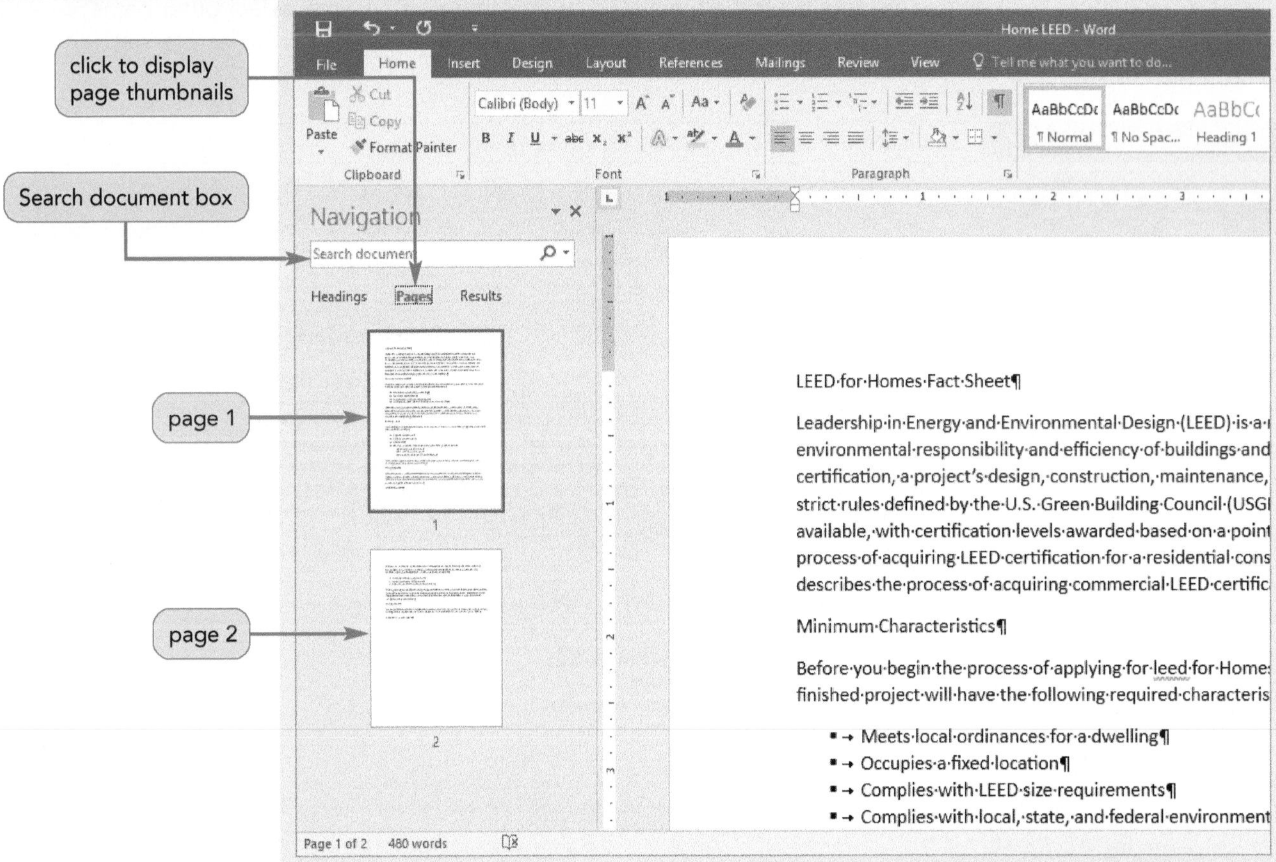

> **4.** In the Navigation pane, click the **page 2** thumbnail. Page 2 is displayed in the document window, with the insertion point blinking at the beginning of the page.

> **5.** In the Navigation pane, click the **page 1** thumbnail to move the insertion point back to the beginning of the document.

Carolina thinks she might have mistakenly used "leed" when she actually meant to use "LEED" in certain parts of the document. She asks you to use the Navigation pane to find all instances of "leed."

To search for "leed" in the document:

> **1.** In the Navigation pane, click the **Results** link, click the **Search document** box, and then type **leed**. You do not have to press the Enter key.

Every instance of the word "leed" is highlighted in yellow in the document. The yellow highlight is only temporary; it will disappear as soon as you begin to perform any other task in the document. A full list of the 20 search results is displayed in the Navigation pane. Some of the search results contain "LEED" (with all uppercase letters), while others contain "leed" (with all lowercase letters). To narrow the search results, you need to tell Word to match the case of the search text.

2. In the Navigation pane, click the **Search for more things** button ![icon]. This displays a two-part menu. In the bottom part, you can select other items to search for, such as graphics or tables. The top part provides more advanced search tools. See Figure 2-13.

Figure 2-13 **Navigation pane with Search for more things menu**

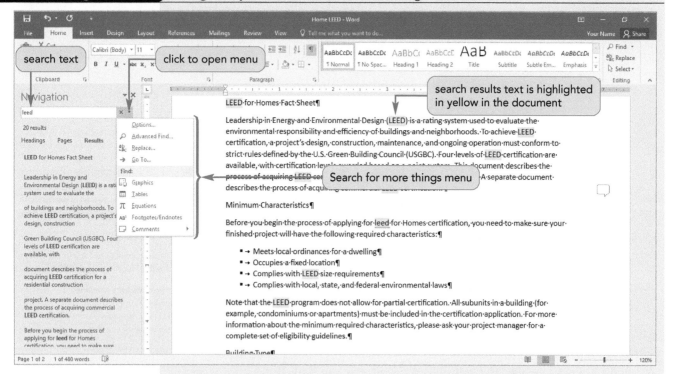

3. At the top of the Search for more things menu, click **Options** to open the Find Options dialog box.

The check boxes in this dialog box allow you to fine-tune your search. For example, to ensure that Word finds the search text only when it appears as a separate word and not when it appears as part of another word, you could select the Find whole words only check box. Right now, you are concerned only with making sure the search results have the same case as the search text.

4. Click the **Match case** check box to select it, and then click the **OK** button to close the Find Options dialog box. Now you can search the document again.

5. Press the **Ctrl+Home** keys to move the insertion point to the beginning of the document, click the **Search document** box in the Navigation pane, and then type **leed**. This time, there are only three search results in the Navigation pane, and they contain the lowercase text "leed."

To move among the search results, you can use the up and down arrows in the Navigation pane.

6. In the Navigation pane, click the **down arrow** button ![icon]. Word selects the first instance of "leed" in the Navigation pane, as indicated by a blue outline. Also, in the document, the first instance has a gray selection highlight over the yellow highlight. See Figure 2-14.

Figure 2-14	Navigation pane with the first search result selected

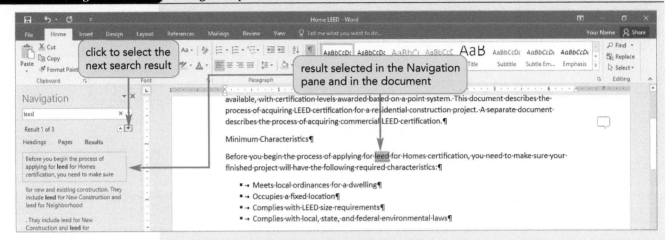

Trouble? If the second instance of "leed" is selected in the Navigation pane, then you pressed the Enter key after typing "leed" in Step 5. Click the up arrow button ▲ to select the first instance.

▶ **7.** In the Navigation pane, click the **down arrow** button ▼. Word selects the second instance of "leed" in the document and in the Navigation pane.

▶ **8.** Click the **down arrow** button ▼ again to select the third search result, and then click the **up arrow** button ▲ to select the second search result again.

You can also select a search result in the document by clicking a search result in the Navigation pane.

▶ **9.** In the Navigation pane, click the third search result (which begins ". They include leed for New Construction…"). The third search result is selected in the document and in the Navigation pane.

After reviewing the search results, Carolina decides she would like to replace the three instances of "leed" with "LEED." You can do that by using the Find and Replace dialog box.

Finding and Replacing Text

To open the Find and Replace dialog box from the Navigation pane, click the Search for more things button, and then click Replace. This opens the **Find and Replace dialog box**, with the Replace tab displayed by default. The Replace tab provides options for finding a specific word or phrase in the document and replacing it with another word or phrase. To use the Replace tab, type the search text in the Find what box, and then type the text you want to substitute in the Replace with box. You can also click the More button on the Replace tab to display the Search Options section, which includes the same options you saw earlier in the Find Options dialog box, including the Find whole words only check box and the Match case check box.

After you have typed the search text and selected any search options, you can click the Find Next button to select the first occurrence of the search text; you can then decide whether to substitute the search text with the replacement text.

REFERENCE

Finding and Replacing Text

- Press the Ctrl+Home keys to move the insertion point to the beginning of the document.
- In the Editing group on the Home tab, click the Replace button; or, in the Navigation pane, click the Search for more things button, and then click Replace.
- In the Find and Replace dialog box, click the More button, if necessary, to expand the dialog box and display the Search Options section of the Replace tab.
- In the Find what box, type the search text.
- In the Replace with box, type the replacement text.
- Select the appropriate check boxes in the Search Options section of the dialog box to narrow your search.
- Click the Find Next button.
- Click the Replace button to substitute the found text with the replacement text and find the next occurrence.
- Click the Replace All button to substitute all occurrences of the found text with the replacement text without reviewing each occurrence. Use this option only if you are absolutely certain that the results will be what you expect.

You'll use the Find and Replace dialog box now to replace three instances of "leed" with "LEED."

To replace three instances of "leed" with "LEED":

1. Press the **Ctrl+Home** keys to move the insertion point to the beginning of the document.

2. In the Navigation pane, click the **Search for more things** button ▼ to open the menu, and then click **Replace**. The Find and Replace dialog box opens with the Replace tab on top.

   The search text you entered earlier in the Navigation pane, "leed," appears in the Find what box. If you hadn't already conducted a search, you would need to type your search text now. Because you selected the Match case check box earlier in the Find Options dialog box, "Match Case" appears below the Find what box.

3. In the lower-left corner of the dialog box, click the **More** button to display the search options. Because you selected the Match case check box earlier in the Find Options dialog box, it is selected here.

   Trouble? If you see the Less button instead of the More button, the search options are already displayed.

4. Click the **Replace with** box, and then type **LEED**.

5. Click the **Find Next** button. Word highlights the first instance of "leed" in the document. See Figure 2-15.

Figure 2-15   **Find and Replace dialog box**

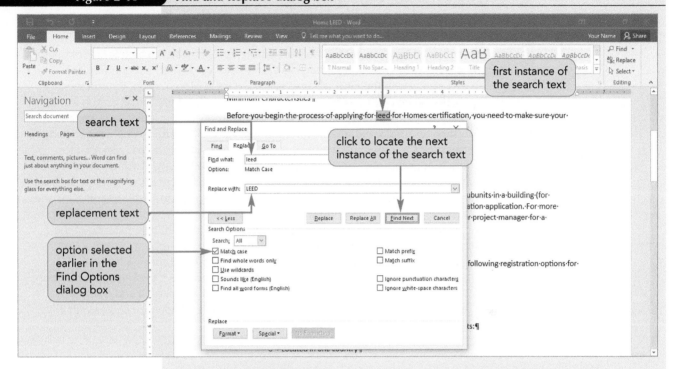

6. Click the **Replace** button. Word replaces "leed" with "LEED," so the text reads "applying for LEED for Homes certification." Then, Word selects the next instance of "leed." If you do not want to make a replacement, you can click the Find Next button to skip the current instance of the search text and move onto the next. In this case, however, you do want to make the replacement.

7. Click the **Replace** button. Word selects the last instance of "leed," which happens to be located in the same sentence.

8. Click the **Replace** button. Word makes the substitution, so the text reads "LEED for Neighborhood Development," and then displays a message box telling you that Word has finished searching the document.

9. Click the **OK** button to close the message box, and then in the Find and Replace dialog box, click the **Close** button.

You are finished with the Navigation pane, so you can close it. But first you need to restore the search options to their original settings. It's a good practice to restore the original search settings so that future searches are not affected by any settings you used for an earlier search.

To restore the search options to their original settings:

1. In the Navigation pane, open the **Find Options** dialog box, deselect the **Match case** check box, and then click the **OK** button to close the Find Options dialog box.

2. Click the **Close** button ⊠ in the upper-right corner of the Navigation pane.

3. Save the document.

Searching for Formatting

You can search for formatting just as you can search for text. For example, you might want to check a document to look for text formatted in bold and the Arial font. To search for formatting from within the Navigation pane, click the Search for more things button to display the menu, and then click Advanced Find. The Find and Replace dialog box opens with the Find tab displayed. Click the More button, if necessary, to display the Search Options section of the Find tab. Click the Format button at the bottom of the Search Options section, click the category of formatting you want to look for (such as Font or Paragraph), and then select the formatting you want to find.

You can look for formatting that occurs only on specific text, or you can look for formatting that occurs anywhere in a document. If you're looking for text formatted in a certain way (such as all instances of "LEED" that are bold), enter the text in the Find what box, and then specify the formatting you're looking for. To find formatting on any text in a document, leave the Find what box empty, and then specify the formatting. Use the Find Next button to move through the document, from one instance of the specified formatting to another.

You can follow the same basic steps on the Replace tab to replace one type of formatting with another. First, click the Find what box and select the desired formatting. Then click the Replace with box and select the desired formatting. If you want, type search text and replacement text in the appropriate boxes. Then proceed as with any Find and Replace operation.

Now that the text in the Home LEED document is final, you will turn your attention to styles and themes, which affect the look of the entire document.

Working with Styles

A style is a set of formatting options that you can apply by clicking an icon in the Style gallery on the Home tab. Each style is designed for a particular use. For example, the Title style is intended for formatting the title at the beginning of a document.

All the text you type into a document has a style applied to it. By default, text is formatted in the Normal style, which applies 11-point Calibri font, left alignment, 1.08 line spacing, and a small amount of extra space between paragraphs. In other words, the Normal style applies the default formatting you learned about when you first began typing a Word document.

Note that some styles apply **paragraph-level formatting**—that is, they are set up to format an entire paragraph, including the paragraph and line spacing. The Normal, Heading, and Title styles all apply paragraph-level formatting. Other styles apply **character-level formatting**—that is, they are set up to format only individual characters or words (for example, emphasizing a phrase by adding italic formatting and changing the font color).

One row of the Style gallery is always visible on the Home tab. To display the entire Style gallery, click the More button in the Styles group. After you begin applying styles in a document, the visible row of the Style gallery changes to show the most recently used styles.

You are ready to use the Style gallery to format the document title.

To display the entire Style gallery and then format the document title with a style:

▸ **1.** Make sure the Home tab is still selected and locate the More button in the Styles group, as shown earlier in the Session 2.1 Visual Overview.

▸ **2.** In the Styles group, click the **More** button. The Style gallery opens, displaying a total of 16 styles arranged in two rows, as shown in Figure 2-16. If your screen is set at a lower resolution than the screenshots in this book, the Style gallery on your screen might contain more than two rows.

Figure 2-16   Displaying the Style gallery

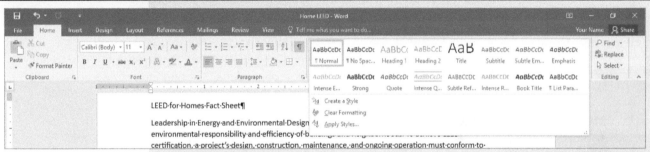

You don't actually need any of the styles in the bottom row now, so you can close the Style gallery.

▸ **3.** Press the **Esc** key to close the Style gallery.

▸ **4.** Click anywhere in the first paragraph, "LEED for Homes Fact Sheet," if necessary, and then point to (but don't click) the **Title** style, which is the fifth style from the left in the top row of the gallery. The ScreenTip "Title" is displayed, and a Live Preview of the style appears in the paragraph containing the insertion point, as shown in Figure 2-17. The Title style changes the font to 28-point Calibri Light.

Figure 2-17   Title style in the Style gallery

▸ **5.** Click the **Title** style. The style is applied to the paragraph. To finish the title, you need to center it.

▸ **6.** In the Paragraph group, click the **Center** button ≡. The title is centered in the document.

Next, you will format the document headings using the heading styles, which have different levels. The highest level, Heading 1, is used for the major headings in a document, and it applies the most noticeable formatting with a larger font than the other heading styles. (In heading styles, the highest, or most important, level has the lowest number.) The Heading 2 style is used for headings that are subordinate to the highest level headings; it applies slightly less dramatic formatting than the Heading 1 style.

The Home LEED handout only has one level of headings, so you will apply only the Heading 1 style.

To format text with the Heading 1 style:

1. Click anywhere in the "Minimum Characteristics" paragraph.

2. On the Home tab, in the Style gallery, click the **Heading 1** style. The paragraph is now formatted in blue, 16-point Calibri Light. The Heading 1 style also inserts some paragraph space above the heading.

3. Scroll down, click anywhere in the "Building Type" paragraph, and then click the **Heading 1** style in the Style gallery.

4. Repeat Step 3 to apply the Heading 1 style to the "Rating Systems" paragraph, the "Certification Levels" paragraph, and the "Getting Started" paragraph. When you are finished, scroll up to the beginning of the document to review the new formatting. See Figure 2-18.

TIP

On most computers, you can press the F4 key to repeat your most recent action.

| Figure 2-18 | Document with Title and Heading 1 styles |

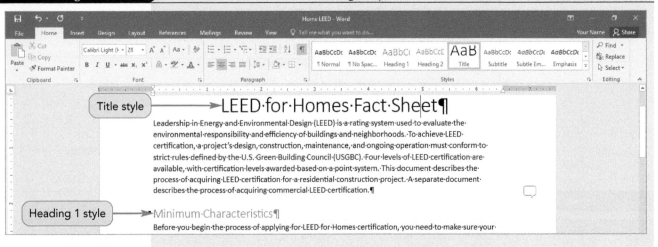

Understanding the Benefits of Heading Styles

By default, the Style gallery offers 16 styles, each designed for a specific purpose. As you gain more experience with Word, you will learn how to use a wider array of styles. You'll also learn how to create your own styles. Styles allow you to change a document's formatting in an instant. But the benefits of heading styles go far beyond attractive formatting. Heading styles allow you to reorganize a document or generate a table of contents with a click of the mouse. Also, heading styles are set up to keep a heading and the body text that follows it together, so a heading is never separated from its body text by a page break. Each Word document includes nine levels of heading styles, although only the Heading 1 and Heading 2 styles are available by default in the Style gallery. Whenever you use the lowest heading style in the Style gallery, the next-lowest level is added to the Style gallery. For example, after you use the Heading 2 style, the Heading 3 style appears in the Styles group in the Style gallery.

After you format a document with a variety of styles, you can alter the look of the document by changing the document's theme.

Working with Themes

A **theme** is a coordinated collection of fonts, colors, and other visual effects designed to give a document a cohesive, polished look. A variety of themes are installed with Word, with more available online at Templates.office.com. When you open a new, blank document in Word, the Office theme is applied by default. To change a document's theme, you click the Themes button, which is located in the Document Formatting group on the Design tab, and then click the theme you want. Pointing to the Themes button displays a ScreenTip that tells you what theme is currently applied to the document.

When applying color to a document, you usually have the option of selecting a color from a palette of colors designed to match the current theme or from a palette of standard colors. For instance, recall that the colors in the Font Color gallery are divided into Theme Colors and Standard Colors. When you select a Standard Color, such as Dark Red, that color remains the same no matter which theme you apply to the document. But when you click one of the Theme Colors, you are essentially telling Word to use the color located in that particular spot on the Theme Colors palette. Then, if you change the document's theme later, Word substitutes a color from the same location on the Theme Colors palette. This ensures that all the colors in a document are drawn from a group of colors coordinated to look good together. So as a rule, if you are going to use multiple colors in a document (perhaps for paragraph shading and font color), it's a good idea to stick with the Theme Colors.

A similar substitution takes place with fonts when you change the theme. However, to understand how this works, you need to understand the difference between headings and body text. Carolina's document includes the headings "Minimum Characteristics," "Building Type," "Rating Systems," "Certification Levels," and "Getting Started"—all of which you have formatted with the Heading1 style. The title of the document, "LEED for Homes Fact Sheet," is now formatted with the Title style, which is also a type of heading style. Everything else in the Home LEED document is body text.

To ensure that your documents have a harmonious look, each theme assigns a font for headings and a font for body text. Typically, in a given theme, the same font is used for both headings and body text, but not always. In the Office theme, for instance, they are slightly different; the heading font is Calibri Light, and the body font is Calibri. These two fonts appear at the top of the Font list as "Calibri Light (Headings)" and "Calibri (Body)" when you click the Font box arrow in the Font group on the Home tab. When you begin typing text in a new document with the Office theme, the text is formatted as body text with the Calibri font by default.

When applying a font to selected text, you can choose one of the two theme fonts at the top of the Font list, or you can choose one of the other fonts in the Font list. If you choose one of the other fonts and then change the document theme, that font remains the same. But if you use one of the theme fonts and then change the document theme, Word substitutes the appropriate font from the new theme. When you paste text into a document that has a different theme, Word applies the theme fonts and colors of the new document. To retain the original formatting, use the Keep Source Formatting option in the Paste Options menu.

Figure 2-19 compares elements of the default Office theme with the Integral theme. The Integral theme was chosen for this example because, like the Office theme, it has different heading and body fonts.

Figure 2-19   Comparing the Office theme to the Integral theme

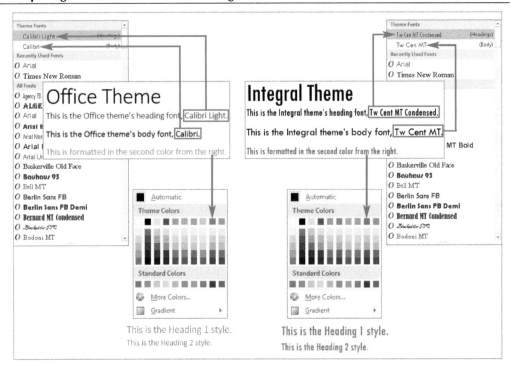

Because Carolina has not yet selected a new theme, the Office theme is currently applied to the Home LEED document. However, she thinks the Berlin theme might be more appropriate for the Home LEED document. She asks you to apply it now.

To change the document's theme:

1. If necessary, press the **Ctrl+Home** keys to move the insertion point to the beginning of the document. With the title and first heading visible, you will more easily see what happens when you change the document's theme.

2. On the ribbon, click the **Design** tab.

3. In the Document Formatting group, point to the **Themes** button. A ScreenTip appears containing the text "Current: Office Theme" as well as general information about themes.

4. In the Document Formatting group, click the **Themes** button. The Themes gallery opens. Because Microsoft occasionally updates the available themes, you might see a different list than the one shown in Figure 2-20.

Figure 2-20   Themes gallery

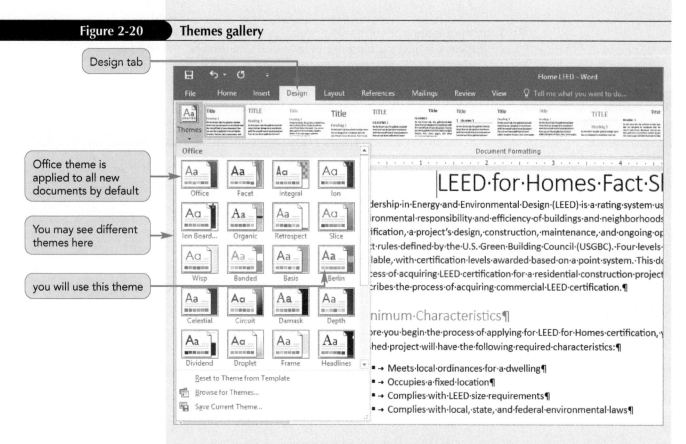

5. Move the mouse pointer (without clicking it) over the various themes in the gallery to see a Live Preview of each theme in the document. The heading and body fonts as well as the heading colors change to reflect the fonts associated with the various themes.

6. In the Themes gallery, click the **Berlin** theme. The text in the Home LEED document changes to the body and heading fonts of the Berlin theme, with the headings formatted in dark orange. To see exactly what the Berlin theme fonts are, you can point to the Fonts button in the Document Formatting group.

    Trouble? If you do not see the Berlin theme in your Themes gallery, click a different theme.

7. In the Document Formatting group, point to the **Fonts** button. A ScreenTip appears, listing the currently selected theme (Berlin), the heading font (Trebuchet MS), and the body font (Trebuchet MS). See Figure 2-21.

Figure 2-21   **Fonts for the Berlin theme**

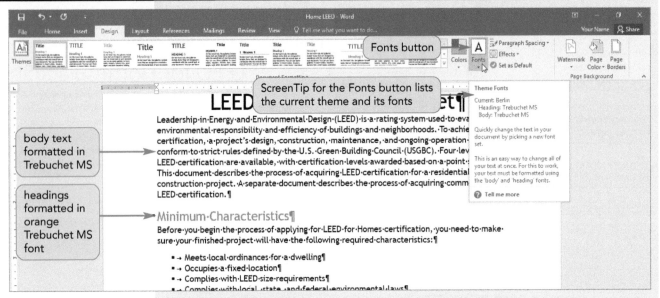

Trouble? If a menu appears, you clicked the Fonts button instead of pointing to it. Press the Esc key, and then repeat Step 7.

8. Save your changes and then close the document.

Carolina's Home LEED document is ready to be handed in to her supervisor. The use of styles, bulleted and numbered lists, and a new theme gives the document a professional look appropriate for use in a business handout.

INSIGHT

Personalizing the Word Interface

The Word Options dialog box allows you to change the look of the Word interface. For starters, you can change the Office Theme from the default setting (Colorful) to Dark Gray or White. Note that in this context, "Office Theme" refers to the colors of the Word interface, and not the colors and fonts used in a Word document. You can also use the Office Background setting to add graphic designs, such as clouds or stars, to the Word interface. To get started, click the File tab, click Options in the navigation bar, and then select the options you want in the Personalize your copy of Microsoft Office section of the Word Options dialog box.

REVIEW

Session 2.1 Quick Check

1. When you reply to a comment, what name appears in the reply?
2. When should you use a numbered list instead of a bulleted list?
3. How can you ensure that the Navigation pane will find instances of "LEED" instead of "leed"?
4. What style is applied to all text in a new document by default?
5. What theme is applied to a new document by default?

Session 2.2 Visual Overview:

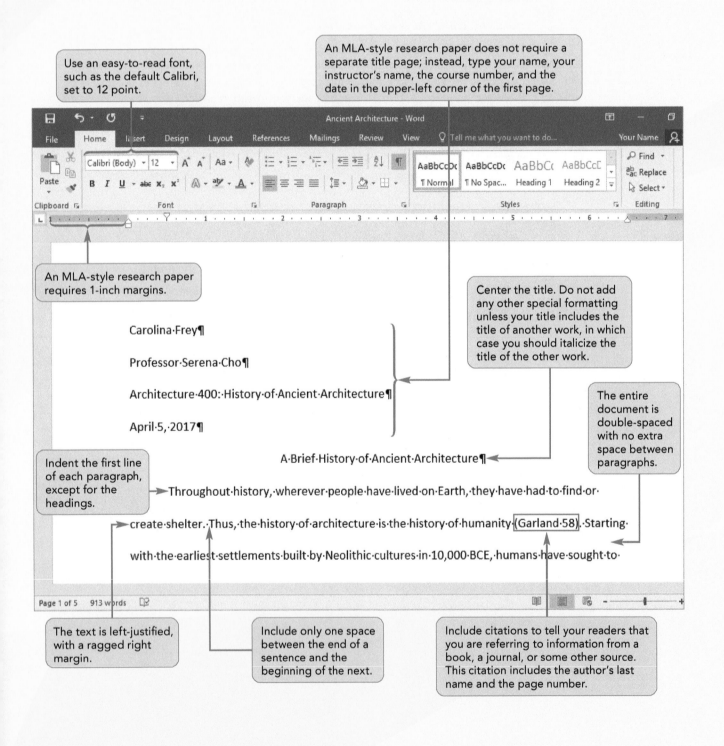

Use an easy-to-read font, such as the default Calibri, set to 12 point.

An MLA-style research paper does not require a separate title page; instead, type your name, your instructor's name, the course number, and the date in the upper-left corner of the first page.

An MLA-style research paper requires 1-inch margins.

Center the title. Do not add any other special formatting unless your title includes the title of another work, in which case you should italicize the title of the other work.

The entire document is double-spaced with no extra space between paragraphs.

Indent the first line of each paragraph, except for the headings.

The text is left-justified, with a ragged right margin.

Include only one space between the end of a sentence and the beginning of the next.

Include citations to tell your readers that you are referring to information from a book, a journal, or some other source. This citation includes the author's last name and the page number.

MLA Formatting Guidelines

The References tab includes options that help you create a research paper.

In the Style box, specify the style of research paper you are creating. For college research papers, the MLA style is commonly used.

After you create all the citations, click the Bibliography button to create a list of all the sources mentioned in your citations. This list is known as a bibliography or, in the MLA style, a works cited list.

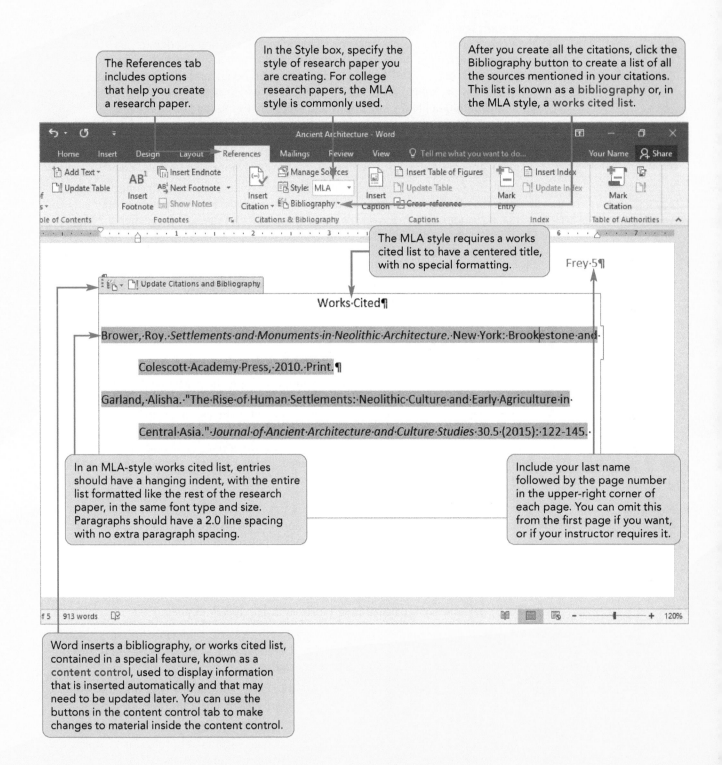

The MLA style requires a works cited list to have a centered title, with no special formatting.

In an MLA-style works cited list, entries should have a hanging indent, with the entire list formatted like the rest of the research paper, in the same font type and size. Paragraphs should have a 2.0 line spacing with no extra paragraph spacing.

Include your last name followed by the page number in the upper-right corner of each page. You can omit this from the first page if you want, or if your instructor requires it.

Word inserts a bibliography, or works cited list, contained in a special feature, known as a content control, used to display information that is inserted automatically and that may need to be updated later. You can use the buttons in the content control tab to make changes to material inside the content control.

Reviewing the MLA Style

A **style guide** is a set of rules that describe the preferred format and style for a certain type of writing. People in different fields use different style guides, with each style guide designed to suit the needs of a specific discipline. For example, journalists commonly use the *Associated Press Stylebook*, which focuses on the concise writing style common in magazines and newspapers. In the world of academics, style guides emphasize the proper way to create **citations**, which are formal references to the work of others. Researchers in the social and behavioral sciences use the **American Psychological Association (APA) style**, which is designed to help readers scan an article quickly for key points and emphasizes the date of publication in citations. Other scientific and technical fields have their own specialized style guides.

In the humanities, the **Modern Language Association (MLA) style** is widely used. This is the style Carolina has used for her research paper. She followed the guidelines specified in the *MLA Handbook for Writers of Research Papers*, published by the Modern Language Association of America. These guidelines focus on specifications for formatting a research document and citing the sources used in research conducted for a paper. The major formatting features of an MLA-style research paper are illustrated in the Session 2.2 Visual Overview. Compared to style guides for technical fields, the MLA style is very flexible, making it easy to include citations without disrupting the natural flow of the writing. MLA-style citations of other writers' works take the form of a brief parenthetical entry, with a complete reference to each item included in the alphabetized bibliography, also known as the works cited list, at the end of the research paper.

INSIGHT

Formatting an MLA-Style Research Paper

The MLA guidelines were developed, in part, to simplify the process of transforming a manuscript into a journal article or a chapter of a book. The style calls for minimal formatting; the simpler the formatting in a manuscript, the easier it is to turn the text into a published document. The MLA guidelines were also designed to ensure consistency in documents, so that all research papers look alike. Therefore, you should apply no special formatting to the text in an MLA-style research paper. Headings should be formatted like the other text in the document, with no bold or heading styles.

Carolina has started writing a research paper on the history of architecture for her class. You'll open the draft of Carolina's research paper and determine what needs to be done to make it meet the MLA style guidelines for a research paper.

To open the document and review it for MLA style:

▶ **1.** Open the document **Ancient** located in the Word2 > Module folder included with your Data Files, and then save the document as **Ancient Architecture** in the location specified by your instructor.

▶ **2.** Verify that the document is displayed in Print Layout view, and that the rulers and nonprinting characters are displayed. Make sure the Zoom level is set to **120%**.

▶ **3.** Review the document to familiarize yourself with its structure. First, notice the parts of the document that already match the MLA style. Carolina included a block of information in the upper-left corner of the first page, giving her name, her instructor's name, the course name, and the date. The title at the top of the first page also meets the MLA guidelines in that it is centered and does not have any special formatting. The headings

("Neolithic Settlements," "Egyptian Construction," "The Civic-Minded Greeks," and "Roman Achievement") have no special formatting; but unlike the title, they are left-aligned. Finally, the body text is left-aligned with a ragged right margin, and the entire document is formatted in the same font, Calibri, which is easy to read.

What needs to be changed in order to make Carolina's paper consistent with the MLA style? Currently, the entire document is formatted using the default settings, which are the Normal style for the Office theme. To transform the document into an MLA-style research paper, you need to complete the checklist shown in Figure 2-22.

Figure 2-22	Checklist for formatting a default Word document to match the MLA style

✓ Double-space the entire document.

✓ Remove paragraph spacing from the entire document.

✓ Increase the font size for the entire document to 12 points.

✓ Indent the first line of each body paragraph .5 inch from the left margin.

✓ Add the page number (preceded by your last name) in the upper-right corner of each page. If you prefer, you can omit this from the first page.

You'll take care of the first three items in the checklist now.

To begin applying MLA formatting to the document:

1. Press the **Ctrl+A** keys to select the entire document.

2. Make sure the Home tab is selected on the ribbon.

3. In the Paragraph group, click the **Line and Paragraph Spacing** button ⟰, and then click **2.0**.

4. Click the **Line and Spacing** button ⟰ again, and then click **Remove Space After Paragraph**. The entire document is now double-spaced, with no paragraph spacing, and the entire document is still selected.

5. In the Font group, click the **Font Size** arrow, and then click **12**. The entire document is formatted in 12-point font.

6. Click anywhere in the document to deselect the text.

7. In the first paragraph of the document, replace Carolina's name with your first and last names, and then save the document.

Now you need to indent the first line of each body paragraph.

Indenting a Paragraph

Word offers a number of options for indenting a paragraph. You can move an entire paragraph to the right, or you can create specialized indents, such as a **hanging indent**, where all lines except the first line of the paragraph are indented from the left margin. As you saw in the Session 2.2 Visual Overview, all the body paragraphs (that is, all the paragraphs except the information in the upper-left corner of the first page, the title, and the headings) have a first-line indent in MLA research papers. Figure 2-23 shows some examples of other common paragraph indents.

Figure 2-23 Common paragraph indents

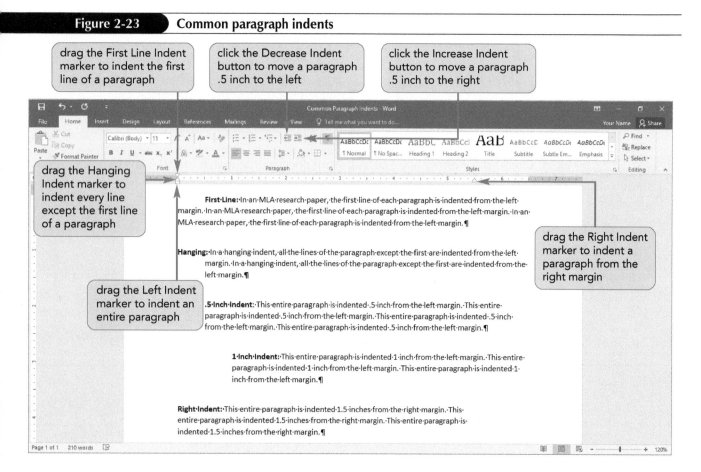

To quickly indent an entire paragraph .5 inch from the left, position the insertion point in the paragraph you want to indent, and then click the Increase Indent button in the Paragraph group on the Home tab. You can continue to indent the paragraph in increments of .5 inch by repeatedly clicking the Increase Indent button. To move an indented paragraph back to the left .5 inch, click the Decrease Indent button.

To create first-line, hanging, or right indents, you can use the indent markers on the ruler. First, click in the paragraph you want to indent or select multiple paragraphs. Then drag the appropriate indent marker to the left or right on the horizontal ruler. The indent markers are small and can be hard to see. As shown in Figure 2-23, the **First Line Indent marker** looks like the top half of an hourglass; the **Hanging Indent marker** looks like the bottom half. The rectangle below the Hanging Indent marker is the **Left Indent marker**. The **Right Indent marker** looks just like the Hanging Indent marker except that it is located on the far-right side of the horizontal ruler.

Note that when you indent an entire paragraph using the Increase Indent button, the three indent markers, shown stacked on top of one another in Figure 2-23, move as a unit along with the paragraphs you are indenting.

In Carolina's paper, you will indent the first lines of the body paragraphs .5 inch from the left margin, as specified by the MLA style.

To indent the first line of each paragraph:

▶ **1.** On the first page of the document, just below the title, click anywhere in the first main paragraph, which begins "Throughout history...."

▶ **2.** On the horizontal ruler, position the mouse pointer over the First Line Indent marker 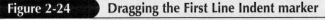. When you see the ScreenTip that reads "First Line Indent," you know the mouse is positioned correctly.

▶ **3.** Press and hold the mouse button as you drag the **First Line Indent** marker 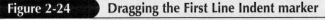 to the right, to the .5-inch mark on the horizontal ruler. As you drag, a vertical guideline appears over the document, and the first line of the paragraph moves right. See Figure 2-24.

Figure 2-24	Dragging the First Line Indent marker

First Line Indent marker

.5-inch mark

guideline appears as you drag the indent marker and the first line of the paragraph moves right

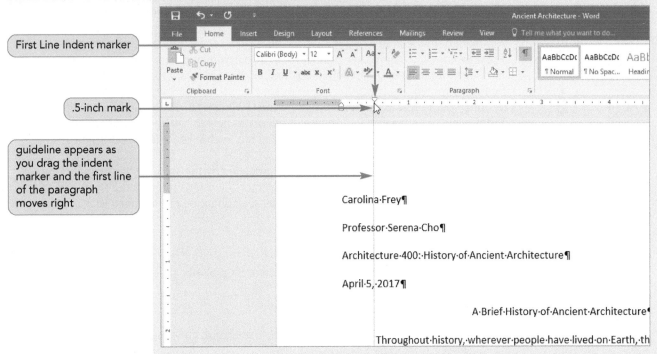

▶ **4.** When the First Line Indent marker 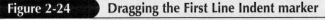 is positioned at the .5-inch mark on the ruler, release the mouse button. The first line of the paragraph containing the insertion point indents .5 inch, and the vertical guideline disappears.

▶ **5.** Scroll down, if necessary, click anywhere in the next paragraph in the document (which begins "In this paper, I will present..."), and then drag the **First Line Indent** marker 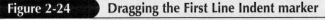 to the right, to the .5-inch mark on the horizontal ruler. As you move the indent marker, you can use the vertical guideline to ensure that you match the first-line indent of the preceding paragraph.

You could continue to drag the indent marker to indent the first line of the remaining body paragraphs, but it's faster to use the Repeat button on the Quick Access Toolbar.

▶ **6.** Scroll down and click in the paragraph below the "Neolithic Settlements" heading, and then on the Quick Access Toolbar, click the **Repeat** button ⟳.

▶ **7.** Click in the next paragraph, at the top of page 2 (which begins "The rise of agriculture introduced..."), and then click the **Repeat** button ⟳.

▶ **8.** Continue using the **Repeat** button ↻ to indent the first line of all of the remaining body paragraphs. Take care not to indent the headings, which in this document are formatted just like the body text.

▶ **9.** Scroll to the top of the document, verify that you have correctly indented the first line of each body paragraph, and then save the document.

Next, you need to insert page numbers.

Inserting and Modifying Page Numbers

When you insert page numbers in a document, you don't have to type a page number on each page. Instead, you can insert a **page number field**, which is an instruction that tells Word to insert a page number on each page, no matter how many pages you eventually add to the document. Word inserts page number fields above the top margin, in the blank area known as the **header**, or below the bottom margin, in the area known as the **footer**. You can also insert page numbers in the side margins, although for business or academic documents, it's customary to place them in the header or footer.

After you insert a page number field, Word switches to Header and Footer view. In this view, you can add your name or other text next to the page number field or use the Header & Footer Tools Design contextual tab to change various settings related to headers and footers.

The MLA style requires a page number preceded by the student's last name in the upper-right corner of each page. If you prefer (or if your instructor requests it), you can omit the page number from the first page by selecting the Different First Page check box on the Design tab.

To add page numbers to the research paper:

▶ **1.** Press the **Ctrl+Home** keys to move the insertion point to the beginning of the document.

▶ **2.** On the ribbon, click the **Insert** tab. The ribbon changes to display the Insert options, including options for inserting page numbers.

> **TIP**
>
> To remove page numbers from a document, click the Remove Page Numbers command on the Page Number menu.

▶ **3.** In the Header & Footer group, click the **Page Number** button to open the Page Number menu. Here you can choose where you want to position the page numbers in your document—at the top of the page, at the bottom of the page, in the side margins, or at the current location of the insertion point.

▶ **4.** Point to **Top of Page**. A gallery of page number styles opens. You can scroll the list to review the many styles of page numbers. Because the MLA style calls for a simple page number in the upper-right corner, you will use the Plain Number 3 style. See Figure 2-25.

Figure 2-25   Gallery of page number styles

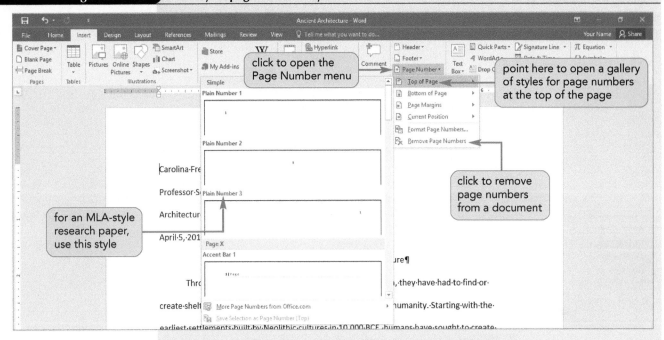

5. In the gallery, click the **Plain Number 3** style. The Word window switches to Header and Footer view, with the page number for the first page in the upper-right corner. The page number has a gray background, indicating that it is actually a page number field and not simply a number that you typed.

   The Header & Footer Tools Design tab is displayed on the ribbon, giving you access to a variety of formatting options. The insertion point blinks to the left of the page number field, ready for you to add text to the header if you wish. Note that in Header and Footer view, you can type only in the header or footer areas. The text in the main document area is a lighter shade of gray, indicating that it cannot be edited in this view.

6. Type your last name, and then press the **spacebar**. If you see a wavy red line below your last name, right-click your name, and then click **Ignore All** on the Shortcut menu.

7. Select your last name and the page number field.

8. In the Mini toolbar, click the **Font Size** button arrow, click **12**, and then click anywhere in the header to deselect it. Now the header's font size matches the font size of the rest of the document. This isn't strictly necessary in an MLA research paper, but some instructors prefer it. The page number no longer has a gray background, but it is still a field, which you can verify by clicking it.

9. Click the **page number field** to display its gray background. See Figure 2-26.

Figure 2-26   **Last name inserted next to the page number field**

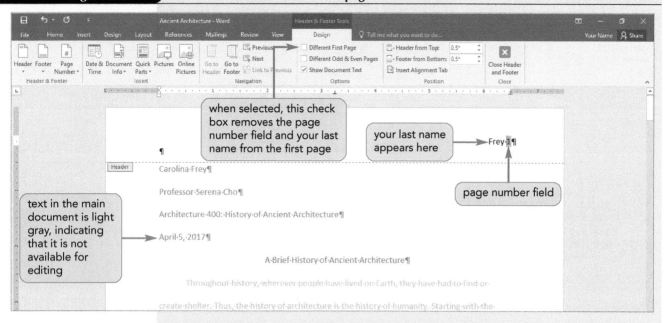

10. Scroll down and observe the page number (with your last name) at the top of pages 2, 3, and 4. As you can see, whatever you insert in the header on one page appears on every page of the document by default.

11. Press the **Ctrl+Home** keys to return to the header on the first page.

12. On the Header & Footer Tools Design tab, in the Options group, click the **Different First Page** check box to insert a check. The page number field and your last name are removed from the first page header. The insertion point blinks at the header's left margin in case you want to insert something else for the first page header. In this case, you don't.

13. In the Close group, click the **Close Header and Footer** button. You return to Print Layout view, and the Header & Footer Tools Design tab is no longer displayed on the ribbon.

14. Scroll down to review your last name and the page number in the headers for pages 2, 3, and 4. In Print Layout view, the text in the header is light gray, indicating that it is not currently available for editing.

TIP

After you insert page numbers, you can reopen Header and Footer view by double-clicking a page number in Print Layout view.

You have finished all the tasks related to formatting the MLA-style research paper. Now Carolina wants your help with creating the essential parts of any research paper—the citations and the bibliography.

Creating Citations and a Bibliography

A bibliography (or, as it is called in the MLA style, the works cited list) is an alphabetical list of all the books, magazine articles, websites, movies, and other works referred to in a research paper. The items listed in a bibliography are known as **sources**. The entry for each source includes information such as the author, the title of the work, the publication date, and the publisher.

Within the research paper itself, you include a parenthetical reference, or citation, every time you quote or refer to a source. Every source included in your citations then has a corresponding entry in the works cited list. A citation should include enough information to identify the quote or referenced material so the reader can easily locate the source in the accompanying works cited list. The exact form for a citation varies depending on the style guide you are using and the type of material you are referencing.

Some style guides are very rigid about the form and location of citations, but the MLA style offers quite a bit of flexibility. Typically, though, you insert an MLA citation at the end of a sentence in which you quote or refer to material from a source. For books or journals, the citation itself usually includes the author's last name and a page number. However, if the sentence containing the citation already includes the author's name, you need to include only the page number in the citation. Figure 2-27 provides some sample MLA citations; the format shown could be used for books or journals. For detailed guidelines, you can consult the *MLA Handbook for Writers of Research Papers, Seventh Edition*, which includes many examples.

Figure 2-27   **MLA guidelines for citing a book or journal**

Citation Rule	Example
If the sentence includes the author's name, the citation should only include the page number.	Peterson compares the opening scene of the movie to a scene from Shakespeare (188).
If the sentence does not include the author's name, the citation should include the author's name and the page number.	The opening scene of the movie has been compared to a scene from Shakespeare (Peterson 188).

Word greatly simplifies the process of creating citations and a bibliography. You specify the style you want to use, and then Word takes care of setting up the citation and the works cited list appropriately. Every time you create a citation for a new source, Word prompts you to enter the information needed to create the corresponding entry in the works cited list. If you don't have all of your source information available, Word also allows you to insert a temporary, placeholder citation, which you can replace later with a complete citation. When you are finished creating your citations, Word generates the bibliography automatically. Note that placeholder citations are not included in the bibliography.

PROSKILLS

Written Communication: Acknowledging Your Sources

A research paper is a means for you to explore the available information about a subject and then present this information, along with your own understanding of the subject, in an organized and interesting way. Acknowledging all the sources of the information presented in your research paper is essential. If you fail to do this, you might be subject to charges of plagiarism, or trying to pass off someone else's thoughts as your own. Plagiarism is an extremely serious accusation for which you could suffer academic consequences ranging from failing an assignment to being expelled from school.

To ensure that you don't forget to cite a source, you should be careful about creating citations in your document as you type. It's very easy to forget to go back and cite all your sources correctly after you've finished typing a research paper. Failing to cite a source could lead to accusations of plagiarism and all the consequences that entails. If you don't have the complete information about a source available when you are typing your paper, you should at least insert a placeholder citation. But take care to go back later and substitute complete citations for any placeholders.

Creating Citations

Before you create citations, you need to select the style you want to use, which in the case of Carolina's paper is the MLA style. Then, to insert a citation, you click the Insert Citation button in the Citations & Bibliography group on the References tab. If you are citing a source for the first time, Word prompts you to enter all the information required for the source's entry in the bibliography or works cited list. If you are citing an existing source, you simply select the source from the Insert Citation menu.

By default, an MLA citation includes only the author's name in parentheses. However, you can use the Edit Citation dialog box to add a page number. You can also use the Edit Citation dialog box to remove, or suppress, the author's name, so only the page number appears in the citation. However, in an MLA citation, Word will replace the suppressed author name with the title of the source, so you need to suppress the title as well, by selecting the Title check box in the Edit Citation dialog box.

REFERENCE

Creating Citations

- On the ribbon, click the References tab. In the Citations & Bibliography group, click the Style button arrow, and then select the style you want.
- Click in the document where you want to insert the citation. Typically, a citation goes at the end of a sentence, before the ending punctuation.
- To add a citation for a new source, click the Insert Citation button in the Citations & Bibliography group, click Add New Source, enter information in the Create Source dialog box, and then click the OK button.
- To add a citation for an existing source, click the Insert Citation button, and then click the source.
- To add a placeholder citation, click the Insert Citation button, click Add New Placeholder, and then, in the Placeholder Name dialog box, type placeholder text, such as the author's last name, that will serve as a reminder about which source you need to cite. Note that a placeholder citation cannot contain any spaces.
- To add a page number to a citation, click the citation in the document, click the Citation Options button, click Edit Citation, type the page number, and then click the OK button.
- To display only the page number in a citation, click the citation in the document, click the Citation Options button, and then click Edit Citation. In the Edit Citation dialog box, select the Author and Title check boxes to suppress this information, and then click the OK button.

So far, Carolina has referenced information from two different sources in her research paper. You'll select a style and then begin adding the appropriate citations.

To select a style for the citation and bibliography:

1. On the ribbon, click the **References** tab. The ribbon changes to display references options.

2. In the Citations & Bibliography group, click the **Style button** arrow, and then click **MLA Seventh Edition** if it is not already selected.

3. Press the **Ctrl+F** keys to open the Navigation pane.

4. Use the Navigation pane to find the phrase "As at least one historian," which appears on page 2, and then click in the document at the end of that sentence (between the end of the word "standing" and the closing period).

5. Close the **Navigation** pane, and then click the **References** tab on the ribbon, if necessary. You need to add a citation that informs the reader that historian Roy Brauer made the observation described in the sentence. See Figure 2-28.

> Be sure to select the correct citation and bibliography style before you begin.

| Figure 2-28 | MLA style selected and insertion point positioned for new citation |

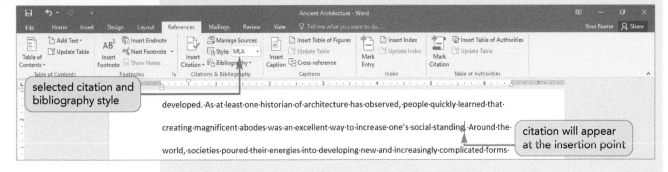

selected citation and bibliography style

developed. As at least one historian of architecture has observed, people quickly learned that creating magnificent abodes was an excellent way to increase one's social standing. Around the world, societies poured their energies into developing new and increasingly complicated forms

citation will appear at the insertion point

6. In the Citations & Bibliography group, click the **Insert Citation** button to open the menu. At this point, you could click Add New Placeholder on the menu to insert a temporary, placeholder citation. However, because you have all the necessary source information, you can go ahead and create a complete citation.

7. On the menu, click **Add New Source**. The Create Source dialog box opens, ready for you to add the information required to create a bibliography entry for Roy Brauer's book.

8. If necessary, click the **Type of Source** arrow, scroll up or down in the list, and then click **Book**.

9. In the Author box, type **Roy Brauer**.

10. Click in the **Title** box, and then type **Settlements and Monuments in Neolithic Architecture**.

11. Click in the **Year** box, and then type **2010**. This is the year the book was published. Next, you need to enter the name and location of the publisher.

12. Click the **City** box, type **New York**, click the **Publisher** box, and then type **Brookstone and Colescott Academy Press**.

Finally, you need to indicate the medium used to publish the book. In this case, Carolina used a printed copy, so the medium is "Print." For books or journals published online, the correct medium would be "Web."

13. Click the **Medium** box, and then type **Print**. See Figure 2-29.

TIP

When entering information in a dialog box, you can press the Tab key to move the insertion point from one box to another.

Figure 2-29	Create Source dialog box with information for the first source

Create Source

Type of Source   Book

Bibliography Fields for MLA

Author   Roy Brauer   Edit
☐ Corporate Author
Title   Settlements and Monuments in Neolithic Architecture
Year   2010
City   New York
Publisher   Brookstone and Colescott Academy Press
Medium   Print

☐ Show All Bibliography Fields
Tag name   Example: Document
Roy10   OK   Cancel

14. Click the **OK** button. Word inserts the parenthetical "(Brauer)" at the end of the sentence in the document.

Although the citation looks like ordinary text, it is actually contained inside a content control, a special feature used to display information that is inserted automatically and that may need to be updated later. You can see the content control itself only when it is selected. When it is unselected, you simply see the citation. In the next set of steps, you will select the content control and then edit the citation to add a page number.

TIP

To delete a citation, click the citation to display the content control, click the tab on the left side of the content control, and then press the Delete key.

To edit the citation:

1. In the document, click the citation **(Brauer)**. The citation appears in a content control, which is a box with a tab on the left and an arrow button on the right. The arrow button is called the Citation Options button.

2. Click the **Citation Options** button ▢. A menu of options related to editing a citation opens, as shown in Figure 2-30.

Figure 2-30   Citation Options menu

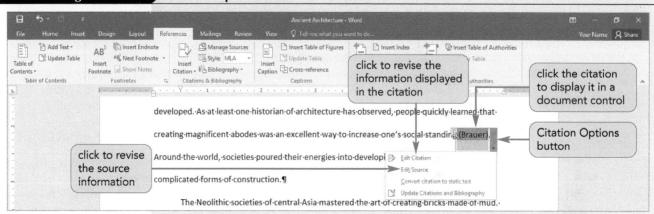

To edit the information about the source, you click Edit Source. To change the information that is displayed in the citation itself, you use the Edit Citation option.

3. On the Citation Options menu, click **Edit Citation**. The Edit Citation dialog box opens, as shown in Figure 2-31.

Figure 2-31   Edit Citation dialog box

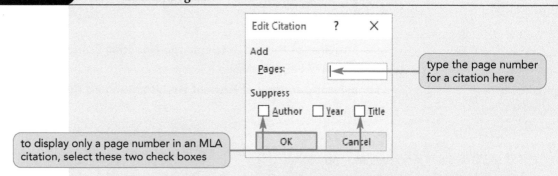

To add a page number for the citation, you type the page number in the Pages box. If you want to display only the page number in the citation (which would be necessary if you already mentioned the author's name in the same sentence in the text), then you would also select the Author and Title check boxes in this dialog box to suppress this information.

4. Type **37** to insert the page number in the Pages box, click the **OK** button to close the dialog box, and then click anywhere in the document outside the citation content control. The revised citation now reads "(Brauer 37)."

Next, you will add two more citations, both for the same journal article.

To insert two more citations:

▶ **1.** Scroll up to display the last paragraph on page 1, and then click at the end of the first sentence in that paragraph (which begins "According to Alisha Garland…"), between the word "animals" and the period. This sentence mentions historian Alisha Garland; you need to add a citation to one of her journal articles.

▶ **2.** In the Citations & Bibliography group, click the **Insert Citation** button to open the Insert Citation menu. Notice that Roy Brauer's book is now listed as a source on this menu. You could click Brauer's book on the menu to add a citation to it, but right now you need to add a new source.

▶ **3.** Click **Add New Source** to open the Create Source dialog box, click the **Type of Source** arrow, and then click **Journal Article**.

The Create Source dialog box displays the boxes, or fields, appropriate for a journal article. The information required to cite a journal article differs from the information you entered earlier for the citation for the Brauer book. For journal articles, you are prompted to enter the page numbers for the entire article. If you want to display a particular page number in the citation, you can add it later.

By default, Word displays boxes, or fields, for the information most commonly included in a bibliography. In this case, you also want to include the volume and issue numbers for Alisha Garland's article, so you need to display more fields.

▶ **4.** In the Create Source dialog box, click the **Show All Bibliography Fields** check box to select this option. The Create Source dialog box expands to allow you to enter more detailed information. Red asterisks highlight the fields that are recommended, but these recommended fields don't necessarily apply to every source.

▶ **5.** Enter the following information, scrolling down to display the necessary boxes:

Author: **Alisha Garland**

Title: **The Rise of Human Settlements: Neolithic Culture and Early Agriculture in Central Asia**

Journal Name: **Journal of Ancient Architecture and Cultural Studies**

Year: **2015**

Pages: **122–145**

Volume: **30**

Issue: **5**

Medium: **Web**

When you are finished, your Create Source dialog box should look like the one shown in Figure 2-32.

| Figure 2-32 | Create Source dialog box with information for the journal article |

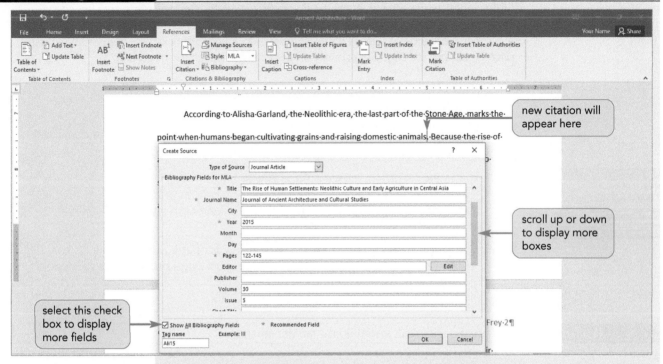

new citation will appear here

scroll up or down to display more boxes

select this check box to display more fields

6. Click the **OK** button. The Create Source dialog box closes, and the citation "(Garland)" is inserted in the text. Because the sentence containing the citation already includes the author's name, you will edit the citation to include the page number and suppress the author's name.

7. Click the **(Garland)** citation to display the content control, click the **Citation Options** button , and then click **Edit Citation** to open the Edit Citation dialog box.

8. In the Pages box, type **142**, and then click the **Author** and **Title** check boxes to select them. You need to suppress both the author's name and the title because otherwise Word will replace the suppressed author name with the title. When using the MLA style, you don't ever have to suppress the year because the year is never included as part of an MLA citation. When working in other styles, however, you might need to suppress the year.

9. Click the **OK** button to close the Edit Citation dialog box, and then click anywhere outside the content control to deselect it. The end of the sentence now reads "...raising domestic animals (142)."

10. Use the Navigation pane to find the sentence that begins "The Neolithic societies of central Asia..." on the second page. Click at the end of the sentence, to the left of the period after "mud," and then close the Navigation pane.

11. On the References tab, in the Citations & Bibliography group, click the **Insert Citation** button, and then click the **Garland, Alisha** source at the top of the menu. You want the citation to refer to the entire article instead of just one page, so you will not edit the citation to add a specific page number.

12. Save the document.

You have entered the source information for two sources.

Inserting a Page Break

Once you have created a citation for a source in a document, you can generate a bibliography. In the MLA style, the bibliography (or works cited list) starts on a new page. So your first step is to insert a manual page break. A **manual page break** is one you insert at a specific location; it doesn't matter if the previous page is full or not. To insert a manual page break, use the Page Break button in the Pages group on the Insert tab.

To insert a manual page break:

1. Press the **Ctrl+End** keys to move the insertion point to the end of the document.

2. On the ribbon, click the **Insert** tab.

TIP

Use the Blank Page button in the Pages group to insert a new, blank page in the middle of a document.

3. In the Pages group, click the **Page Break** button. Word inserts a new, blank page at the end of the document, with the insertion point blinking at the top. Note that you could also use the Ctrl+Enter keyboard shortcut to insert a manual page break.

4. Scroll up to see the dotted line with the words "Page Break" at the bottom of the text on page 4. You can delete a manual page break just as you would delete any other nonprinting character, by clicking immediately to its left and then pressing the Delete key. See Figure 2-33.

Figure 2-33 **Manual page break inserted into the document**

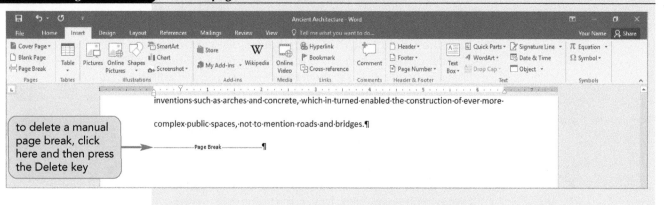

to delete a manual page break, click here and then press the Delete key

Now you can insert the bibliography on the new page 5.

Generating a Bibliography

When you generate a bibliography, Word scans all the citations in the document, collecting the source information for each citation, and then it creates a list of information for each unique source. The format of the entries in the bibliography will reflect the style you specified when you created your first citation, which in this case is the MLA style. The bibliography itself is a **field**, similar to the page number field you inserted earlier in this session. In other words, it is really an instruction that tells Word to display the source information for all the citations in the document. Because it is a field and not actual text, you can easily update the bibliography later to reflect any new citations you might add.

You can choose to insert a bibliography as a field directly in the document, or you can insert a bibliography enclosed within a content control that also includes the heading "Bibliography" or "Works Cited." Inserting a bibliography enclosed in a content control is best because the content control includes a useful button that you can use to update your bibliography if you make changes to the sources.

To insert the bibliography:

1. Scroll down so you can see the insertion point at the top of page 5.

2. On the ribbon, click the **References** tab.

3. In the Citations & Bibliography group, click the **Bibliography** button. The Bibliography menu opens, displaying three styles with preformatted headings—"Bibliography," "References," and "Works Cited." The Insert Bibliography command at the bottom inserts a bibliography directly in the document as a field, without a content control and without a preformatted heading. See Figure 2-34.

Figure 2-34   **Bibliography menu**

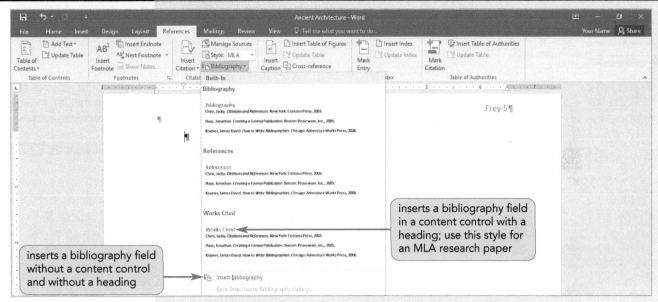

inserts a bibliography field without a content control and without a heading

inserts a bibliography field in a content control with a heading; use this style for an MLA research paper

---

4. Click **Works Cited**. Word inserts the bibliography, with two entries, below the "Works Cited" heading. The bibliography text is formatted in Calibri, the default font for the Office theme. The "Works Cited" heading is formatted with the Heading 1 style.

   To see the content control that contains the bibliography, you need to select it.

5. Click anywhere in the bibliography. Inside the content control, the bibliography is highlighted in gray, indicating that it is a field and not regular text. The content control containing the bibliography is also now visible in the form of a rectangular border and a tab with two buttons. See Figure 2-35.

Figure 2-35 | **Bibliography displayed in a content control**

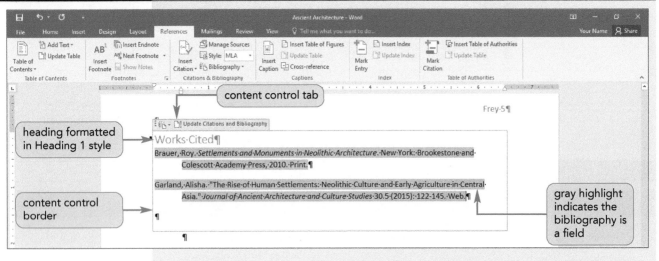

As Carolina looks over the works cited list, she realizes that she misspelled the last name of one of the authors. You'll correct the error now and then update the bibliography.

Managing Sources

When you create a source, Word adds it to a Master List of all the sources created on your computer. Word also adds each new source to the Current List of sources for that document. Both the Master List and the Current List are accessible via the Source Manager dialog box, which you open by clicking the Manage Sources button in the Citations & Bibliography group on the References tab. Using this dialog box, you can copy sources from the Master List into the Current List and vice versa. As you begin to focus on a particular academic field and turn repeatedly to important works in your chosen field, you'll find this ability to reuse sources very helpful.

Modifying an Existing Source

To modify information about a source, you click a citation to that source in the document, click the Citation Options button on the content control, and then click Edit Source. Depending on how your computer is set up, after you are finished editing the source, Word may prompt you to update the Master List and the source information in the current document. In almost all cases, you should click Yes to ensure that the source information is correct in all the places it is stored on your computer.

To edit a source in the research paper:

1. Click in the blank paragraph below the bibliography content control to deselect the bibliography.

2. Scroll up to display the first paragraph on page 2, and then click the **(Brauer 37)** citation you entered earlier in the second-to-last sentence in the paragraph. The content control appears around the citation.

3. Click the **Citation Options** button ▢, and then click **Edit Source**. The Edit Source dialog box opens. Note that Word displays the author's last name first in the Author box, just as it would appear in a bibliography.

4. In the **Author** box, double-click **Brauer** to select the author's last name, and then type **Brower**. The author's name now reads "Brower, Roy."

5. Click the **OK** button. The revised author name in the citation now reads "(Brower 37)."

   Trouble? If you see a message dialog box asking if you want to update the master source list and the current document, click the Yes button.

6. Click anywhere on the second page to deselect the citation content control. The revised author name in the citation now reads "(Brower 37)."

7. Save the document.

You've edited the document text and the citation to include the correct spelling of "Brower," but now you need to update the bibliography to correct the spelling.

Updating and Finalizing a Bibliography

The bibliography does not automatically change to reflect edits you make to existing citations or to show new citations. To incorporate the latest information stored in the citations, you need to update the bibliography. To update a bibliography in a content control, click the bibliography, and then, in the content control tab, click Update Citations and Bibliography. To update a bibliography field that is not contained in a content control, right-click the bibliography, and then click Update Field on the shortcut menu.

To update the bibliography:

1. Scroll down to page 5 and click anywhere in the works cited list to display the content control.

2. In the content control tab, click **Update Citations and Bibliography**. The works cited list is updated, with "Brauer" changed to "Brower" in the first entry.

Carolina still has a fair amount of work to do on her research paper. After she finishes writing it and adding all the citations, she will update the bibliography again to include all her cited sources. At that point, you might think the bibliography would be finished. However, a few steps remain to ensure that the works cited list matches the MLA style. To finalize Carolina's works cited list to match the MLA style, you need to make the changes shown in Figure 2-36.

Figure 2-36	Steps for finalizing a Word bibliography to match MLA guidelines for the works cited list

1. Format the "Works Cited" heading to match the formatting of the rest of the text in the document.

2. Center the "Works Cited" heading.

3. Double-space the entire works cited list, including the heading, and remove extra space after the paragraphs.

4. Change the font size for the entire works cited list to 12 points.

To format the bibliography as an MLA-style works cited list:

▶ **1.** Click in the **Works Cited** heading, and then click the **Home** tab on the ribbon.

▶ **2.** In the Styles group, click the **Normal** style. The "Works Cited" heading is now formatted in Calibri body font like the rest of the document. The MLA style for a works cited list requires this heading to be centered.

▶ **3.** In the Paragraph group, click the **Center** button ≣.

▶ **4.** Select the entire works cited list, including the heading. Change the font size to **12** points, change the line spacing to **2.0**, and then remove the paragraph spacing after each paragraph.

▶ **5.** Click below the content control to deselect the works cited list, and then review your work. See Figure 2-37.

Figure 2-37   MLA-style Works Cited list

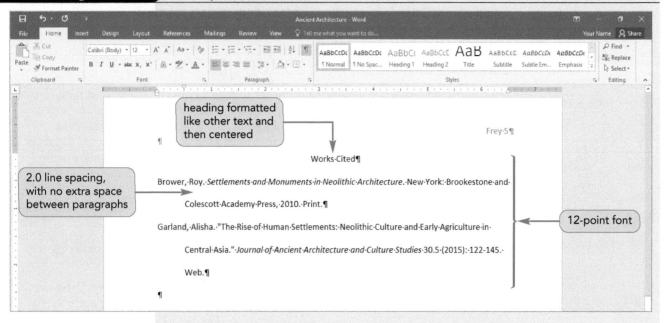

▶ **6.** Save the document and close it.

Carolina's research paper now meets the MLA style guidelines.

Session 2.2 Quick Check

REVIEW

1. List the five tasks you need to perform to make a default Word document match the MLA style.

2. How can you quickly repeat the action you just performed?

3. Explain how to remove a page number from the first page of a document.

4. What is the default form of an MLA citation in Word?

5. Explain how to edit a citation to display only the page number.

6. Explain how to generate a works cited list.

Review Assignments

PRACTICE

Data Files needed for the Review Assignments: Commercial.docx, Modern.docx

Because the Home LEED document turned out so well, Carolina has been asked to create a handout describing LEED certification for commercial buildings. Carolina asks you to help her revise and format the document. She also asks you to create a document listing projects that are suitable for this type of LEED certification. Finally, as part of her architecture history class, Carolina is working on a research paper on the history of modern architecture. She asks you to help her format the paper according to the MLA style and to create some citations and a bibliography. She has inserted the uppercase word "CITATION" wherever she needs to insert a citation. Complete the following steps:

1. Open the document **Commercial** located in the Word2 > Review folder included with your Data Files, and then save the document as **Commercial LEED** in the location specified by your instructor.

2. Read the first comment, which provides an overview of the changes you will be making to the document in the following steps. Perform the task described in the second comment, and then delete both comments.

3. In the middle of page 1, revise the text "SPECIAL PROJECTS" so that only the first letter of each word is capitalized. Attach a comment to this paragraph that explains the change.

4. Near the end of page 2, move the "Getting Started" heading up to position it before the paragraph that begins "Talk to your project manager…."

5. Replace the second instance of "Design" with "design," being sure to match the case.

6. On page 1, format the list of suitable projects as a bulleted list with square bullets, starting with "Schools, including…" and ending with "Clinics, hospitals, and other healthcare facilities." Do the same for the list of special projects, starting with "Mixed-use projects…" and ending with "No larger than 25,000 square feet.") Then indent the three requirements for multiple structures so they are formatted with an open circle bullet.

7. At the top of page 2, format the three steps for developing a certification plan as a numbered list, using the "1), 2), 3)" numbering style.

8. In the numbered list, move paragraph 3 ("Establish target certification level…") up to make it paragraph 2.

9. Format the title "Commercial LEED Fact Sheet" using the Title style. Format the following headings with the Heading 1 style: "Suitable Projects," "Special Projects," "Location," "Developing a Certification Plan," and "Getting Started."

10. Change the document theme to the Ion theme. If the Ion theme isn't included in your Themes gallery, choose a different theme.

11. Display the Clipboard task pane. On page 1, copy the bulleted list of suitable projects (which begins "Schools, including entire college campuses…") to the Clipboard, and then copy the "Suitable Projects" heading to the Clipboard. To ensure that you copy the heading formatting, be sure to select the paragraph mark after "Suitable Projects" before you click the Copy button.

12. Open a new, blank document, and then save the document as **Suitable Projects** in the location specified by your instructor.

13. At the beginning of the document, paste the heading "Suitable Projects," and then, from the Paste Options menu, apply the Keep Source Formatting option. Below the heading, paste the list of suitable projects.

14. At the end of the document, insert a new paragraph, and then type **Prepared by:** followed by your first and last names.

15. Save the Suitable Projects document and close it.

16. In the Commercial LEED document, clear the contents of the Clipboard task pane, close the Clipboard task pane, save the document, and then close it.

17. Open the document **Modern** located in the Word2 > Review folder included with your Data Files.

18. Save the document as **Modern Architecture** in the location specified by your instructor.

19. In the first paragraph, replace Carolina's name with your own.

20. Adjust the font size, line spacing, paragraph spacing, and paragraph indents to match the MLA style.

21. Insert your last name and a page number on every page except the first. Use the same font size as in the rest of the document.

22. If necessary, select MLA Seventh Edition as the citations and bibliography style.

23. Use the Navigation pane to highlight all instances of the uppercase word "CITATION." Keep the Navigation pane open so you can continue to use it to find the locations where you need to insert citations in Steps 24–28.

24. Delete the first instance of "CITATION" and the space before it, and then create a new source with the following information:
    Type of Source: **Book**
    Author: **Lincoln Mayfield**
    Title: **Very Modern Architecture: A History in Words and Photos**
    Year: **2014**
    City: **Cambridge**
    Publisher: **Boston Pines Press**
    Medium: **Print**

25. Edit the citation to add **105** as the page number. Display only the page number in the citation.

26. Delete the second instance of "CITATION" and the space before it, and then create a new source with the following information:
    Type of Source: **Journal Article**
    Author: **Odessa Robinson**
    Title: **Modern Architecture in the Modern World**
    Journal Name: **Atlantis Architecture Quarterly: Criticism and Comment**
    Year: **2015**
    Pages: **68–91**
    Volume: **11**
    Issue: **2**
    Medium: **Web**

27. Edit the citation to add **80** as the page number.

28. Delete the third instance of "CITATION" and the space before it, and then insert a citation for the book by Lincoln Mayfield.

29. At the end of the document, start a new page and insert a bibliography in a content control with the heading "Works Cited."

30. In the second source you created, change "**Robinson**" to "**Robbins**" and then update the bibliography.

31. Finalize the bibliography to create an MLA-style works cited list.

32. Save the Modern Architecture document, and close it.

33. Close any other open documents.

Case Problem 1

APPLY

Data File needed for this Case Problem: Field.docx

Hilltop Elementary School   Crystal Martinez, a fourth-grade teacher at Hilltop Elementary School, created a flyer to inform parents and guardians about an upcoming field trip. It's your job to format the flyer to make it look professional and easy to read. Crystal included comments in the document explaining what she wants you to do. Complete the following steps:

1. Open the document **Field** located in the Word2 > Case1 folder included with your Data Files, and then save the file as **Field Trip Flyer** in the location specified by your instructor.

2. Format the document as directed in the comments. After you complete a task, delete the relevant comment. Respond "Yes" to the comment asking if October 20 is the correct date. When you are finished with the formatting, the comment with the question and the comment with your reply should be the only remaining comments.

3. Move up the second bulleted item (which begins "Email me at...") to make it the first bulleted item in the list.

4. Change the theme to the Slice theme, and then attach a comment to the title listing the heading and body fonts applied by the Slice theme.

5. Save the document, and then close it.

Case Problem 2

APPLY

Data File needed for this Case Problem: Comedy.docx

Frederick Douglass College   Liam Shelton is a student at Frederick Douglass College. He's working on a research paper, which is only partly finished, about the types of comedy used in plays and films. He inserted the uppercase word "CITATION" wherever he needs to insert a citation. Liam asks you to help him format this early draft to match the MLA style. He also asks you to help him create some citations and a first attempt at a bibliography. He will update the bibliography later, after he finishes writing the research paper. Complete the following steps:

1. Open the document **Comedy** located in the Word2 > Case2 folder included with your Data Files, and then save the document as **Comedy Paper** in the location specified by your instructor.

2. In the first paragraph, replace "Liam Shelton" with your name, and then adjust the font size, line spacing, paragraph spacing, and paragraph indents to match the MLA style.

3. Insert your last name and a page number in the upper-right corner of every page except the first page in the document. Use the same font size as in the rest of the document.

4. If necessary, select MLA Seventh Edition as the citations and bibliography style.

5. Use the Navigation pane to find three instances of the uppercase word "CITATION."

6. Delete the first instance of "CITATION" and the space before it, and then create a new source with the following information:
   Type of Source: **Book**
   Author: **Danyl Taylor**
   Title: **Comedy: The Happy Art**
   Year: **2013**
   City: **Chicago**
   Publisher: **Singleton University Press**
   Medium: **Print**

7. Edit the citation to add **135** as the page number. Suppress the author's name and the title.

8. Delete the second instance of "CITATION" and the space before it, and then create a new source with the following information:

    Type of Source: **Sound Recording**

    Performer: **Anne Golden**

    Title: **Slapstick Sample**

    Album Title: **Sounds of the Renaissance**

    Production Company: **Foley Studio Productions**

    Year: **1995**

    Medium: **CD**

    City: **Los Angeles**

9. Edit the citation to suppress the Author and the Year, so that it displays only the title.

10. Delete the third instance of "CITATION" and the space before it, and then insert a second reference to the book by Danyl Taylor.

11. Edit the citation to add **65** as the page number.

12. At the end of the document, start a new page, and then insert a bibliography with the preformatted heading "Works Cited."

13. Edit the last source you created, changing the date to **2000**.

14. Update the bibliography so it shows the revised date.

15. Finalize the bibliography so that it matches the MLA style.

16. Save the Comedy Paper document, and close it.

Case Problem 3

CREATE

Data Files needed for this Case Problem: Maliha.docx, Nursing.docx

Emergency Room Nurse   Maliha Shadid has more than a decade of experience as a nurse in several different settings. After moving to a new city, she is looking for a job as an emergency room nurse. She has asked you to edit and format her resume. As part of the application process, she will have to upload her resume to employee recruitment websites at a variety of hospitals. Because these sites typically request a simple page design, Maliha plans to rely primarily on heading styles and bullets to organize her information. When the resume is complete, she wants you to remove any color applied by the heading styles. She also needs help formatting a document she created for a nursing organization for which she volunteers. Complete the following steps:

1. Open the document **Maliha** located in the Word2 > Case3 folder included with your Data Files, and then save the file as **Maliha Resume** in the location specified by your instructor.

2. Read the comment included in the document, and then perform the task it specifies.

3. Respond to the comment with the response **I think that's a good choice for the theme.**, and then mark Maliha's comment as done.

4. Replace all occurrences of "Lawrencekansas" with **Lawrence, Kansas**.

5. Format the resume as shown in Figure 2-38. To ensure that the resume fits on one page, pay special attention to the paragraph spacing settings specified in Figure 2-38.

6. In the email address, replace "Maliha Shadid" with your first and last names, separated by an underscore, and then save the document and close it.

Figure 2-38   **Formatting for Maliha Shadid's resume**

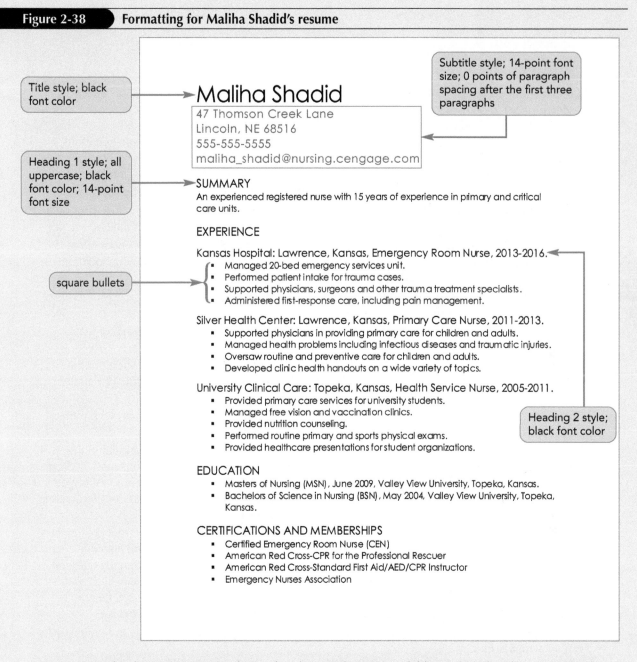

7. Open the document **Nursing** located in the Word2 > Case3 folder included with your Data Files, and then save the file as **Nursing Foundation** in the location specified by your instructor. Search for the text "Your Name", and then replace it with your first and last names.

8. Select the three paragraphs below your name, and then decrease the indent for the selected paragraphs so that they align at the left margin. Create a .5-inch hanging indent for the selected paragraphs.

9. Change the document theme to Facet, and then add a comment to the first word in the document that reads "**I changed the theme to Facet.**" (If Facet is not an option in your Themes gallery, choose a different theme, and then include that theme name in the comment.)

10. Use the Advanced Find dialog box to search for bold formatting. Remove the bold formatting from the fourth bold element in the document, and then add a comment to that element that reads "**I assumed bold here was a mistake, so I removed it.**"

11. Save and close the document.

CHALLENGE

Case Problem 4

Data File needed for this Case Problem: Louis.docx

Elliot Community College Maria Taketou is a student at Elliot Community College. She's working on a research paper about Louis Armstrong for Music History 201, taught by Professor Delphine Chabot. The research paper is only partly finished, but before she does more work on it, she asks you to help format this early draft to match the MLA style. She also asks you to help her create some citations, add a placeholder citation, and manage her sources. Complete the following steps:

1. Open the document **Louis** located in the Word2 > Case4 folder included with your Data Files, and then save the document as **Louis Armstrong Paper** in the location specified by your instructor.

2. Revise the paper to match the MLA style, seventh edition. Instead of Maria's name, use your own. Also, use the current date. Use the same font size for the header as for the rest of the document.

3. Locate the sentences in which the authors Philip Brewster and Sylvia Cohen are mentioned. At the end of the appropriate sentence, add a citation for page 123 in the following book and one for page 140 in the following journal article:

   Brewster, Philip. Louis Armstrong in America: King of Music, King of Our Hearts. New York: Jazz Notes Press, 2010. Print.

   Cohen, Sylvia. "The New Orleans Louis Armstrong Loved." North American Journal of Jazz Studies (2015): 133–155. Web.

4. At the end of the second-to-last sentence in the document, insert a placeholder citation that reads "Feldman." At the end of the last sentence in the document, insert a placeholder citation that reads "Harrison."

⊕ **Explore** 5. Use Word Help to look up the topic "Create a bibliography," and then, within that article, read the sections titled "Find a source" and "Edit a citation placeholder."

⊕ **Explore** 6. Open the Source Manager, and search for the name "Brewster." From within the Current List in the Source Manager, edit the Philip Brewster citation to delete "in America" from the title, so that the title reads "Louis Armstrong: King of Music, King of Our Hearts." After you make the change, if you are asked, update the source in both lists. When you are finished, delete "Brewster" from the Search box to redisplay all the sources in both lists.

⊕ **Explore** 7. From within the Source Manager, copy a source not included in the current document from the Master List to the Current List. Examine the sources in the Current List, and note the checkmarks next to the two sources for which you have already created citations and the question marks next to the placeholder sources. Sources in the Current list that are not actually cited in the text have no symbol next to them in the Current List. For example, if you copied a source from the Master List into your Current List, that source has no symbol next to it in the Current List.

8. Close the Source Manager, create a bibliography with a "Works Cited" heading, and note which works appear in it.

⊕ **Explore** 9. Open the Source Manager, and then edit the Feldman placeholder source to include the following information about a journal article:

   Feldman, Jamal. "King Joe Oliver, Music Master." Jazz International Journal (2015): 72–89. Web.

10. Update the bibliography.

⊕ **Explore** 11. Open Microsoft Edge, and use the web to research the difference between a works cited list and a works consulted list. If necessary, open the Source Manager, and then delete any uncited sources from the Current List to ensure that your document contains a true works cited list, as specified by the MLA style, and not a works consulted list. (Maria will create a full citation for the "Harrison" placeholder later.)

12. Update the bibliography, finalize it so it matches the MLA style, save the document, and close it.

OBJECTIVES

Session 3.1
- Review document headings in the Navigation pane
- Reorganize document text using the Navigation pane
- Collapse and expand body text in a document
- Create and edit a table
- Sort rows in a table
- Modify a table's structure
- Format a table

Session 3.2
- Set tab stops
- Turn on automatic hyphenation
- Create footnotes and endnotes
- Divide a document into sections
- Create a SmartArt graphic
- Create headers and footers
- Insert a cover page
- Change the document's theme
- Review a document in Read Mode

Creating Tables and a Multipage Report

Writing a Recommendation

Case | *Vista Grande Neighborhood Center*

Hillary Sanchez is the managing director of the Vista Grande Neighborhood Center, a nonprofit organization that provides social services and community programming for the Vista Grande neighborhood in Tucson, Arizona. Hillary hopes to begin offering exercise and nutrition classes at the center. She has written a multiple-page report for the center's board of directors summarizing basic information about the proposed classes. She has asked you to finish formatting the report. Hillary also needs your help adding a table and a diagram to the end of the report.

In this module, you'll use the Navigation pane to review the document headings and reorganize the document. You will also insert a table, modify it by changing the structure and formatting, set tab stops, create footnotes and endnotes, hyphenate the document, and insert a section break. In addition, you'll create a SmartArt graphic and add headers and footers. Finally, you will insert a cover page and review the document in Read Mode.

STARTING DATA FILES

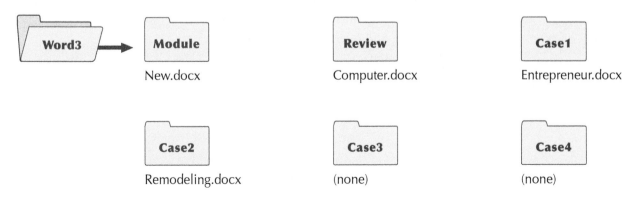

Word3 → Module
New.docx

Review
Computer.docx

Case1
Entrepreneur.docx

Case2
Remodeling.docx

Case3
(none)

Case4
(none)

Session 3.1 Visual Overview:

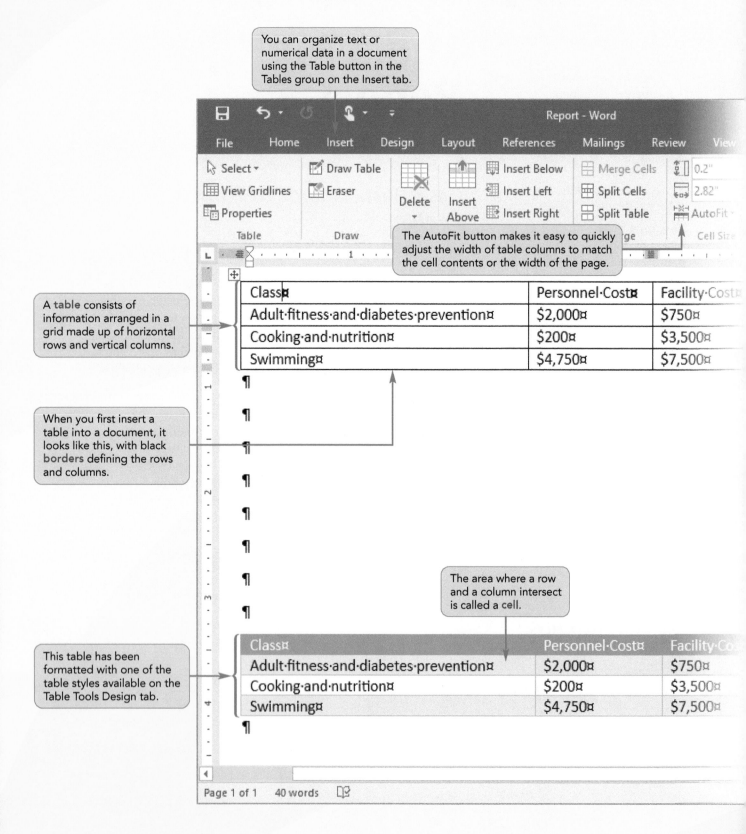

You can organize text or numerical data in a document using the Table button in the Tables group on the Insert tab.

The AutoFit button makes it easy to quickly adjust the width of table columns to match the cell contents or the width of the page.

A table consists of information arranged in a grid made up of horizontal rows and vertical columns.

When you first insert a table into a document, it looks like this, with black borders defining the rows and columns.

The area where a row and a column intersect is called a cell.

This table has been formatted with one of the table styles available on the Table Tools Design tab.

Class¤	Personnel·Cost¤	Facility·Cost¤
Adult·fitness·and·diabetes·prevention¤	$2,000¤	$750¤
Cooking·and·nutrition¤	$200¤	$3,500¤
Swimming¤	$4,750¤	$7,500¤

Class¤	Personnel·Cost¤	Facility·Cost¤
Adult·fitness·and·diabetes·prevention¤	$2,000¤	$750¤
Cooking·and·nutrition¤	$200¤	$3,500¤
Swimming¤	$4,750¤	$7,500¤

Page 1 of 1   40 words

Organizing Information in Tables

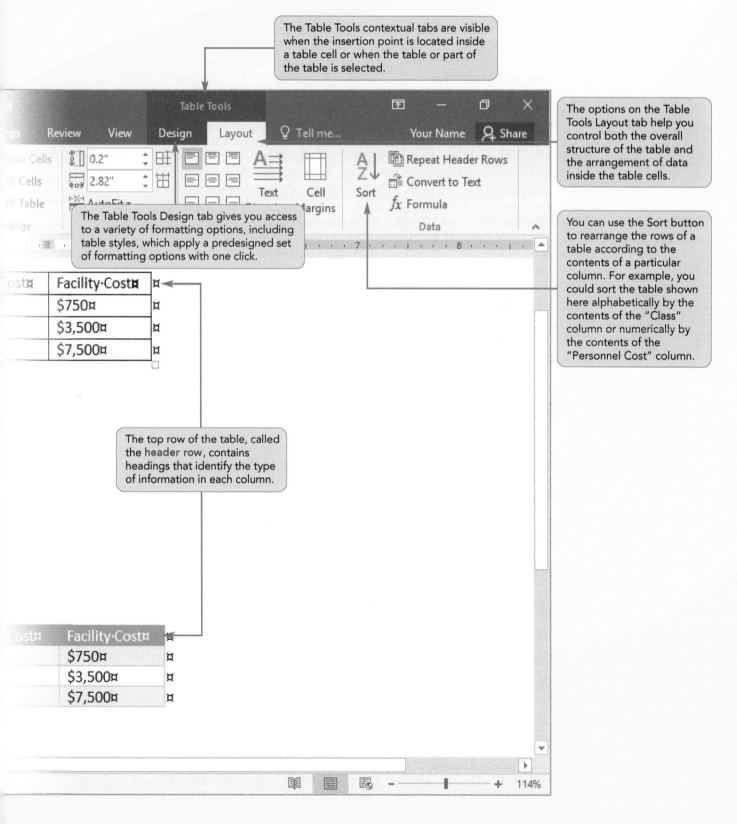

The Table Tools contextual tabs are visible when the insertion point is located inside a table cell or when the table or part of the table is selected.

The options on the Table Tools Layout tab help you control both the overall structure of the table and the arrangement of data inside the table cells.

The Table Tools Design tab gives you access to a variety of formatting options, including table styles, which apply a predesigned set of formatting options with one click.

You can use the Sort button to rearrange the rows of a table according to the contents of a particular column. For example, you could sort the table shown here alphabetically by the contents of the "Class" column or numerically by the contents of the "Personnel Cost" column.

The top row of the table, called the header row, contains headings that identify the type of information in each column.

Working with Headings in the Navigation Pane

When used in combination with the Navigation pane, Word's heading styles make it easier to navigate through a long document and to reorganize a document. You start by formatting the document headings with heading styles, displaying the Navigation pane, and then clicking the Headings link. This displays a hierarchy of all the headings in the document, allowing you to see, at a glance, an outline of the document headings.

Paragraphs formatted with the Heading 1 style are considered the highest-level headings and are aligned at the left margin of the Navigation pane. Paragraphs formatted with the Heading 2 style are considered **subordinate** to Heading 1 paragraphs and are indented slightly to the right below the Heading 1 paragraphs. Subordinate headings are often referred to as **subheadings**. Each successive level of heading styles (Heading 3, Heading 4, and so on) is indented farther to the right. To simplify your view of the document outline in the Navigation pane, you can choose to hide lower-level headings from view, leaving only the major headings visible.

From within the Navigation pane, you can **promote** a subordinate heading to the next level up in the heading hierarchy. For example, you can promote a Heading 2 paragraph to a Heading 1 paragraph. You can also do the opposite—that is, you can **demote** a heading to a subordinate level. You can also click and drag a heading in the Navigation pane to a new location in the document's outline. When you do so, any subheadings—along with their subordinate body text—move to the new location in the document.

REFERENCE

Working with Headings in the Navigation Pane

- Format the document headings using Word's heading styles.
- On the ribbon, click the Home tab.
- In the Editing group, click the Find button, or press the Ctrl+F keys, to display the Navigation pane.
- In the Navigation pane, click the Headings link to display a list of the document headings, and then click a heading to display that heading in the document window.
- In the Navigation pane, click a heading, and then drag it up or down in the list of headings to move that heading and the body text below it to a new location in the document.
- In the Navigation pane, right-click a heading, and then click Promote to promote the heading to the next-highest level. To demote a heading, right-click it, and then click Demote.
- To hide subheadings in the Navigation pane, click the Collapse arrow next to the higher level heading above them. To redisplay the subheadings, click the Expand arrow next to the higher-level heading.

Hillary saved the draft of her report as a Word document named New. You will use the Navigation pane to review the outline of Hillary's report and make some changes to its organization.

To review the document headings in the Navigation pane:

▶ **1.** Open the document **New** located in the Word3 > Module folder included with your Data Files, and then save the file with the name **New Classes Report** in the location specified by your instructor.

▶ **2.** Verify that the document is displayed in Print Layout view and that the rulers and nonprinting characters are displayed.

3. Make sure the Zoom level is set to **120%**, and that the Home tab is selected on the ribbon.

4. Press the **Ctrl+F** keys. The Navigation pane opens to the left of the document.

5. In the Navigation pane, click the **Headings** link. The document headings are displayed in the Navigation pane, as shown in Figure 3-1. The blue highlighted heading ("Summary") indicates that part of the document currently contains the insertion point.

Figure 3-1   **Headings displayed in the Navigation pane**

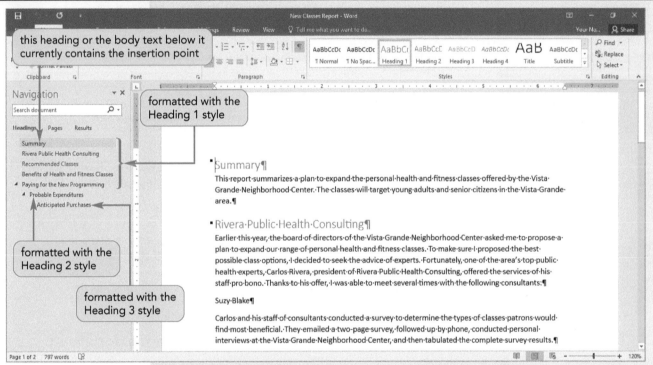

this heading or the body text below it currently contains the insertion point

formatted with the Heading 1 style

formatted with the Heading 2 style

formatted with the Heading 3 style

6. In the Navigation pane, click the **Recommended Classes** heading. Word displays the heading in the document window, with the insertion point at the beginning of the heading. The "Recommended Classes" heading is highlighted in blue in the Navigation pane.

7. In the Navigation pane, click the **Paying for the New Programming** heading. Word displays the heading in the document window. In the Navigation pane, you can see that there are subheadings below this heading.

8. In the Navigation pane, click the **Collapse** arrow ◢ next to the "Paying for the New Programming" heading. The subheadings below this heading are no longer visible in the Navigation pane. This has no effect on the text in the actual document. See Figure 3-2.

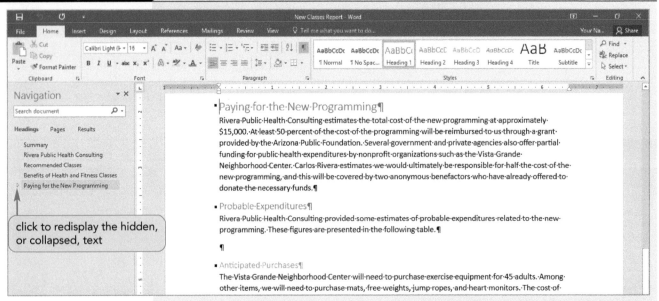

Figure 3-2   **Heading 2 and Heading 3 text hidden in Navigation pane**

▶ **9.** In the Navigation pane, click the **Expand** arrow ▷ next to the "Paying for the New Programming" heading. The subheadings are again visible in the Navigation pane.

Now that you have had a chance to review the report, you need to make a few organizational changes. Hillary wants to promote the Heading 3 text "Anticipated Purchases" to Heading 2 text. Then she wants to move the "Anticipated Purchases" heading and its body text up, so it precedes the "Probable Expenditures" section.

To use the Navigation pane to reorganize text in the document:

▶ **1.** In the Navigation pane, right-click the **Anticipated Purchases** heading to display the shortcut menu.

▶ **2.** Click **Promote**. The heading moves to the left in the Navigation pane, aligning below the "Probable Expenditures" heading. In the document window, the text is now formatted with the Heading 2 style, with its slightly larger font.

▶ **3.** In the Navigation pane, click and drag the **Anticipated Purchases** heading up. As you drag the heading, the pointer changes to ▷, and a blue guideline is displayed. You can use the guideline to position the heading in its new location.

▶ **4.** Position the guideline directly below the "Paying for the New Programming" heading, as shown in Figure 3-3.

Figure 3-3   Moving a heading in the Navigation pane

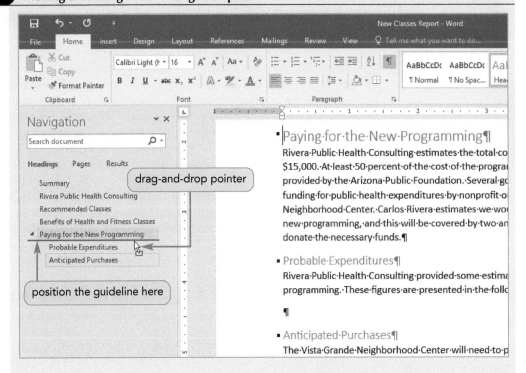

5. Release the mouse button. The "Anticipated Purchases" heading is displayed in its new position in the Navigation pane, as the second-to-last heading in the outline. The heading and its body text are displayed in their new location in the document, before the "Probable Expenditures" heading. See Figure 3-4.

Figure 3-4   Heading and body text in new location

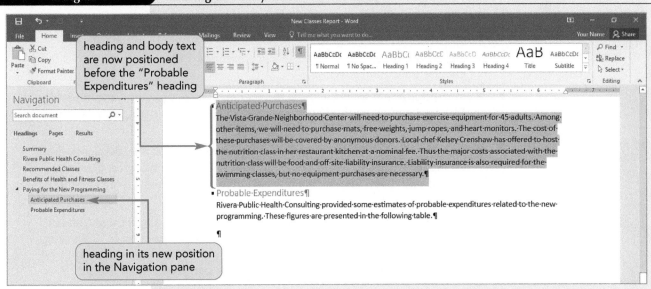

6. Click anywhere in the document to deselect the text, and then save the document.

Hillary also wants you to move the "Recommended Classes" heading and its accompanying body text. You'll do that in the next section, using a different method.

Promoting and Demoting Headings

When you promote or demote a heading, Word applies the next higher- or lower-level heading style to the heading paragraph. You could accomplish the same thing by using the Style gallery to apply the next higher- or lower-level heading style, but it's easy to lose track of the overall organization of the document that way. By promoting and demoting headings from within the Navigation pane, you ensure that the overall document outline is right in front of you as you work.

You can also use Outline view to display, promote, and demote headings and to reorganize a document. Turn on Outline view by clicking the View tab, and then clicking the Outline button in the Views group to display the Outlining contextual tab on the ribbon. To hide the Outlining tab and return to Print Layout view, click the Close Outline View button on the ribbon or the Print Layout button in the status bar.

Collapsing and Expanding Body Text in the Document

Because the Navigation pane gives you an overview of the entire document, dragging headings within the Navigation pane is the best way to reorganize a document. However, you can also reorganize a document from within the document window, without using the Navigation pane, by first hiding, or collapsing, the body text below a heading in a document. After you collapse the body text below a heading, you can drag the heading to a new location in the document. When you do, the body text moves along with the heading, just as if you had dragged the heading in the Navigation pane. You'll use this technique now to move the "Recommended Classes" heading and its body text.

To collapse and move a heading in the document window:

▶ 1. In the Navigation pane, click the **Recommended Classes** heading to display it in the document window.

▶ 2. In the document window, place the mouse pointer over the **Recommended Classes** heading to display the gray Collapse button ◢ to the left of the heading.

▶ 3. Point to the gray **Collapse** button ◢ until it turns blue, and then click the **Collapse** button ◢. The body text below the "Recommended Classes" heading is now hidden. The Collapse button is replaced with an Expand button.

▶ 4. Collapse the body text below the "Benefits of Health and Fitness Classes" heading. The body text below that heading is no longer visible. Collapsing body text can be helpful when you want to hide details in a document temporarily, so you can focus on a particular part. See Figure 3-5.

Figure 3-5   **Body text collapsed in the document**

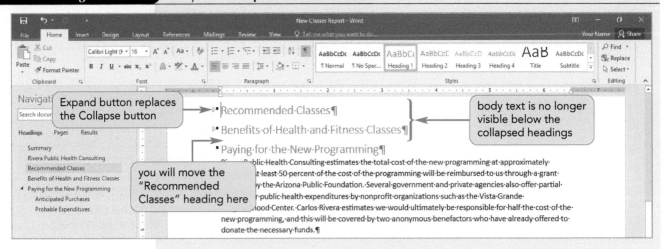

> **5.** In the document, select the **Recommended Classes** heading, including the paragraph mark at the end of the paragraph.

> **6.** Click and drag the heading down. As you drag, a dark black insertion point moves along with the mouse pointer.

> **7.** Position the dark black insertion point to the left of the "P" in the "Paying for the New Programming" heading, and then release the mouse button. The "Recommended Classes" heading and its body text move to the new location, before the "Paying for the New Programming" heading.

> Finally, you need to expand the body text below the two collapsed headings.

> **8.** Click anywhere in the document to deselect the text.

> **9.** Point to the **Expand** button ▷ to the left of the "Recommended Classes" heading until it turns blue, and then click the **Expand** button ▶ to redisplay the body text below the heading.

> **10.** Point to the **Expand** button ▷ to the left of the "Benefits of Health and Fitness Classes" heading until it turns blue, and then click the **Expand** button ▶ to redisplay the body text below the heading.

> **11.** Save the document.

The document is now organized the way Hillary wants it. Next, you need to create a table summarizing her data on probable expenditures.

Inserting a Blank Table

TIP

The terms "table," "field," and "record" are also used to discuss information stored in database programs, such as Microsoft Access.

A table is a useful way to present information that is organized into categories, or **fields**. For example, you could use a table to organize contact information for a list of clients. For each client, you could include information in the following fields: first name, last name, street address, city, state, and ZIP code. The complete set of information about a particular client is called a **record**. In a typical table, each column is a separate field, and each row is a record. A header row at the top contains the names of each field.

The sketch in Figure 3-6 shows what Hillary wants the table in her report to look like.

Figure 3-6   **Table sketch**

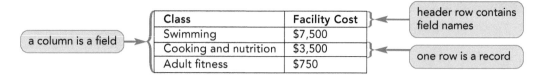

Hillary's table includes two columns, or fields—"Class" and "Facility Cost." The header row contains the names of these two fields. The three rows below contain the records.

Creating a table in Word is a three-step process. First, you use the Table button on the Insert tab to insert a blank table structure. Then you enter information into the table. Finally, you format the table to make it easy to read.

Before you begin creating the table, you'll insert a page break before the "Probable Expenditures" heading. This will move the heading and its body text to a new page, with plenty of room below for the new table. As a general rule, you should not use page breaks to position a particular part of a document at the top of a page. If you add or remove text from the document later, you might forget that you inserted a manual page break, and you might end up with a document layout you didn't expect. By default, Word heading styles are set up to ensure that a heading always appears on the same page as the body text paragraph below it, so you'll never need to insert a page break just to move a heading to the same page as its body text. However, in this case, a page break is appropriate because you need the "Probable Expenditures" heading to be displayed at the top of a page with room for the table below.

To insert a page break and insert a blank table:

▶ **1.** In the Navigation pane, click **Probable Expenditures** to display the heading in the document, with the insertion point to the left of the "P" in "Probable."

▶ **2.** Close the Navigation pane, and then press the **Ctrl+Enter** keys to insert a page break. The "Probable Expenditures" heading and the body text following it move to a new, third page.

▶ **3.** Scroll to position the "Probable Expenditures" heading at the top of the Word window, and then press the **Ctrl+End** keys to move the insertion point to the blank paragraph at the end of the document.

▶ **4.** On the ribbon, click the **Insert** tab.

TIP

You can use the Quick Tables option to choose from preformatted tables that contain placeholder text.

▶ **5.** In the Tables group, click the **Table** button. A table grid opens, with a menu at the bottom.

▶ **6.** Use the mouse pointer to point to the **upper-left cell** of the grid, and then move the mouse pointer down and across the grid to highlight two columns and four rows. (The outline of a cell turns orange when it is highlighted.) As you move the pointer across the grid, Word indicates the size of the table (columns by rows) at the top of the grid. A Live Preview of the table structure is displayed in the document. See Figure 3-7.

Figure 3-7   Inserting a blank table

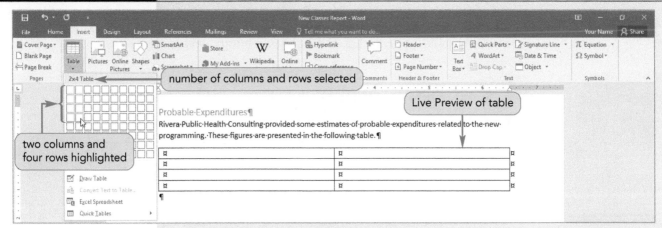

7. When the table size is 2×4, click the lower-right cell in the block of selected cells. An empty table consisting of two columns and four rows is inserted in the document, with the insertion point in the upper-left cell. See Figure 3-8.

Figure 3-8   Blank table inserted in document

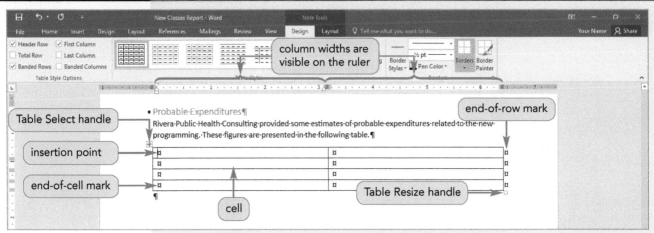

The two columns are of equal width. Because nonprinting characters are displayed in the document, each cell contains an end-of-cell mark, and each row contains an end-of-row mark, which are important for selecting parts of a table. The Table Select handle ⊞ is displayed at the table's upper-left corner. You can click the Table Select handle ⊞ to select the entire table, or you can drag it to move the table. You can drag the Table Resize handle □, which is displayed at the lower-right corner, to change the size of the table. The Table Tools Design and Layout contextual tabs are displayed on the ribbon.

Trouble? If you inserted a table with the wrong number of rows or columns, click the Undo button ⟲ on the Quick Access Toolbar to remove the table, and then repeat Steps 4 through 7.

The blank table is ready for you to begin entering information.

Entering Data in a Table

You can enter data in a table by moving the insertion point to a cell and typing. If the data takes up more than one line in the cell, Word automatically wraps the text to the next line and increases the height of that row. To move the insertion point to another cell in the table, you can click in that cell, use the arrow keys, or use the Tab key.

To enter information in the header row of the table:

▶ **1.** Verify that the insertion point is located in the upper-left cell of the table.

▶ **2.** Type **Class**. As you type, the end-of-cell mark moves right to accommodate the text.

▶ **3.** Press the **Tab** key to move the insertion point to the next cell to the right.

   Trouble? If Word created a new paragraph in the first cell rather than moving the insertion point to the second cell, you pressed the Enter key instead of the Tab key. Press the Backspace key to remove the paragraph mark, and then press the Tab key to move to the second cell in the first row.

▶ **4.** Type **Facility Cost** and then press the **Tab** key to move to the first cell in the second row.

You have finished entering the header row—the row that identifies the information in each column. Now you can enter the information about the various expenditures.

To continue entering information in the table:

▶ **1.** Type **swimming** and then press the **Tab** key to move to the second cell in the second row. Notice that the "s" in "swimming" is capitalized, even though you typed it in lowercase. By default, AutoCorrect capitalizes the first letter in a cell entry.

▶ **2.** Type **$7,500** and then press the **Tab** key to move the insertion point to the first cell in the third row.

▶ **3.** Enter the following information in the bottom two rows, pressing the **Tab** key to move from cell to cell:

   Cooking and nutrition; **$3,500**

   Adult fitness; **$750**

At this point, the table consists of a header row and three records. Hillary realizes that she needs to add one more row to the table. You can add a new row to the bottom of a table by pressing the Tab key when the insertion point is in the rightmost cell in the bottom row.

To add a row to the table:

▶ **1.** Verify that the insertion point is in the lower-right cell (which contains the value "$750"), and then press the **Tab** key. A new, blank row is added to the bottom of the table.

▶ **2.** Type **Diabetes prevention**, press the **Tab** key, type **$400**, and then save the document. When you are finished, your table should look like the one shown in Figure 3-9.

Figure 3-9   Table with all data entered

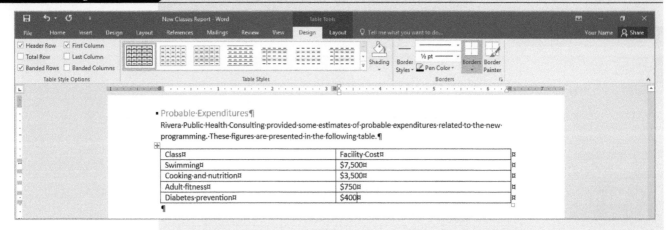

Trouble? If a new row is added to the bottom of your table, you pressed the Tab key after entering "$400". Click the Undo button ↶ on the Quick Access Toolbar to remove the extra row from the table.

The table you've just created presents information about expenditures in an easy-to-read format. To make it even easier to read, you can format the header row in bold so it stands out from the rest of the table. To do that, you need to first select the header row.

Selecting Part of a Table

TIP

To merge multiple cells into one cell, select the cells you want to merge, and then click the Merge Cells button in the Merge group on the Table Tools Layout tab.

When selecting part of a table, you need to make sure you select the end-of-cell mark in a cell or the end-of-row mark at the end of a row. If you don't, the formatting changes you make next might not have the effect you expect. The foolproof way to select part of a table is to click in the cell, row, or column you want to select; click the Select button on the Table Tools Layout contextual tab; and then click the appropriate command—Select Cell, Select Column, or Select Row. (You can also click Select Table to select the entire table.) To select a row, you can also click in the left margin next to the row. Similarly, you can click just above a column to select it. After you've selected an entire row, column, or cell, you can drag the mouse to select adjacent rows, columns, or cells.

Note that in the following steps, you'll position the mouse pointer until it takes on a particular shape so that you can then perform the task associated with that type of pointer. Pointer shapes are especially important when working with tables and graphics; in many cases, you can't perform a task until the pointer is the right shape. It takes some patience to get accustomed to positioning the pointer until it takes on the correct shape, but with practice you'll grow to rely on the pointer shapes as a quick visual cue to the options currently available to you.

To select and format the header row:

▶ **1.** Position the mouse pointer in the selection bar, to the left of the header row. The pointer changes to a right-facing arrow ⬈.

▶ **2.** Click the mouse button. The entire header row, including the end-of-cell mark in each cell and the end-of-row mark, is selected. See Figure 3-10.

| Figure 3-10 | **Header row selected** |

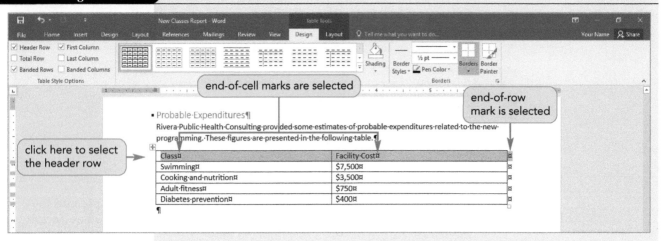

▶ **3.** Press the **Ctrl+B** keys to apply bold to the text in the header row. You can also use the formatting options on the Home tab to format selected text in a table, including adding italic formatting, changing the font, aligning text within cells, or applying a style.

▶ **4.** Click anywhere in the table to deselect the header row, and then save the document.

INSIGHT

Formatting a Multipage Table

In some documents, you might have a long table that extends across multiple pages. To make a multipage table easier to read, you can format the table header row to appear at the top of every page. To do so, click in the header row, click the Table Tools Layout tab, and then click the Properties button in the Table group. In the Table Properties dialog box, click the Row tab, and then select the "Repeat as header row at the top of each page" check box.

Now that you have created a very basic table, you can sort the information in it and improve its appearance.

Sorting Rows in a Table

The term **sort** refers to the process of rearranging information in alphabetical, numerical, or chronological order. You can sort a series of paragraphs, including the contents of a bulleted list, or you can sort the rows of a table.

When you sort a table, you arrange the rows based on the contents of one of the columns. For example, you could sort the table you just created based on the contents of the "Class" column—either in ascending alphabetical order (from A to Z) or in descending alphabetical order (from Z to A). Alternatively, you could sort the table based on the contents of the "Facility Cost" column—either in ascending numerical order (lowest to highest) or in descending numerical order (highest to lowest).

Clicking the Sort button in the Data group on the Table Tools Layout tab opens the Sort dialog box, which provides a number of options for fine-tuning the sort, including options for sorting a table by the contents of more than one column. This is useful if, for example, you want to organize the table rows by last name and then by first name within each last name. By default, Word assumes your table includes a header row that should remain at the top of the table—excluded from the sort.

REFERENCE

Sorting the Rows of a Table

- Click anywhere within the table.
- On the ribbon, click the Table Tools Layout tab.
- In the Data group, click the Sort button.
- In the Sort dialog box, click the Sort by arrow, and then select the header for the column you want to sort by.
- In the Type box located to the right of the Sort by box, select the type of information stored in the column you want to sort by; you can choose Text, Number, or Date.
- To sort in alphabetical, chronological, or numerical order, verify that the Ascending option button is selected. To sort in reverse order, click the Descending option button.
- To sort by a second column, click the Then by arrow, and then select a column header. If necessary, specify the type of information stored in the Then by column, and then confirm the sort order.
- At the bottom of the Sort dialog box, make sure the Header row option button is selected. This indicates that the table includes a header row that should not be included in the sort.
- Click the OK button.

Hillary would like you to sort the contents of the table in ascending numerical order based on the contents of the "Facility Cost" column.

To sort the information in the table:

▶ **1.** Make sure the insertion point is located somewhere in the table.

▶ **2.** On the ribbon, click the **Table Tools Layout** tab.

▶ **3.** In the Data group, click the **Sort** button. The Sort dialog box opens. Take a moment to review its default settings. The leftmost column in the table, the "Class" column, is selected in the Sort by box, indicating the sort will be based on the contents in this column. Because the "Class" column contains text, "Text" is selected in the Type box. The Ascending option button is selected by default, indicating that Word will sort the contents of the "Class" column from A to Z. The Header row option button is selected in the lower-left corner of the dialog box, ensuring the header row will not be included in the sort.

You want to sort the column by the contents of the "Facility Cost" column, so you need to change the Sort by setting.

4. Click the **Sort by** button arrow, and then click **Facility Cost**. Because the "Facility Cost" column contains numbers, the Type box now displays "Number". The Ascending button is still selected, indicating that Word will sort the numbers in the "Facility Cost" column from lowest to highest. See Figure 3-11.

Figure 3-11   **Sort dialog box**

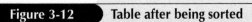

type of data in the "Facility Cost" column

sort based on the contents of the "Facility Cost" column

sort order

header row will be excluded from the sort

5. Click the **OK** button to close the Sort dialog box, and then click anywhere in the table to deselect it. Rows 2 through 5 are now arranged numerically, according to the numbers in the "Facility Cost" column, with the "Swimming" row at the bottom. See Figure 3-12.

Figure 3-12   **Table after being sorted**

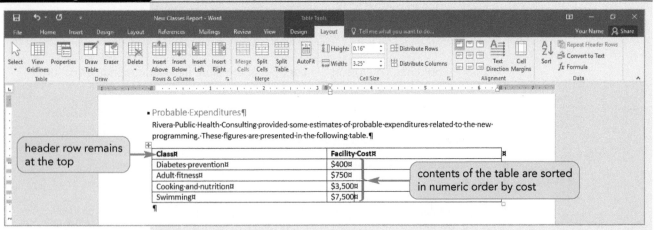

header row remains at the top

contents of the table are sorted in numeric order by cost

6. Save the document.

Hillary decides that the table should also include the personnel cost for each item. She asks you to insert a "Personnel Cost" column.

Inserting Rows and Columns in a Table

To add a column to a table, you can use the tools in the Rows & Columns group on the Table Tools Layout tab, or you can use the Add Column button in the document window. To use the Add Column button, make sure the insertion point is located somewhere within the table. When you position the mouse pointer at the top of the table, pointing to the border between two columns, the Add Column button is displayed. When you click that button, a new column is inserted between the two existing columns.

To insert a column in the table:

▶ **1.** Verify that the insertion point is located anywhere in the table.

▶ **2.** Position the mouse pointer at the top of the table, so that it points to the border between the two columns. The Add Column button ⊕ appears at the top of the border. A blue guideline shows where the new column will be inserted. See Figure 3-13.

Figure 3-13 Inserting a column

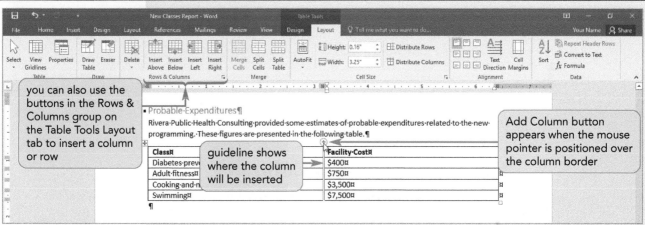

you can also use the buttons in the Rows & Columns group on the Table Tools Layout tab to insert a column or row

Add Column button appears when the mouse pointer is positioned over the column border

guideline shows where the column will be inserted

▪ Probable·Expenditures¶

Rivera·Public·Health·Consulting·provided·some·estimates·of·probable·expenditures·related·to·the·new·programming.·These·figures·are·presented·in·the·following·table.¶

Class¤	Facility·Cost¤
Diabetes·prev	$400¤
Adult·fitness¤	$750¤
Cooking·and·n	$3,500¤
Swimming¤	$7,500¤

▶ **3.** Click the **Add Column** button ⊕. A new, blank column is inserted between the "Class" and "Facility Cost" columns. The three columns in the table are narrower than the original two columns, but the overall width of the table remains the same.

▶ **4.** Click in the top cell of the new column, and then enter the following header and data. Use the ↓ key to move the insertion point down through the column.

Personnel Cost

$500

$2,000

$200

$4,750

Your table should now look like the one in Figure 3-14.

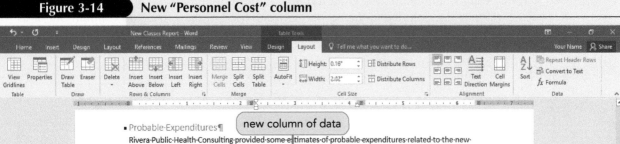

Figure 3-14   New "Personnel Cost" column

> Because you selected the entire header row when you formatted the original headers in bold, the newly inserted header, "Personnel Cost," is also formatted in bold.

Hillary just learned that the costs listed for adult fitness actually cover both adult fitness and diabetes prevention. Therefore, she would like you to delete the "Diabetes prevention" row from the table.

Deleting Rows and Columns

When you consider deleting a row, you need to be clear about whether you want to delete just the contents of the row, or both the contents and the structure of the row. You can delete the contents of a row by selecting the row and pressing the Delete key. This removes the information from the row but leaves the row structure intact. The same is true for deleting the contents of an individual cell, a column, or the entire table. To delete the structure of a row, a column, or the entire table—including its contents—you select the row (or column or the entire table), and then use the Delete button on the Mini toolbar or in the Rows & Columns group on the Table Tools Layout tab. To delete multiple rows or columns, start by selecting all the rows or columns you want to delete.

Before you delete the "Diabetes prevention" row, you need to edit the contents in the third cell in the first column to indicate that the items in that row are for adult fitness and diabetes prevention.

To delete the "Diabetes prevention" row:

▶ **1.** In the cell containing the text "Adult fitness," click to the right of the final "s," press the **spacebar**, and then type **and diabetes prevention**. The cell now reads "Adult fitness and diabetes prevention." Part of the text wraps to a second line within the cell.

   Next, you can delete the "Diabetes prevention" row, which is no longer necessary.

▶ **2.** Click in the selection bar to the left of the **Diabetes prevention** row. The row is selected, with the Mini toolbar displayed on top of the selected row.

> **3.** On the Mini toolbar, click the **Delete** button. The Delete menu opens, displaying options for deleting cells, columns, rows, or the entire table. See Figure 3-15.

Figure 3-15	Deleting a row

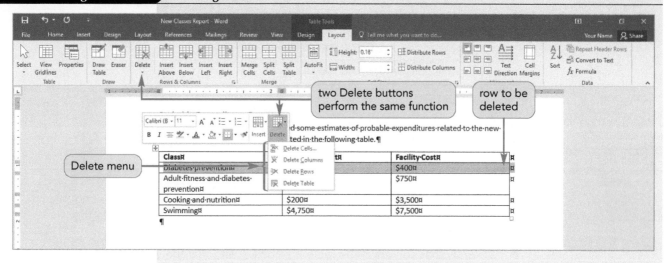

> **4.** Click **Delete Rows**. The "Diabetes prevention" row is removed from the table, and the Mini toolbar disappears.

> **5.** Save your work.

The table now contains all the information Hillary wants to include. Next, you'll adjust the widths of the three columns.

Changing Column Widths

TIP

To change the height of a row, position the mouse pointer over the bottom row border and drag the border up or down.

Columns that are too wide for the material they contain can make a table hard to read. You can change a column's width by dragging the column's right border to a new position. Or, if you prefer, you can double-click a column border to make the column width adjust automatically to accommodate the widest entry in the column. To adjust the width of all the columns to match their widest entries, click anywhere in the table, click the AutoFit button in the Cell Size group on the Table Tools Layout tab, and then click AutoFit Contents. To adjust the width of the entire table to span the width of the page, click the AutoFit button and then click AutoFit Window.

You'll adjust the columns in Hillary's table by double-clicking the right column border. You need to start by making sure that no part of the table is selected. Otherwise, when you double-click the border, only the width of the selected part of the table will change.

To change the width of the columns in the table:

When resizing a column, be sure that no part of the table is selected. Otherwise, you'll resize just the selected part.

> **1.** Verify that no part of the table is selected, and then position the mouse pointer over the right border of the "Personnel Cost" column until the pointer changes to +‖+. See Figure 3-16.

Figure 3-16　　**Adjusting the column width**

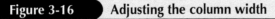

Figure 3-16　　**Adjusting the column width**

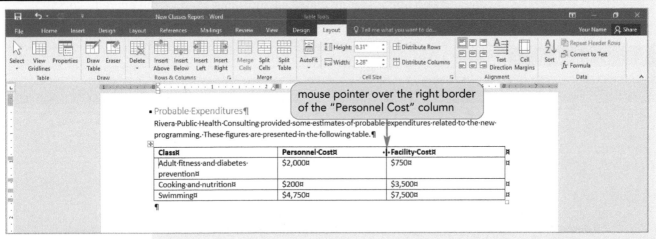

▶ **2.** Double-click the mouse button. The right column border moves left so that the "Personnel Cost" column is just wide enough to accommodate the widest entry in the column.

▶ **3.** Verify that no part of the table is selected, and that the insertion point is located in any cell in the table.

▶ **4.** Make sure the Table Tools Layout tab is selected on the ribbon.

▶ **5.** In the Cell Size group, click the **AutoFit** button, and then click **AutoFit Contents**. All of the table columns adjust so that each is just wide enough to accommodate its widest entry. The text "Adult fitness and diabetes prevention" in row 2 no longer wraps to a second line.

To finish the table, you will add some formatting to improve the table's appearance.

Formatting Tables with Styles

To adjust a table's appearance, you can use any of the formatting options available on the Home tab. To change a table's appearance more dramatically, you can use table styles, which allow you to apply a collection of formatting options, including shading, color, borders, and other design elements, with a single click.

By default, a table is formatted with the Table Grid style, which includes only black borders between the rows and columns, no paragraph spacing, no shading, and the default black font color. You can select a more colorful table style from the Table Styles group on the Table Tools Design tab. Whatever table style you choose, you'll give your document a more polished look if you use the same style consistently in all the tables in a single document.

Some table styles format rows in alternating colors, called **banded rows**, while others format the columns in alternating colors, called **banded columns**. You can choose a style that includes different formatting for the header row than for the rest of the table. Or, if the first column in your table is a header column—that is, if it contains headers identifying the type of information in each row—you can choose a style that instead applies different formatting to the first column.

REFERENCE

Formatting a Table with a Table Style

- Click in the table you want to format.
- On the ribbon, click the Table Tools Design tab.
- In the Table Styles group, click the More button to display the Table Styles gallery.
- Position the mouse pointer over a style in the Table Styles gallery to see a Live Preview of the table style in the document.
- In the Table Styles gallery, click the style you want.
- To apply or remove style elements (such as special formatting for the header row, banded rows, or banded columns), select or deselect check boxes as necessary in the Table Style Options group.

Hillary wants to use a table style that emphasizes the header row with special formatting, does not include column borders, and uses color to separate the rows.

To apply a table style to the Probable Expenditures table:

1. Click anywhere in the table, and then scroll to position the table at the very bottom of the Word window. This will make it easier to see the Live Preview in the next few steps.

2. On the ribbon, click the **Table Tools Design** tab. In the Table Styles group, the plain Table Grid style is highlighted, indicating that it is the table's current style.

3. In the Table Styles group, click the **More** button. The Table Styles gallery opens. The default Table Grid style now appears under the heading "Plain Tables." The more elaborate styles appear below, in the "Grid Tables" section of the gallery.

4. Use the gallery's vertical scroll bar to view the complete collection of table styles. When you are finished, scroll up until you can see the "Grid Tables" heading again.

5. Move the mouse pointer over the style located in the fourth row of the Grid Tables section, first column on the right. See Figure 3-17.

Figure 3-17 Table Styles gallery

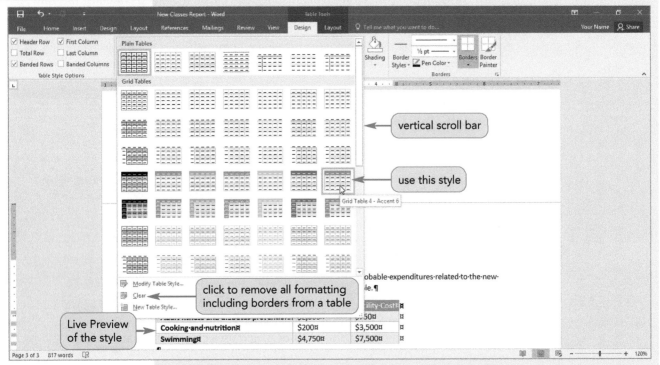

A ScreenTip displays the style's name, "Grid Table 4 - Accent 6." The style consists of a dark green heading row, with alternating rows of light green and white below. A Live Preview of the style is visible in the document.

6. Click the **Grid Table 4 - Accent 6** style. The Table Styles gallery closes.

7. Scroll to position the table at the top of the Word window, so you can review it more easily. The table's header row is formatted with dark green shading and white text. The rows below appear in alternating colors of light green and white.

The only problem with the newly formatted table is that the text in the first column is formatted in bold. In tables where the first column contains headers, bold would be appropriate—but this isn't the case with Hillary's table. You'll fix this by deselecting the First Column check box in the Table Style Options group on the Table Tools Design tab.

To remove the bold formatting from the first column:

1. In the Table Style Options group, click the **First Column** check box to deselect this option. The bold formatting is removed from the entries in the "Class" column. Note that the Header Row check box is selected. This indicates that the table's header row is emphasized with special formatting (dark green shading with white text). The Banded Rows check box is also selected because the table is formatted with banded rows of green and white. Figure 3-18 shows the finished table.

Figure 3-18   **Completed table**

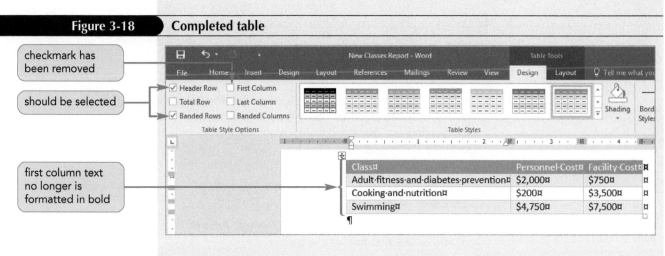

checkmark has been removed

should be selected

first column text no longer is formatted in bold

2. Save the document.

After you apply a table style, it's helpful to know how to remove it in case you want to start over from scratch. The Clear option on the menu below the Table Styles gallery removes the current style from a table, including the borders between cells. When a table has no borders, the rows and columns are defined by **gridlines**, which are useful as guidelines but do not appear when you print the table.

In the following steps, you'll experiment with clearing the table's style, displaying and hiding the gridlines, and removing the table's borders.

To experiment with table styles, gridlines, and borders:

1. In the Table Styles group, click the **More** button, and then click **Clear** in the menu below the gallery. Next, you need to make sure the table gridlines are displayed.

2. On the ribbon, click the **Table Tools Layout** tab.

3. In the Table group, click the **View Gridlines** button, if necessary, to select it. The table now looks much simpler, with no shading or font colors. Instead of the table borders, dotted gridlines separate the rows and columns. The text in the table is spaced farther apart because removing the table style restored the default paragraph and line spacing of the Normal style. The bold formatting that you applied earlier, which is not part of a table style, is visible again.

   It is helpful to clear a table's style and view only the gridlines if you want to use a table to lay out text and graphics on a page, but you want no visible indication of the table itself. You'll have a chance to try this technique in the Case Problems at the end of this module.

   Another option is to remove only the table borders, leaving the rest of the table style applied to the table. To do this, you have to select the entire table. But first you need to undo the style change.

▶ **4.** On the Quick Access Toolbar, click the **Undo** button ↶ to restore the Grid Table 4 - Accent 6 style, so that your table looks like the one in Figure 3-18.

▶ **5.** In the upper-left corner of the table, click the **Table Select** handle ⊕ to select the entire table, and then click the **Table Tools Design** tab.

▶ **6.** In the Borders group, click the **Borders button arrow** to open the Borders gallery, click **No Border**, and then click anywhere in the table to deselect it. The borders are removed from the table, leaving only the nonprinting gridlines to separate the rows and columns. To add borders of any color to specific parts of a table, you can use the Border Painter.

▶ **7.** In the Borders group, click the **Border Painter** button, and then click the **Pen Color** button to open the Pen Color gallery.

▶ **8.** In the Pen Color gallery, click the **Orange, Accent 2** square in the sixth column of the first row of the gallery.

▶ **9.** Use the Border Painter pointer to click any gridline in the table. An orange border is added to the cell where you clicked.

▶ **10.** Continue experimenting with the Border Painter pointer, and then press the **Esc** key to turn off the Border Painter pointer when you are finished.

▶ **11.** Reapply the Grid Table 4 - Accent 6 table style to make your table match the one shown earlier in Figure 3-18.

▶ **12.** Save the document and then close it.

PROSKILLS

Problem Solving: Fine-Tuning Table Styles

After you apply a table style to a table, you might like the look of the table but find that it no longer effectively conveys your information or is not quite as easy to read. To solve this problem, you might be inclined to go back to the Table Styles gallery to find another style that might work better. Another method to correct problems with a table style is to identify the table elements with problematic formatting, and then manually make formatting adjustments to only those elements using the options on the Table Tools Design tab. For example, you can change the thickness and color of the table borders using the options in the Borders group, and you can add shading using the Shading button in the Table Styles group. Also, if you don't like the appearance of table styles in your document, consider changing the document's theme and previewing the table styles again. The table styles have a different appearance in each theme. When applying table styles, remember there are many options for attractively formatting the table without compromising the information being conveyed.

In the next session, you'll complete the rest of the report by organizing information using tab stops, creating footnotes and endnotes, dividing the document into sections, inserting headers and footers, and, finally, inserting a cover page.

REVIEW

Session 3.1 Quick Check

1. What kind of style must you apply to a paragraph to make the paragraph appear as a heading in the Navigation pane?

2. What are the three steps involved in creating a table in Word?

3. Explain how to insert a new column in a table.

4. After you enter data in the last cell in the last row in a table, how can you insert a new row?

5. When sorting a table, is the header row included by default?

6. To adjust the width of a table's column to span the width of the page, would you use the AutoFit Contents option or the AutoFit Window option?

Session 3.2 Visual Overview:

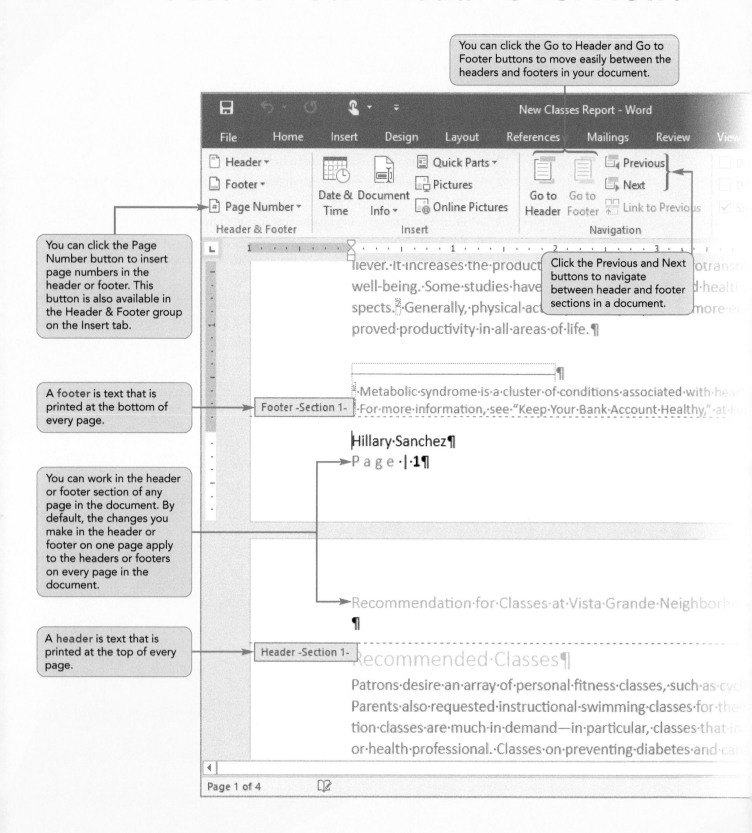

You can click the Go to Header and Go to Footer buttons to move easily between the headers and footers in your document.

You can click the Page Number button to insert page numbers in the header or footer. This button is also available in the Header & Footer group on the Insert tab.

Click the Previous and Next buttons to navigate between header and footer sections in a document.

A footer is text that is printed at the bottom of every page.

You can work in the header or footer section of any page in the document. By default, the changes you make in the header or footer on one page apply to the headers or footers on every page in the document.

A header is text that is printed at the top of every page.

Working with Headers and Footers

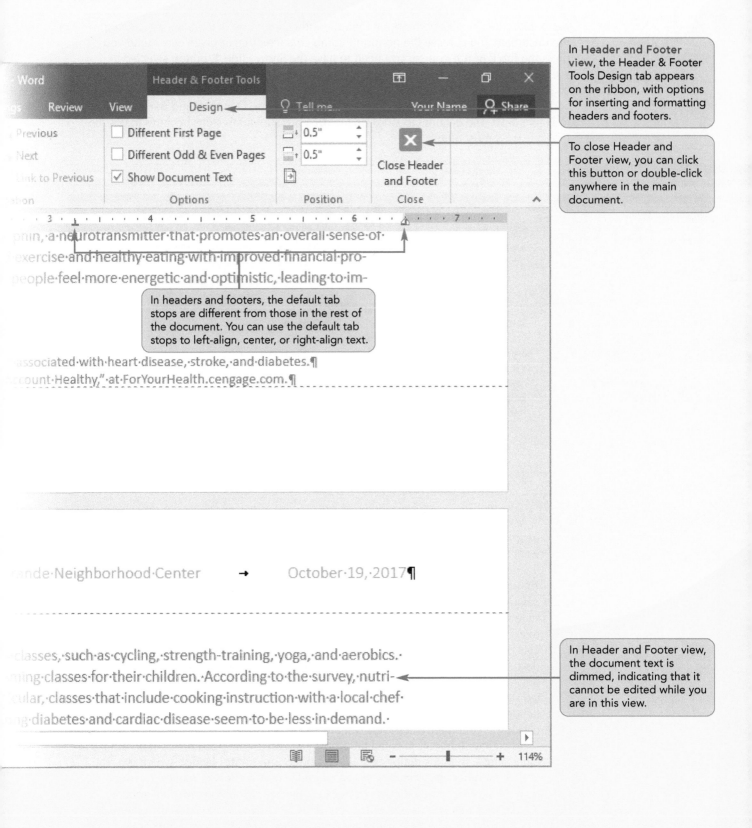

In Header and Footer view, the Header & Footer Tools Design tab appears on the ribbon, with options for inserting and formatting headers and footers.

To close Header and Footer view, you can click this button or double-click anywhere in the main document.

In headers and footers, the default tab stops are different from those in the rest of the document. You can use the default tab stops to left-align, center, or right-align text.

In Header and Footer view, the document text is dimmed, indicating that it cannot be edited while you are in this view.

Setting Tab Stops

A **tab stop** (often called a **tab**) is a location on the horizontal ruler where the insertion point moves when you press the Tab key. You can use tab stops to align small amounts of text or data. By default, a document contains tab stops every one-half inch on the horizontal ruler. There's no mark on the ruler indicating these default tab stops, but in the document you can see the nonprinting Tab character that appears every time you press the Tab key. (Of course, you need to have the Show/Hide ¶ button selected to see these nonprinting characters.) A nonprinting tab character is just like any other character you type; you can delete it by pressing the Backspace key or the Delete key.

The five major types of tab stops are Left, Center, Right, Decimal, and Bar, as shown in Figure 3-19. The default tab stops on the ruler are all left tab stops because that is the tab style used most often.

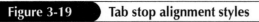

Figure 3-19 Tab stop alignment styles

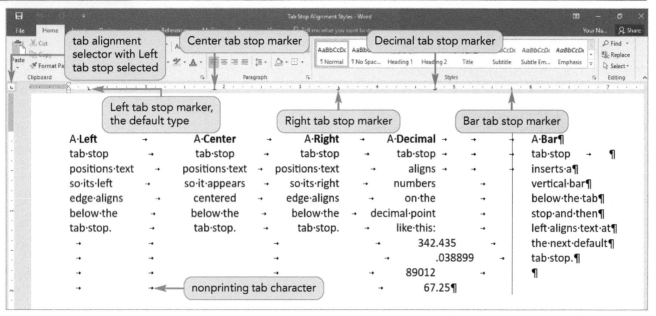

You can use tab stops a few different ways. The simplest is to press the Tab key until the insertion point is aligned where you want it, and then type the text you want to align. Each time you press the Tab key, the insertion point moves right to the next default tab stop, with the left edge of the text aligning below the tab stop. To use a different type of tab stop, or to use a tab stop at a location other than the default tab stop locations (every half-inch on the ruler), first select an alignment style from the tab alignment selector, located at the left end of the horizontal ruler, and then click the horizontal ruler where you want to insert the tab stop. This process is called setting a tab stop. When you set a new tab stop, all of the default tab stops to its left are removed. This means you have to press the Tab key only once to move the insertion point to the newly created tab stop. To set a new tab stop in text you have already typed, select the text, including the nonprinting tab stop characters, and then set the tab stop by selecting an alignment style and clicking on the ruler where you want to set the tab stop.

To create more complicated tab stops, you can use the Tabs dialog box. Among other things, the Tabs dialog box allows you to insert a **dot leader**, which is a row of dots (or other characters) between tabbed text. A dot leader makes it easier to read a long list of tabbed material because the eye can follow the dots from one item to the next. You've probably seen dot leaders used in the table of contents in a book, where the dots separate the chapter titles from the page numbers.

To create a left tab stop with a dot leader, click the Dialog Box Launcher in the Paragraph group on the Home tab, click the Indents and Spacing tab, if necessary, and then click the Tabs button at the bottom of the dialog box. In the Tab stop position box in the Tabs dialog box, type the location on the ruler where you want to insert the tab. For example, to insert a tab stop at the 4-inch mark, type 4. Verify that the Left option button is selected in the Alignment section, and then, in the Leader section, click the option button for the type of leader you want. Click the Set button, and then click the OK button.

REFERENCE

Setting, Moving, and Clearing Tab Stops

- To set a tab stop, click the tab alignment selector on the horizontal ruler until the appropriate tab stop alignment style is displayed, and then click the horizontal ruler where you want to position the tab stop.
- To move a tab stop, drag it to a new location on the ruler. If you have already typed text that is aligned by the tab stop, select the text before dragging the tab stop to a new location.
- To clear a tab stop, drag it off the ruler.

In the New Classes Report document you have been working on, you need to type the list of consultants and their titles. You can use tab stops to quickly format this small amount of information in two columns. As you type, you'll discover whether Word's default tab stops are appropriate for this document or whether you need to set a new tab stop. Before you get started working with tabs, you'll take a moment to explore Word's Resume Reading feature.

To enter the list of consultants using tabs:

▶ **1.** Open the **New Classes Report** document. The document opens with the "Summary" heading at the top of the Word window. In the lower-right corner, a "Welcome back!" message is displayed briefly and is then replaced with the Resume Reading button ⟦▣⟧.

▶ **2.** Point to the **Resume Reading** button ⟦▣⟧ to expand its "Welcome back!" message. See Figure 3-20.

Figure 3-20   **"Welcome back!" message displayed in re-opened document**

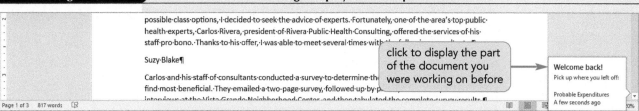

possible·class·options,·I·decided·to·seek·the·advice·of·experts.·Fortunately,·one·of·the·area's·top·public·
health·experts,·Carlos·Rivera,·president·of·Rivera·Public·Health·Consulting,·offered·the·services·of·his·
staff·pro·bono.·Thanks·to·his·offer,·I·was·able·to·meet·several·times·with···········

Suzy·Blake¶

click to display the part of the document you were working on before

Welcome back!
Pick up where you left off:

Carlos·and·his·staff·of·consultants·conducted·a·survey·to·determine·the
find·most·beneficial.·They·emailed·a·two-page·survey,·followed·up·by·p
interviews·at·the·Vista·Grande·Neighborhood·Center,·and·then·tabulated·the·complete·survey·results.¶

Probable Expenditures
A few seconds ago

Page 1 of 3   817 words

▶ **3.** Click the **Welcome back!** message. The document window scrolls down to display the table, which you were working on just before you closed the document.

▶ **4.** Scroll up to display the "Rivera Public Health Consulting" heading on page 1.

▶ **5.** Confirm that the ruler and nonprinting characters are displayed, and that the document is displayed in **Print Layout** view, zoomed to **120%**.

6. Click to the right of the last "e" in "Suzy Blake."

7. Press the **Tab** key. An arrow-shaped tab character appears, and the insertion point moves to the first tab stop after the last "e" in "Blake." This tab stop is the default tab located at the 1-inch mark on the horizontal ruler. See Figure 3-21.

Figure 3-21   Tab character

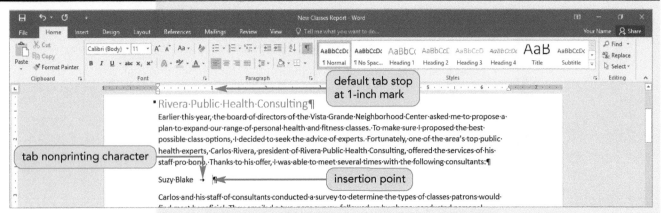

8. Type **Senior Consultant**, and then press the **Enter** key to move the insertion point to the next line.

9. Type **Emmanuel Iglesias**, and then press the **Tab** key. The insertion point moves to the next available tab stop, this time located at the 1.5-inch mark on the ruler.

10. Type **Senior Consultant**, and then press the **Enter** key to move to the next line. Notice that Emmanuel Iglesias's title does not align with Suzy Blake's title on the line above it. You'll fix this after you type the last name in the list.

11. Type **Carolina Sheffield-Bassinger**, press the **Tab** key, and then type **Project Manager**. See Figure 3-22.

Figure 3-22   List of consultants

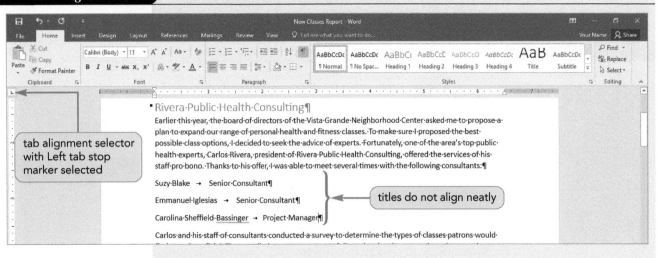

The list of names and titles is not aligned properly. You can fix this by inserting a new tab stop.

To add a new tab stop to the horizontal ruler:

▶ **1.** Make sure the Home tab is displayed on the ribbon, and then select the list of consultants and their titles.

▶ **2.** On the horizontal ruler, click at the 2.5-inch mark. Because the current tab stop alignment style is Left tab, Word inserts a left tab stop at that location. Remember that when you set a new tab stop, all the default tab stops to its left are removed. The column of titles shifts to the new tab stop. See Figure 3-23.

Figure 3-23 | Titles aligned at new tab stop

To complete the list, you need to remove the paragraph spacing after the first two paragraphs in the list, so the list looks like it's all one paragraph. You can quickly reduce paragraph and line spacing to 0 points by clicking the No Spacing style in the Styles group. In this case, you want to reduce only the paragraph spacing to 0 points, so you'll use the Line and Paragraph Spacing button instead.

▶ **3.** Select the first two paragraphs in the list, which contain the names and titles for Suzy and Emmanuel.

▶ **4.** In the Paragraph group, click the **Line and Paragraph Spacing** button, and then click **Remove Space After Paragraph**.

▶ **5.** Click anywhere in the document to deselect the list, and then save your work.

Decision Making: Choosing Between Tabs and Tables

When you have information that you want to align in columns in your document, you need to decide whether to use tabs or tables. Whatever you do, don't try to align columns of data by adding extra spaces with the spacebar. Although the text might seem precisely aligned on the screen, it probably won't be aligned when you print the document. Furthermore, if you edit the text, the spaces you inserted to align your columns will be affected by your edits; they get moved just like regular text, ruining your alignment.

So what is the most efficient way to align text in columns? It depends. Inserting tabs works well for aligning small amounts of information in just a few columns and rows, such as two columns with three rows, but tabs become cumbersome when you need to organize a lot of data over multiple columns and rows. In that case, using a table to organize columns of information is better. Unlike with tabbed columns of data, it's easy to add data to tables by inserting columns. You might also choose tables over tab stops when you want to take advantage of the formatting options available with table styles. As mentioned earlier, if you don't want the table structure itself to be visible in the document, you can clear its table style and then hide its gridlines.

Hillary would like to add two footnotes that provide further information about topics discussed in her report. You will do that next.

Creating Footnotes and Endnotes

A **footnote** is an explanatory comment or reference that appears at the bottom of a page. When you create a footnote, Word inserts a small, superscript number (called a **reference marker**) in the text. The term **superscript** means that the number is raised slightly above the line of text. Word then inserts the same number in the page's bottom margin and positions the insertion point next to it so you can type the text of the footnote. **Endnotes** are similar, except that the text of an endnote appears at the end of a section or, in the case of a document without sections, at the end of the document. (You'll learn about dividing a document into sections later in this module.) By default, the reference marker for an endnote is a lowercase Roman numeral, and the reference marker for a footnote is an ordinary, Arabic numeral.

Word automatically manages the reference markers for you, keeping them sequential from the beginning of the document to the end, no matter how many times you add, delete, or move footnotes or endnotes. For example, if you move a paragraph containing footnote 4 so that it falls before the paragraph containing footnote 1, Word renumbers all the footnotes in the document to keep them sequential.

Inserting a Footnote or an Endnote

- Click the location in the document where you want to insert a footnote or an endnote.
- On the ribbon, click the References tab.
- In the Footnotes group, click the Insert Footnote button or the Insert Endnote button.
- Type the text of the footnote in the bottom margin of the page, or type the text of the endnote at the end of the document.
- When you are finished typing the text of a footnote or an endnote, click in the body of the document to continue working on the document.

Hillary asks you to insert a footnote that provides more information about some studies mentioned in the report.

To add a footnote to the report:

1. Use the Navigation pane to find the phrase "improved financial prospects" on page 1, and then click to the right of the period after "prospects."

2. Close the Navigation pane.

3. On the ribbon, click the **References** tab.

4. In the Footnotes group, click the **Insert Footnote** button. A superscript "1" is inserted to the right of the period after "prospects." Word also inserts the number "1" in the bottom margin below a separator line. The insertion point is now located next to the number in the bottom margin, ready for you to type the text of the footnote.

5. Type **For more information, see "Keep Your Bank Account Healthy," at ForYourHealth.cengage.com.** See Figure 3-24.

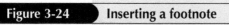

Figure 3-24   Inserting a footnote

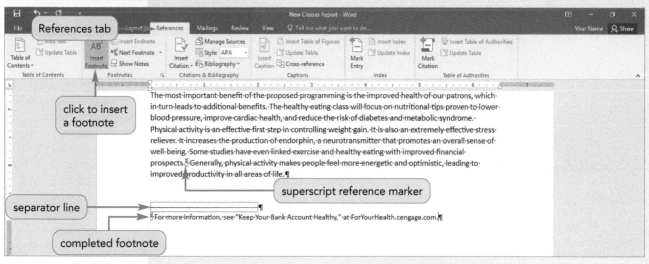

Now, Hillary would like you to insert a second footnote.

To insert a second footnote:

1. At the end of the third line of the same paragraph, click at the end of the second sentence to position the insertion point to the right of the period after "syndrome."

2. In the Footnotes group, click the **Insert Footnote** button, and then type **Metabolic syndrome is a cluster of conditions associated with heart disease, stroke, and diabetes.** Because this footnote is placed earlier in the document than the one you just created, Word inserts a superscript "1" for this footnote and then renumbers the other footnote as "2." See Figure 3-25.

Figure 3-25 ▶ **Inserting a second footnote**

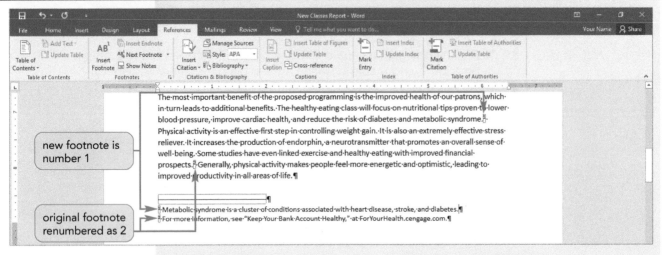

> ▶ **3.** Save the document.

Understanding Endnotes, Footnotes, and Citations

It's easy to confuse footnotes with endnotes, and endnotes with citations. Remember, a footnote appears at the bottom, or foot, of a page and always on the same page as its reference marker. You might have one footnote at the bottom of page 3, three footnotes at the bottom of page 5, and one at the bottom of page 6. By contrast, an endnote appears at the end of the document or section, with all the endnotes compiled into a single list. Both endnotes and footnotes can contain any kind of information you think might be useful to your readers. Citations, however, are only used to list specific information about a book or other source you refer to or quote from in the document. A citation typically appears in parentheses at the end of the sentence containing information from the source you are citing, and the sources for all of the document's citations are listed in a bibliography, or a list of works cited, at the end of the document.

Now you're ready to address some other issues with the document. First, Hillary has noticed that the right edges of most of the paragraphs in the document are uneven, and she'd like you to try to smooth them out. You'll correct this problem in the next section.

Hyphenating a Document

By default, hyphenation is turned off in Word documents. That means if you are in the middle of typing a word and you reach the end of a line, Word moves the entire word to the next line instead of inserting a hyphen and breaking the word into two parts. This can result in ragged text on the right margin. To ensure a smoother right margin, you can turn on automatic hyphenation—in which case, any word that ends within the last .25 inch of a line will be hyphenated.

To turn on automatic hyphenation in the document:

▶ **1.** Review the paragraph above the footnotes on page 1. The text on the right side of this paragraph is uneven. Keeping an eye on this paragraph will help you see the benefits of hyphenation.

▶ **2.** On the ribbon, click the **Layout** tab.

▶ **3.** In the Page Setup group, click the **Hyphenation** button to open the Hyphenation menu, and then click **Automatic**. The Hyphenation menu closes. Throughout the document, the text layout shifts to account for the insertion of hyphens in words that break near the end of a line. For example, in the last paragraph on page 1, the word "Physical" is now hyphenated. See Figure 3-26.

| Figure 3-26 | Hyphenated document |

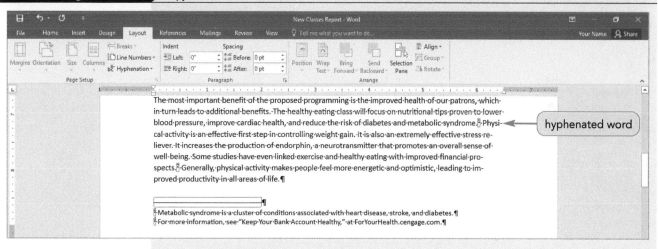

▶ **4.** Save the document.

Hillary plans to post a handout on the bulletin board at the neighborhood center to illustrate the benefits of the new classes, and she wants to include a sample handout in the report. Before you can add the sample of the handout, you need to divide the document into sections.

Formatting a Document into Sections

A **section** is a part of a document that can have its own page orientation, margins, headers, footers, and so on. In other words, each section is like a document within a document. To divide a document into sections, you insert a **section break**. You can select from a few different types of section breaks. One of the most useful is a Next page section break, which inserts a page break and starts the new section on the next page. Another commonly used kind of section break, a Continuous section break, starts the section at the location of the insertion point without changing the page flow. To insert a section break, you click the Breaks button in the Page Setup group on the Layout tab and then select the type of section break you want to insert.

Hillary wants to format the handout in landscape orientation, but the report is currently formatted in portrait orientation. To format part of a document in an orientation different from the rest of the document, you need to divide the document into sections.

To insert a section break below the table:

▶ **1.** Press the **Ctrl+End** keys to move the insertion point to the end of the document, just below the table.

▶ **2.** In the Page Setup group, click the **Breaks** button. The Breaks gallery opens, as shown in Figure 3-27.

Figure 3-27   **Breaks gallery**

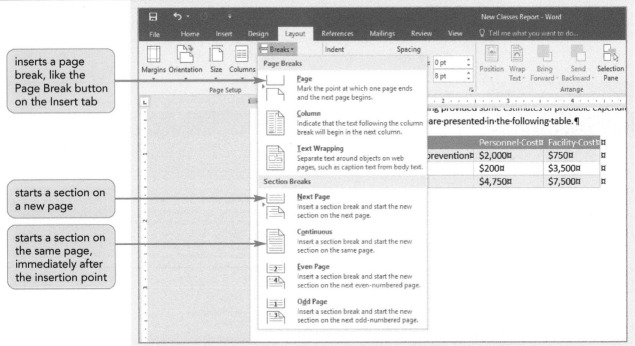

inserts a page break, like the Page Break button on the Insert tab

starts a section on a new page

starts a section on the same page, immediately after the insertion point

The Page Breaks section of the gallery includes options for controlling how the text flows from page to page. The first option, Page, inserts a page break. It has the same effect as pressing the Page Break button on the Insert tab or pressing the Ctrl+Enter keys. The Section Breaks section of the gallery includes four types of section breaks. The two you'll use most often are Next Page and Continuous.

▶ **3.** Under "Section Breaks," click **Next Page**. A section break is inserted in the document, and the insertion point moves to the top of the new page 4.

▶ **4.** Scroll up, if necessary, until you can see the double dotted line and the words "Section Break (Next Page)" below the table on page 3. This line indicates that a new section begins on the next page.

▶ **5.** Save the document.

TIP

To delete a section break, click to the left of the line representing the break, and then press the Delete key.

You've created a new page that is a separate section from the rest of the report. The sections are numbered consecutively. The first part of the document is section 1, and the new page is section 2. Now you can format section 2 in landscape orientation without affecting the rest of the document.

To format section 2 in landscape orientation:

▶ **1.** Scroll down and verify that the insertion point is positioned at the top of the new page 4.

▶ **2.** On the ribbon, click the **View** tab.

▶ **3.** In the Zoom group, click the **Multiple Pages** button, and then change the Zoom level to **30%** so you can see all four pages of the document displayed side by side.

▶ **4.** On the ribbon, click the **Layout** tab.

▶ **5.** In the Page Setup group, click the **Orientation** button, and then click **Landscape**. Section 2, which consists solely of page 4, changes to landscape orientation, as shown in Figure 3-28. Section 1, which consists of pages 1 through 3, remains in portrait orientation.

Figure 3-28	Page 4 formatted in landscape orientation

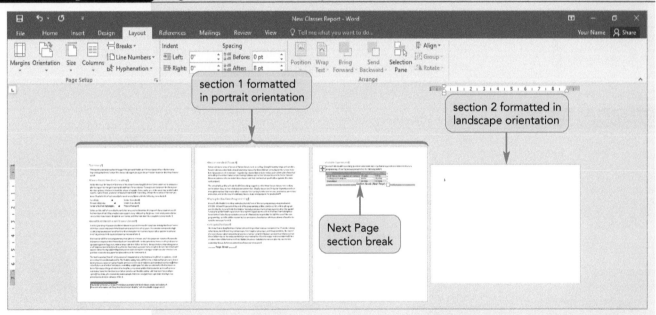

▶ **6.** Change the Zoom level back to **120%**, and then save the document.

Page 4 is now formatted in landscape orientation, ready for you to create Hillary's handout, which will consist of a graphic that shows the benefits of exercise. You'll use Word's SmartArt feature to create the graphic.

Creating SmartArt

A **SmartArt** graphic is a diagram of shapes, such as circles, squares, or arrows. A well-designed SmartArt graphic can illustrate concepts that might otherwise require several paragraphs of explanation. To create a SmartArt graphic, you switch to the Insert tab and then, in the Illustrations group, click the SmartArt button. This opens the Choose a SmartArt Graphic dialog box, where you can select from eight categories of graphics, including graphics designed to illustrate relationships, processes, and hierarchies. Within each category, you can choose from numerous designs. Once inserted into your document, a SmartArt graphic contains placeholder text that you replace with your own text. When a SmartArt graphic is selected, the SmartArt Tools Design and Format tabs appear on the ribbon.

To create a SmartArt graphic:

▶ **1.** Verify that the insertion point is located at the top of page 4, which is blank.

▶ **2.** On the ribbon, click the **Insert** tab.

▶ **3.** In the Illustrations group, click the **SmartArt** button. The Choose a SmartArt Graphic dialog box opens, with categories of SmartArt graphics in the left panel. The middle panel displays the graphics associated with the category currently selected in the left panel. The right panel displays a larger image of the graphic that is currently selected in the middle panel, along with an explanation of the graphic's purpose. By default, All is selected in the left panel.

▶ **4.** Explore the Choose a SmartArt Graphic dialog box by selecting categories in the left panel and viewing the graphics displayed in the middle panel.

▶ **5.** In the left panel, click **Relationship**, and then scroll down in the middle panel and click the **Converging Radial** graphic (in the first column, seventh row from the top), which shows three rectangles with arrows pointing to a circle. In the right panel, you see an explanation of the Converging Radial graphic. See Figure 3-29.

Figure 3-29	Selecting a SmartArt graphic

▶ **6.** Click the **OK** button. The Converging Radial graphic, with placeholder text, is inserted at the top of page 4. The graphic is surrounded by a rectangular border, indicating that it is selected. The SmartArt Tools contextual tabs appear on the ribbon. To the right of the graphic, you also see the Text pane, a small window with a title bar that contains the text "Type your text here." See Figure 3-30.

Figure 3-30   SmartArt graphic with Text pane displayed

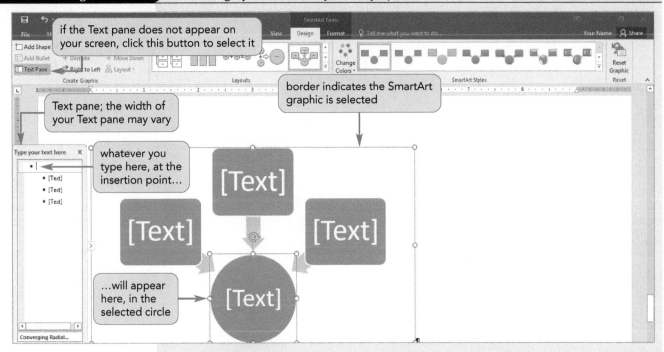

Trouble? If you do not see the Text pane, click the Text Pane button in the Create Graphic group on the SmartArt Tools Design tab to select it.

The insertion point is blinking next to the first bullet in the Text pane, which is selected with an orange rectangle. The circle at the bottom of the SmartArt graphic is also selected, as indicated by the border with handles. At this point, anything you type next to the selected bullet in the Text pane will also appear in the selected circle in the SmartArt graphic.

Trouble? If you see the Text pane but the first bullet is not selected as shown in Figure 3-30, click next to the first bullet in the Text pane to select it.

Now you are ready to add text to the graphic.

To add text to the SmartArt graphic:

▶ 1. Type **Better Physical and Mental Health**. The new text is displayed in the Text pane and in the circle in the SmartArt graphic. Now you need to insert text in the three rectangles.

▶ 2. Press the ↓ key to move the insertion point down to the next placeholder bullet in the Text pane, and then type **Exercise**. The new text is displayed in the Text pane and in the blue rectangle on the left. See Figure 3-31.

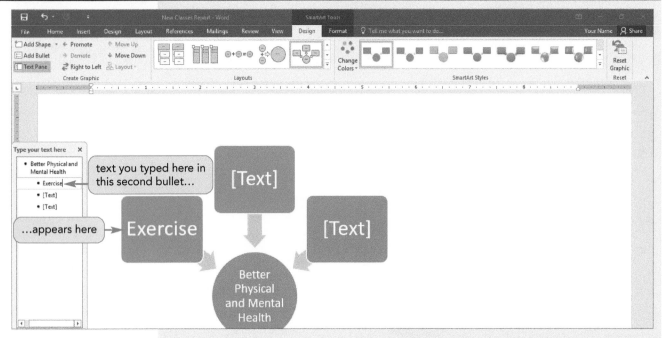

Figure 3-31 New text in Text pane and in SmartArt graphic

3. Press the ↓ key to move the insertion point down to the next placeholder bullet in the Text pane, and then type **Good Nutrition**. The new text appears in the middle rectangle and in the Text pane. You don't need the third rectangle, so you'll delete it.

TIP

To add a shape to a SmartArt graphic, click a shape in the SmartArt graphic, click the Add Shape arrow in the Create Graphic group on the SmartArt Tools Design tab, and then click a placement option.

4. Press the ↓ key to move the insertion point down to the next placeholder bullet in the Text pane, and then press the **Backspace** key. The rectangle on the right is deleted from the SmartArt graphic. The two remaining rectangles and the circle enlarge and shift position.

5. Make sure the SmartArt Tools Design tab is still selected on the ribbon.

6. In the Create Graphic group, click the **Text Pane** button to deselect it. The Text pane closes.

7. Click in the white area inside the SmartArt border.

Next, you need to resize the SmartArt graphic so it fills the page.

To adjust the size of the SmartArt graphic:

1. Zoom out so you can see the entire page. As you can see on the ruler, the SmartArt is currently 6 inches wide. You could drag the SmartArt border to resize it, just as you can with any graphic, but you will get more precise results using the Size button on the SmartArt Tools Format tab.

2. On the ribbon, click the **SmartArt Tools Format** tab.

3. On the right side of the SmartArt Tools Format tab, click the **Size** button to display the Height and Width boxes.

4. Click the **Height** box, type **6.5**, click the **Width** box, type **9**, and then press the **Enter** key. The SmartArt graphic resizes, so that it is now 9 inches wide and 6.5 inches high, taking up most of the page. See Figure 3-32.

Figure 3-32 **Resized SmartArt**

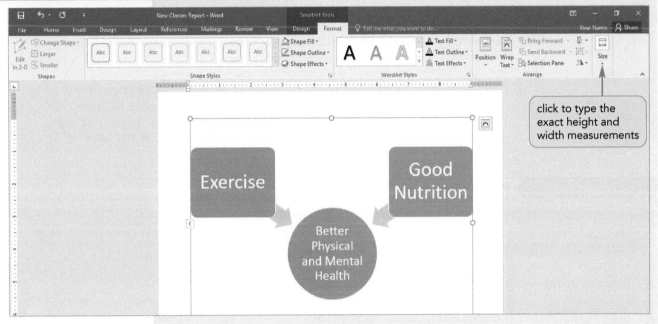

click to type the exact height and width measurements

Trouble? If one of the shapes in the SmartArt graphic was resized, rather than the entire SmartArt graphic, the insertion point was located within the shape rather than in the white space. On the Quick Access Toolbar, click the Undo button 🔄, click in the white area inside the SmartArt border, and then repeat Steps 3 and 4.

▶ **5.** Click outside the SmartArt border to deselect it, and then review the graphic centered on the page.

Next, you need to insert a header at the top of each page in the report and a footer at the bottom of each page in the report.

Adding Headers and Footers

The first step to working with headers and footers is to open Header and Footer view. You can do that in three ways: (1) insert a page number using the Page Number button in the Header & Footer group on the Insert tab; (2) double-click in the header area (in a page's top margin) or in the footer area (in a page's bottom margin); or (3) click the Header button or the Footer button on the Insert tab.

By default, Word assumes that when you add something to the header or footer on any page of a document, you want the same text to appear on every page of the document. To create a different header or footer for the first page, you select the Different First Page check box in the Options group on the Header & Footer Tools Design tab. When a document is divided into sections, like the New Classes Report document, you can create a different header or footer for each section.

For a simple header or footer, double-click the header or footer area, and then type the text you want directly in the header or footer area, formatting the text as you would any other text in a document. To choose from a selection of predesigned header or footer styles, use the Header and Footer buttons on the Header & Footer Tools Design tab (or on the Insert tab). These buttons open galleries that you can use to select from a number of header and footer styles, some of which include page numbers and graphic elements such as horizontal lines or shaded boxes.

Some styles also include document controls that are similar to the kinds of controls that you might encounter in a dialog box. Any information that you enter in a document control is displayed in the header or footer as ordinary text, but it is also stored in the Word file so that Word can easily reuse it in other parts of the document. For example, later in this module you will create a cover page for the report. Word's predefined cover pages include document controls similar to those found in headers and footers. So if you use a document control to enter the document title in the header, the same document title will show up on the cover page; there's no need to retype it.

In the following steps, you'll create a footer for the whole document (sections 1 and 2) that includes the page number and your name. As shown in Hillary's plan in Figure 3-33, you'll also create a header for section 1 only (pages 1 through 3) that includes the document title and the date. You'll leave the header area for section 2 blank.

| Figure 3-33 | Plan for headers and footers in Hillary's report |

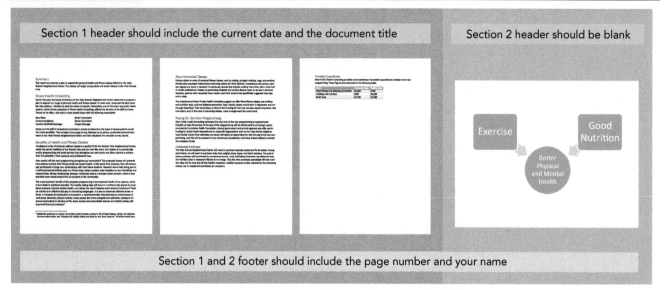

First you will create the footer on page 1, so you can see how the footer fits below the footnotes at the bottom of the page.

To create a footer for the entire document:

1. Change the Zoom level to **120%**, and then scroll up until you can see the bottom of page 1 and the top of page 2.

2. Double-click in the white space at the bottom of page 1. The document switches to Header and Footer view. The Header & Footer Tools Design tab is displayed on the ribbon. The insertion point is positioned on the left side of the footer area, ready for you to begin typing. The label "Footer -Section 1-" tells you that the insertion point is located in the footer for section 1. The document text is gray, indicating that you cannot edit it in Header and Footer view. The header area for section 1 is also visible on top of page 2. The default footer tab stops (which are different from the default tab stops in the main document) are visible on the ruler. See Figure 3-34.

Figure 3-34   **Creating a footer**

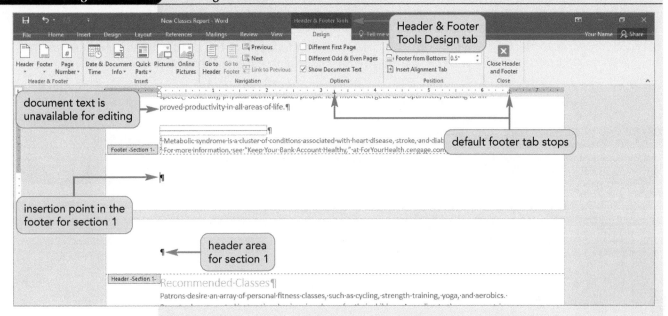

3. Type your first and last names, and then press the **Enter** key. The insertion point moves to the second line in the footer, aligned along the left margin. This is where you will insert the page number.

4. In the Header & Footer group, click the **Page Number** button. The Page Number menu opens. Because the insertion point is already located where you want to insert the page number, you'll use the Current Position option.

5. Point to **Current Position**. A gallery of page number styles opens. Hillary wants to use the Accent Bar 2 style.

6. Click the **Accent Bar 2** style (the third style from the top). The word "Page," a vertical bar, and the page number are inserted in the footer.

   Next, you'll check to make sure that the footer you just created for section 1 also appears in section 2. To move between headers or footers in separate sections, you can use the buttons in the Navigation group on the Header & Footer Tools Design tab.

7. In the Navigation group, click the **Next** button. Word displays the footer for the next section in the document—that is, the footer for section 2, which appears at the bottom of page 4. The label at the top of the footer area reads "Footer -Section 2-" and it contains the same text (your name and the page number) as in the section 1 footer. Word assumes, by default, that when you type text in one footer, you want it to appear in all the footers in the document.

TIP

To change the numbering style or to specify a number to use as the first page number, click the Page Number button in the Header & Footer group, and then click Format Page Numbers.

Now you need to create a header for section 1. Hillary does not want to include a header in section 2 because it would distract attention from the SmartArt graphic. So you will first separate the header for section 1 from the header for section 2.

To separate the headers for section 1 and section 2:

▶ **1.** Verify that the insertion point is located in the section 2 footer area at the bottom of page 4 and that the Header & Footer Tools Design tab is selected on the ribbon. To switch from the footer to the header in the current section, you can use the Go to Header button in the Navigation group.

▶ **2.** In the Navigation group, click the **Go to Header** button. The insertion point moves to the section 2 header at the top of page 4. See Figure 3-35.

Figure 3-35	Section 2 header is currently the same as the previous header, in section 1

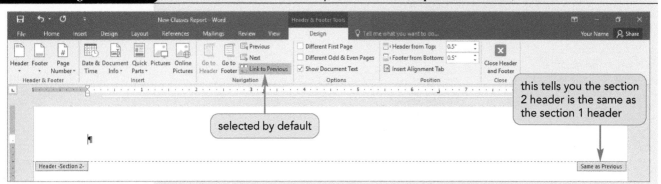

Notice that in the Navigation group, the Link to Previous button is selected. In the header area in the document window, the gray tab on the right side of the header border contains the message "Same as Previous," indicating that the section 2 header is set up to display the same text as the header in the previous section, which is section 1. To make the section 2 header a separate entity, you need to break the link between the section 1 and section 2 headers.

TIP

When you create a header for a section, it doesn't matter what page you're working on as long as the insertion point is located in a header in that section.

▶ **3.** In the Navigation group, click the **Link to Previous** button to deselect it. The Same as Previous tab is removed from the right side of the section 2 header border.

▶ **4.** In the Navigation group, click the **Previous** button. The insertion point moves up to the nearest header in the previous section, which is the section 1 header at the top of page 3. The label "Header -Section 1-" identifies this as a section 1 header.

▶ **5.** In the Header & Footer group, click the **Header** button. A gallery of header styles opens.

▶ **6.** Scroll down and review the various header styles, and then click the **Grid** style (eighth style from the top). The placeholder text "[Document title]" is aligned at the left margin. The placeholder text "[Date]" is aligned at the right margin.

▶ **7.** Click the **[Document title]** placeholder text. The placeholder text is now selected within a document control. See Figure 3-36.

Figure 3-36   **Adding a header to section 1**

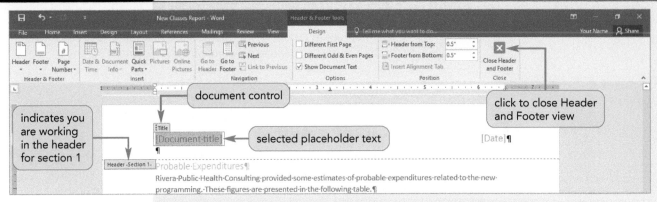

8. Type **Recommendation for Classes at Vista Grande Neighborhood Center**. The text you just typed is displayed in the document control instead of the placeholder text. Next, you need to add the date. The header style you selected includes a date picker document control, which allows you to select the date from a calendar.

9. Click the **[Date]** placeholder text to display an arrow in the document control, and then click the arrow. A calendar for the current month appears, as shown in Figure 3-37. In the calendar, the current date is outlined in dark blue.

Figure 3-37   **Adding a date to the section 1 header**

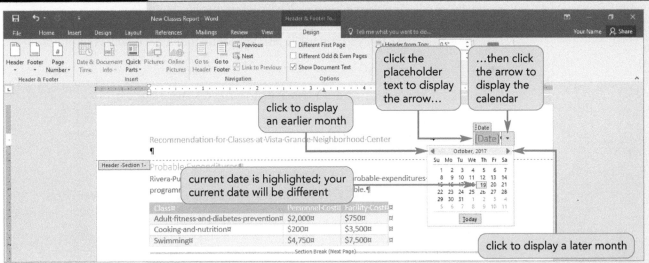

10. Click the current date. The current date, including the year, is inserted in the document control.

11. Scroll up slightly and click anywhere in the Section 1 footer (on the preceding page) to deselect the date document control. You are finished creating the header and footer for Hillary's report, so you can close Header and Footer view and return to Print Layout view.

12. In the Close group, click the **Close Header and Footer** button, or double-click anywhere in the main document, and then save your work.

13. On the ribbon, click the **View** tab.

> **14.** In the Zoom group, click the **Multiple Pages** button, and then change the Zoom level to **30%** so you can see all four pages of the document, including the header at the top of pages 1 through 3 and the footer at the bottom of pages 1 through 4. Take a moment to compare your completed headers and footers with Hillary's plan for the headers and footers shown earlier in Figure 3-33.

Finally, you need to insert a cover page for the report.

Inserting a Cover Page

A document's cover page typically includes the title and the name of the author. Some people also include a summary of the report on the cover page, which is commonly referred to as an abstract. In addition, you might include the date, the name and possibly the logo of your company or organization, and a subtitle. A cover page should not include the document header or footer.

To insert a preformatted cover page at the beginning of the document, you use the Cover Page button on the Insert tab. You can choose from a variety of cover page styles, all of which include document controls in which you can enter the document title, the document's author, the date, and so on. These document controls are linked to any other document controls in the document. For example, you already entered "Recommendation for Classes at Vista Grande Neighborhood Center" into a document control in the header of Hillary's report. So if you use a cover page that contains a similar document control, "Recommendation for Classes at Vista Grande Neighborhood Center" will be displayed on the cover page automatically. Note that document controls sometimes display information entered when either Word or Windows was originally installed on your computer. If your computer has multiple user accounts, the information displayed in some document controls might reflect the information for the current user. In any case, you can easily edit the contents of a document control.

To insert a cover page at the beginning of the report:

> **1.** Verify that the document is still zoomed so that you can see all four pages, and then press the **Ctrl+Home** keys. The insertion point moves to the beginning of the document.

> **2.** On the ribbon, click the **Insert** tab.

> **3.** In the Pages group, click the **Cover Page** button. A gallery of cover page styles opens.
>
> Notice that the names of the cover page styles match the names of the preformatted header styles you saw earlier. For example, the list includes a Grid cover page, which is designed to match the Grid header used in this document. To give a document a uniform look, it's helpful to use elements with the same style throughout.

> **4.** Scroll down the gallery to see the cover page styles, and then locate the Grid cover page style.

> **5.** Click the **Grid** cover page style. The new cover page is inserted at the beginning of the document.

> **6.** Change the Zoom level to **120%**, and then scroll down to display the report title in the middle of the cover page. The only difference between the title "Recommendation for Classes at Vista Grande Neighborhood Center" here and the title you entered in the document header is that here the title is

TIP

To delete a cover page that you inserted from the Cover Page gallery, click the Cover Page button in the Pages group, and then click Remove Current Cover Page.

displayed in all uppercase. The cover page also includes document controls for a subtitle and an abstract. See Figure 3-38.

Figure 3-38   **Newly inserted cover page**

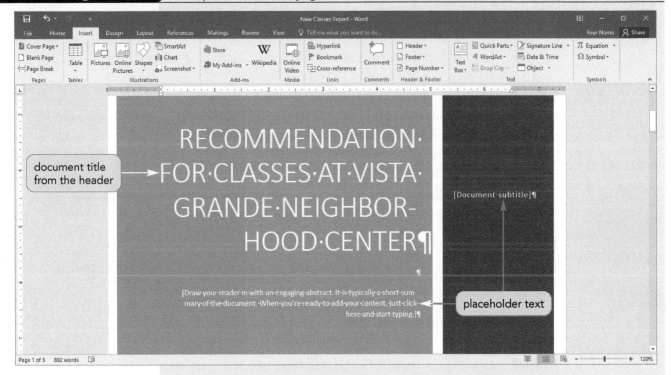

document title from the header →

RECOMMENDATION· FOR·CLASSES·AT·VISTA· GRANDE·NEIGHBOR- HOOD·CENTER¶

[Document·subtitle]¶

[Draw·your·reader·in·with·an·engaging·abstract.·It·is·typically·a·short·sum- mary·of·the·document.·When·you're·ready·to·add·your·content,·just·click· here·and·start·typing.]¶ ← placeholder text

The word "NEIGHBORHOOD" is hyphenated, which looks awkward in a title. You can fix that by changing the document's hyphenation settings.

7. On the ribbon, click the **Layout** tab.

8. In the Page Setup group, click the **Hyphenation** button, and then click **Hyphenation Options**.

9. In the Hyphenation dialog box, click the **Hyphenate words in CAPS** check box to remove the checkmark, and then click the **OK** button. The word "NEIGHBORHOOD" moves to its own line, so the hyphen is no longer necessary.

Next, you need to type a subtitle in the subtitle document control on the right side of the page.

10. Click the **[Document subtitle]** placeholder text, and then type **Rivera Public Health Consulting**. Next, you will remove the abstract document control because you do not need an abstract for this report.

11. Below the document title, right-click the placeholder text that begins **[Draw your reader in...** to display the shortcut menu, and then click **Remove Content Control**. The content control is removed from the cover page.

12. Save the document.

Changing the Theme

The report now contains several formatting elements that are controlled by the document's theme, so changing the theme will affect the document's overall appearance. Hillary suggests that you apply a different theme to the document.

To change the document's theme:

▶ **1.** Change the Zoom level to **40%** so you can see the first four pages side by side, with part of the fifth page visible on the bottom.

▶ **2.** On the ribbon, click the **Design** tab.

▶ **3.** Click the **Themes** button, select any theme you want, and then review the results in the document.

▶ **4.** Apply three or four more different themes of your choice, and review the results of each in the document.

▶ **5.** Apply the **Facet** theme, and then save the document. The cover page is now green and dark gray, the headings and the header text are green, and the table is formatted with a brown header row and brown shading.

Your work on the report is finished. You should preview the report before closing it.

To preview the report:

▶ **1.** On the ribbon, click the **File** tab.

▶ **2.** In the navigation bar, click the **Print** tab. The cover page of the report is displayed in the document preview in the right pane.

▶ **3.** Examine the document preview, using the arrow buttons at the bottom of the pane to display each page.

▶ **4.** If you need to make any changes to the report, return to Print Layout view, edit the document, preview the document again, and then save the document.

▶ **5.** Display the document in Print Layout view.

▶ **6.** Change the Zoom level back to **120%**, and then press the **Ctrl+Home** keys to make sure the insertion point is located on the first page.

Reviewing a Document in Read Mode

The members of the board of directors might choose to print the report, but some might prefer to read it on their computers instead. In that case, they can take advantage of **Read Mode**, a document view designed to make reading on a screen as easy as possible. Unlike Print Layout view, which mimics the look of the printed page with its margins and page breaks, Read Mode focuses on the document's content. Read Mode displays as much content as possible on the screen at a time, with buttons that allow you to display more. Note that you can't edit text in Read Mode. To do that, you need to switch back to Page Layout view.

To display the document in Read Mode:

1. In the status bar, click the **Read Mode** button ▦. The document switches to Read Mode, with a reduced version of the cover page on the left and the first part of the document text on the right. On the left edge of the status bar, the message "Screens 1-2 of 6" explains that you are currently viewing the first two screens out of a total of 6.

Trouble? If your status bar indicates that you have a different number of screens, change the Zoom level as needed so that the document is split into 6 screens.

The title page on the left is screen 1. The text on the right is screen 2. To display more of the document, you can click the arrow button on the right. See Figure 3-39.

Figure 3-39   Document displayed in Read Mode

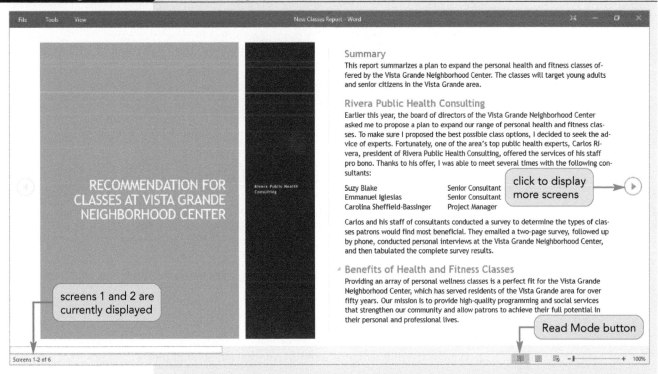

Trouble? If the pages on your screen are not laid out as shown in Figure 3-39, click View on the menu bar, point to Layout, and then click Column Layout.

2. Click the **right arrow** button ⊙ on the right to display screens 3 and 4. A left arrow button is now displayed on the left side of the screen. You could click it to move back to the previous screens.

3. Click the **right arrow** button ⊙ to display screens 5 and 6.

4. Click the **left arrow** button ⊙ on the left as necessary to return to screens 1 and 2, and then click the **Print Layout** button ▤ in the status bar to return to Page Layout view.

5. Close the document.

TIP

To zoom in on a SmartArt graphic, you can double-click it. Click anywhere outside the object zoom window to return to the Read Mode screens.

You now have a draft of the New Classes Report document, including a cover page, the report text, a nicely formatted table, and the SmartArt graphic (in landscape orientation).

PROSKILLS

Written Communication: Taking Notes

The process of writing a report or other long document usually involves taking notes. It's essential to organize your notes in a way that allows you to write about your topic logically and coherently. It's also important to retain your notes after you finish a first draft, so that you can incorporate additional material from your notes in subsequent drafts.

Clicking the Linked Notes button on the Review tab opens Microsoft OneNote in a window on the right side of the screen. (If you don't see the Linked Notes button, click the File tab to display Backstage view. Click Options in the navigation bar, and then click Add-ins. Click the arrow button in the Manage box, select Com Add-ins, if necessary, and then click the Go button. In the Com Add-ins dialog box, select OneNote Linked Notes Add-In, and then click the OK button.) In the Microsoft OneNote window, you can take notes that are linked to your Microsoft Word account. Every time you start Word and click the Linked Notes button, your notes are displayed in the OneNote window. You can copy material from a Word document and paste it in OneNote, and vice versa.

To get started, open a Word document, save it, make sure you are logged into your Microsoft account, click the Review tab, and then, in the OneNote group, click the Linked Notes button. This opens the Select Location in OneNote dialog box, where you can select a notebook. OneNote works best if you use a notebook stored on OneDrive, so unless you have a compelling reason to do otherwise, select a notebook stored on OneDrive. Now you're ready to take notes. Start by typing a title for your notebook page at the insertion point, then click in the blank space below the title, and start taking notes. To display the OneNote ribbon, with a selection of tools for working with notes, click the ellipses at the top of the OneNote window. Click the Close button in the upper-right corner of the OneNote window pane when you are finished.

REVIEW

Session 3.2 Quick Check

1. What is the default tab stop style?

2. What is the difference between a footnote and an endnote?

3. Explain how to configure Word to hyphenate a document automatically.

4. What is the first thing you need to do if you want to format part of a document in an orientation different from the rest of the document?

5. Explain how to create separate headers for a document with two sections.

6. Explain how to insert a preformatted cover page.

Review Assignments

Data File needed for the Review Assignments: Computer.docx

The new exercise and nutrition classes at the Vista Grande Neighborhood Center were a success. Now, Hillary Sanchez is organizing a series of computer literacy classes for the neighborhood center staff. She has begun working on a report for the board that outlines basic information about the classes. You need to format the report, add a table containing a preliminary schedule, and create a sample graphic that Hillary could use in a handout announcing the classes. Complete the following steps:

1. Open the document **Computer** located in the Word3 > Review folder included with your Data Files, and then save it as **Computer Classes Report** in the location specified by your instructor.

2. Promote the "Schedule" and "Facility Requirements" headings from Heading 2 text to Heading 1 text, and then move the "Facility Requirements" heading and its body text up above the "Schedule" heading.

3. Insert a page break before the "Schedule" heading. Insert a blank paragraph at the end of the new page 2, and then insert a table using the information shown in Figure 3-40. Format the header row in bold.

Figure 3-40   **Information for training schedule table**

Date	Topic
April 21	Spreadsheets
January 16	The Internet
April 28	Database concepts
April 6	Social media
March 3	Computer maintenance

4. Sort the table by the contents of the "Date" column in ascending order.

5. In the appropriate location in the table, insert a new row for a **Word processing** class on **February 23**.

6. Delete the "Social media" row from the table.

7. Modify the widths of both columns to accommodate the widest entry in each.

8. Apply the Grid Table 4 - Accent 1 style to the table, and then remove the special formatting for the first column.

9. On page 1, replace the text "[instructor names]" with a tabbed list of instructors and their specialties, using the following information: **Casey Sharpless-Dunaway**, **Word processing**; **Marcolo Jimenez**, **Computer maintenance**; **Jin-Hua Lee**, **Database concepts**; **Tommy Halverson**, **Spreadsheets**; **Katrina Yackel**, **The Internet**. Insert a tab after each name, and don't include any punctuation in the list.

10. Use a left tab stop to align the instructors' specialties 2.5 inches from the left margin, and then adjust the list's paragraph spacing so it appears to be a single paragraph.

11. Locate the first sentence below the "Facility Requirements" heading. At the end of that sentence, insert a footnote that reads **Some board members mentioned the possibility of holding classes in the gym, but the instructors prefer the multipurpose room, where microphones are unnecessary.**

12. Turn on automatic hyphenation.

13. After the schedule table on page 2, insert a section break that starts a new, third page, and then format the new page in landscape orientation.

14. Insert a SmartArt graphic that illustrates the requirements of computer literacy. Use the Circle Process graphic from the Process category, and, from left to right, include the following text in the SmartArt diagram: **Hardware Knowledge**, **Software Knowledge**, and **Computer Literacy**. Do not include any punctuation in the SmartArt. Size the SmartArt graphic to fill the page.

15. Create a footer for sections 1 and 2 that aligns your first and last names at the left margin. Insert the page number, without any design elements and without the word "Page," below your name.

16. Separate the section 1 header from the section 2 header, and then create a header for section 1 using the Retrospect header style. Enter **NEW COMPUTER LITERACY CLASSES** as the document title, and select the current date. Note that the document title will be displayed in all uppercase no matter how you type it.

17. Insert a cover page using the Retrospect style. If you typed the document title in all uppercase in the header, it will be displayed in all uppercase here. If you used a mix of uppercase and lowercase in the header, you'll see a mix here. Revise the document title as necessary to make it all uppercase, and then add the following subtitle: **A REPORT FOR THE VISTA GRANDE NEIGHBORHOOD CENTER BOARD OF DIRECTORS**. In the Author document control, replace Hillary Sanchez's name with yours, and then delete the Company Name and Company Address document controls, as well as the vertical bar character between them.

18. Change the document theme to Integral, save and preview the report, and then close it.

Case Problem 1

Data File needed for this Case Problem: Entrepreneur.docx

Boise Entrepreneurs Consortium   You are the assistant business manager of the Boise Entrepreneurs Consortium, a professional organization for technology entrepreneurs and investors in Boise, Idaho. You have been asked to help prepare an annual report for the board of directors. The current draft is not complete, but it contains enough for you to get started. Complete the following steps:

1. Open the document **Entrepreneur** located in the Word3 > Case1 folder included with your Data Files, and then save it as **Entrepreneur Report** in the location specified by your instructor.

2. Adjust the heading levels so that the "Investment Fair" and "Tech Fest" headings are formatted with the Heading 2 style.

3. Move the "Membership Forecast" heading and its body text down to the end of the report.

4. Format the Board of Directors list using a left tab stop with a dot leader at the 2.2-inch mark. (*Hint:* Use the Dialog Box Launcher in the Paragraph group on the Layout tab to open the Paragraph dialog box, and then click the Tabs button at the bottom of the Indents and Spacing tab to open the Tabs dialog box.)

5. At the end of the first paragraph below the "Monthly Technology Lunches" heading, insert the following footnote: **The monthly technology lunches are open to the public.**

6. Locate the "Purpose" heading on page 1. At the end of the body text below that heading, insert the following footnote: **We recently signed a five-year contract renewal with our website host, Boise Web and Media.**

7. Insert a page break that moves the "Membership Forecast" heading to the top of a new page, and then, below the body text on the new page, insert a table consisting of three columns and four rows.

8. In the table, enter the information shown in Figure 3-41. Format the column headings in bold.

Figure 3-41   **Information for membership forecast table**

Membership Type	2017	Projected 2018
Vendor	340	400
Entrepreneur	205	255
Investor	175	200

9. Sort the table in ascending order by membership type.

10. In the appropriate location in the table, insert a row for a **Student** membership type, with **150** members in 2017, and **170** projected members in 2018.

11. Adjust the column widths so each column accommodates the widest entry.

12. Format the table using the Grid Table 4 - Accent 6 table style without banded rows or bold formatting in the first column.

13. Turn on automatic hyphenation.

14. Insert a Blank footer, and then type your name to replace the selected placeholder text in the footer's left margin. In the right margin, insert a page number using the Large Color style. (*Hint*: Press the Tab key twice to move the insertion point to the right margin before inserting the page number, and then insert the page number at the current location.)

15. Insert a cover page using the Sideline style. Enter the company name, **Boise Entrepreneurs Consortium**, and the title, **Annual Report**, in the appropriate document controls. In the subtitle document control, enter **Prepared by [Your Name]** (but replace "[Your Name]" with your first and last names). Delete the Author document control, which might contain a default name inserted by Word, and then insert the current date in the Date document control.

16. Change the document theme to Facet.

17. Save, preview, and then close the document.

Case Problem 2

Data File needed for this Case Problem: Remodeling.docx

Customer Evaluation Report   Kitchen Design Magic is a construction and design firm that specializes in high-end, energy-efficient kitchens. Hope Richardson has begun writing a report summarizing the most recent crop of customer evaluation forms. She asks you to review her incomplete draft and fix some problems. Complete the following steps:

1. Open the document **Remodeling** located in the Word3 > Case2 folder included with your Data Files, and then save it as **Remodeling Evaluation Report** in the location specified by your instructor.

⚙ **Troubleshoot** 2. Adjust the document so that the following are true:
- The "Problems Acquiring Building Permits" heading, its body text, and the SmartArt graphic appear on the last page in landscape orientation, with the rest of the report in portrait orientation.
- In section 1, the "Summary" heading is displayed at the top of page 2.
- The document header contains your first and last names but not a content control for the document title.
- Neither the header nor the footer is displayed on page 1.
- The footer is not displayed on the last page of the document. (*Hint*: After you break the link between sections, you'll need to delete the contents of the footer in one section.)

⚙ **Troubleshoot** 3. On pages 2 and 3, promote headings as necessary so all the headings are on the same level.

4. Increase the paragraph spacing before the first paragraph, "Kitchen Design Magic," on page 1 as much as necessary so that the paragraph is located at about the 3-inch mark on the vertical ruler. When you're finished, the text should be centered vertically on the page, so it looks like a cover page.

⚙ **Troubleshoot** 5. On page 2, remove any extra rows and columns in the table, and sort the information in a logical way. When you are finished, format it with a style that applies blue (Accent 5) shading to the header row, with banded rows below, and remove any unnecessary bold formatting.

6. Add a fourth shape to the SmartArt Graphic with the text **Submit completed forms, designs, and fee to permit office.** Resize the graphic to fill the white space below the document text.

7. Save the document, review it in Read Mode, preview it, and then close it.

Case Problem 3

CREATE

There are no Data Files needed for this Case Problem.

Tim's Total T's Online Retailer Tim Washburn recently started a new business, Tim's Total T's, which sells athletic team t-shirts online. A friend has just emailed him a list of potential customers. Tim asks you to create and format a table containing the list of customers. When you're finished with that project, you'll create a table detailing some of his recent repair expenses in his new production facility. Complete the following steps:

1. Open a new, blank document, and then save it as **Customer Table** in the location specified by your instructor.

2. Create the table shown in Figure 3-42.

Figure 3-42   **Advertiser table**

Organization	Contact	Phone
Franklin Metropolitan School District	Sasha Malee	555-555-5555
Haverford Swim Club	Crystal Grenier	555-555-5555
Kingford Bowling	Joyce Garcia	555-555-5555
Tri County Rec League	Terrence O'Hern	555-555-5555

For the table style, start with the Grid Table 4 - Accent 6 table style, and then make any necessary changes. Use the Green, Accent 6, Darker 50% pen color to create a darker border around the outside of the table. The final table should be about 6.5 inches wide and 2 inches tall, as measured on the horizontal and vertical rulers. (*Hint*: Remember that you can drag the Table Resize handle to increase the table's overall size.)

3. Replace "Sasha Malee" with your first and last names.

4. Save, preview, and then close the Customer Table document.

5. Open a new, blank document, and then save it as **Repair Table** in the location specified by your instructor.

6. Create the table shown in Figure 3-43.

Figure 3-43   **Expense table**

Repair	Completion Date	Expense
Replace bathroom fan	3/5/17	$350.00
Install deadbolt lock	3/16/17	$85.00
Replace broken window pane	3/26/17	$25.50
	Total	$460.50

For the table style, start with the Grid Table 4 - Accent 6 table style, and then make any necessary changes. Use the Green, Accent 6, Darker 50% pen color to create a darker border around the outside of the table. Note that in the bottom row, you'll need to merge two cells and right-align text within the new, merged cell.

7. For the total, use a formula instead of simply typing the amount. (*Hint*: Click in the cell where you want to insert a formula to sum the values, go to the Table Tools Layout tab, click the Formula button in the Data group to open the Formula dialog box, and then click the OK button.)

8. Save, preview, and then close the Repair Table document.

Case Problem 4

There are no Data Files needed for this Case Problem.

Sun Star Fund-Raisers   Janita Roush coordinates fund-raising events for the Sun Star Bike and Pedestrian Path in Bloomington, Illinois. She needs a flyer to hand out at an upcoming neighborhood festival, where she hopes to recruit more volunteers. You can use Word's table features to lay out the flyer as shown in Janita's sketch in Figure 3-44. At the very end, you'll remove the table borders.

CHALLENGE

Figure 3-44   **Sketch for Sun Star flyer**

Sun Star Fund-Raisers

Bike for Fun!

Sun Star Path Ride
- First Saturday in May
- 50-mile ride
- $20 entrance fee
- Free t-shirt

Sun Star Bike Swap
- First Saturday in April
- $15 swap fee
- Midwest's largest event
- All types of bike gear

Mission
Friends of the Sun Star Path is a nonprofit volunteer organization devoted to supporting the Sun Star Bike and Pedestrian Path through fund-raising and volunteer efforts.

Contact
Janita Roush, **janita@sunstar.cengage.com**, 555-555-5555.

Complete the following steps:

1. Open a new, blank document, and then save it as **Sun Star Flyer** in the location specified by your instructor.

2. Change the document's orientation to landscape.

⊕ **Explore** 3. Use the Table button on the Insert tab to access the Insert Table menu, and then click Draw Table at the bottom of the menu to activate the Draw Table pointer (which looks like a pencil). Click in the upper-left corner of the document (near the paragraph mark), and, using the rulers as guides, drag down and to the right to draw a rectangle that is 9 inches wide and 6 inches high. After you draw the rectangle, you can adjust its height and width using the Height and Width boxes in the Cell Size group on the Table Tools Layout tab, if necessary. (*Hint*: If the Draw Table pointer disappears after you change the table's height and width, you can turn it back on by clicking the Draw Table button in the Draw group on the Table Tools Layout tab.)

⊕ **Explore** 4. Use the Draw Table pointer to draw the columns and rows shown in Figure 3-44. For example, to draw the column border for the "Sun Star Fund-Raisers" column, click the top of the rectangle at the point where you want the right column border to be located, and then drag down to the bottom of the rectangle. Use the same technique to draw rows. (*Hint*: To delete a border, click the Eraser button in the Draw group on the Table Tools Layout tab, click anywhere on the border you want to erase, and then click the Eraser button again to turn it off.)

5. When you are finished drawing the table, turn off the Draw Table pointer by pressing the Esc key.

⊕ **Explore** 6. In the left column, type the text **Sun Star Fund-Raisers**. With the pointer still in that cell, click the Table Tools Layout tab, and then in the Alignment group, click the Text Direction button twice to position the text vertically so that it reads from bottom to top. Using the formatting options on the Home tab, format the text in 36-point font. Use the Align Center button in the Alignment group on the Table Tools Layout tab to center the text in the cell. (*Hint*: You will probably have to adjust and readjust the row and column borders throughout these steps until all the elements of the table are positioned properly.)

7. Type the remaining text as shown in Figure 3-44. To prevent problems with formatting the bulleted lists, press Enter after the text "Free-t-shirt" and after "All types of bike gear," and then remove the bulleted list formatting from the new paragraph, so that an end-of-cell mark appears on a separate line below each bulleted list. Replace "Janita Roush" with your own name, remove the hyperlink formatting from the email address, and format it in bold. Change the font size for "Bike for Fun!" to 36 points, and center-align the text in that cell. Use the Heading 1 style for the following text—"Sun Star Path Ride," "Sun Star Bike Swap," "Mission," and "Contact." Change the font size for this text to 20 points. Center-align the "Sun Star Path Ride" and "Sun Star Bike Swap" headings in their cells. Change the font size for the bulleted lists and the paragraphs below the "Mission" and "Contact" headings to 16 points. If the table expands to two pages, drag a row border up slightly to reduce the row's height. Repeat as necessary until the table fits on one page.

⊕ **Explore** 8. On the Insert tab, use the Shapes button in the Illustrations group to draw the Sun shape (from the Basic Shapes section of the Shapes gallery), similar to the way you drew the table rectangle, by dragging the pointer. Draw the sun in the blank cell in the top row. If the sun isn't centered neatly in the cell, click the Undo button, and try again until you draw a sun that has the same proportions as the one in Figure 3-44. Until you change the theme in the next step, the sun will be blue.

9. Change the document theme to Retrospect.

10. Remove the table borders. When you are finished, your flyer should match the table shown in Figure 3-44, but without the table borders.

11. Save your work, preview the document, and then close it.

MODULE 4

Enhancing Page Layout and Design

Creating a Newsletter

Case | *Aria Occupational Therapy*

Avanti Saro is a public relations consultant who has been hired to create a newsletter for Aria Occupational Therapy, a clinic that provides rehabilitation services in Portland, Oregon. He has written the text of a newsletter describing the services provided by the clinic's therapists. Now he needs you to transform the text into an eye-catching publication with a headline, photos, drop caps, and other desktop-publishing elements. Avanti's budget doesn't allow him to hire a professional graphic designer to create the document using desktop-publishing software. But there's no need for that because you can do the work for him using Word's formatting, graphics, and page layout tools. After you finish the newsletter, Avanti wants you to save the newsletter as a PDF so he can email it to the printing company. You also need to make some edits to a document that is currently available only as a PDF.

OBJECTIVES

Session 4.1
- Use continuous section breaks for page layout
- Format text in columns
- Insert symbols and special characters
- Distinguish between inline and floating objects
- Wrap text around an object
- Insert and format text boxes
- Insert drop caps

Session 4.2
- Create and modify WordArt
- Insert and crop a picture
- Search for Online Pictures
- Rotate and adjust a picture
- Remove a photo's background
- Balance columns
- Add a page border
- Save a document as a PDF
- Open a PDF in Word

STARTING DATA FILES

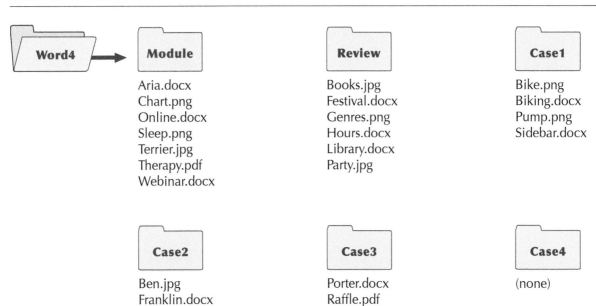

Word4 → Module

Aria.docx
Chart.png
Online.docx
Sleep.png
Terrier.jpg
Therapy.pdf
Webinar.docx

Review

Books.jpg
Festival.docx
Genres.png
Hours.docx
Library.docx
Party.jpg

Case1

Bike.png
Biking.docx
Pump.png
Sidebar.docx

Case2

Ben.jpg
Franklin.docx
Treaty.docx

Case3

Porter.docx
Raffle.pdf

Case4

(none)

Session 4.1 Visual Overview:

Desktop publishing is the process of preparing commercial-quality printed material, such as the newsletter shown here, using a desktop or laptop computer. Using Word, you can create documents that have elements of desktop publishing, such as special font treatments, graphics, and page layout options, as well as design elements such as page borders.

This specially formatted text is an example of WordArt, which is created using the WordArt button in the Text group on the Insert tab.

These are examples of text boxes, which are like mini documents within a document.

This photo and the drawing of the person in bed were inserted from files, but you can also use the Online Pictures button in the Illustrations group on the Insert tab to search for photos and drawings on the web.

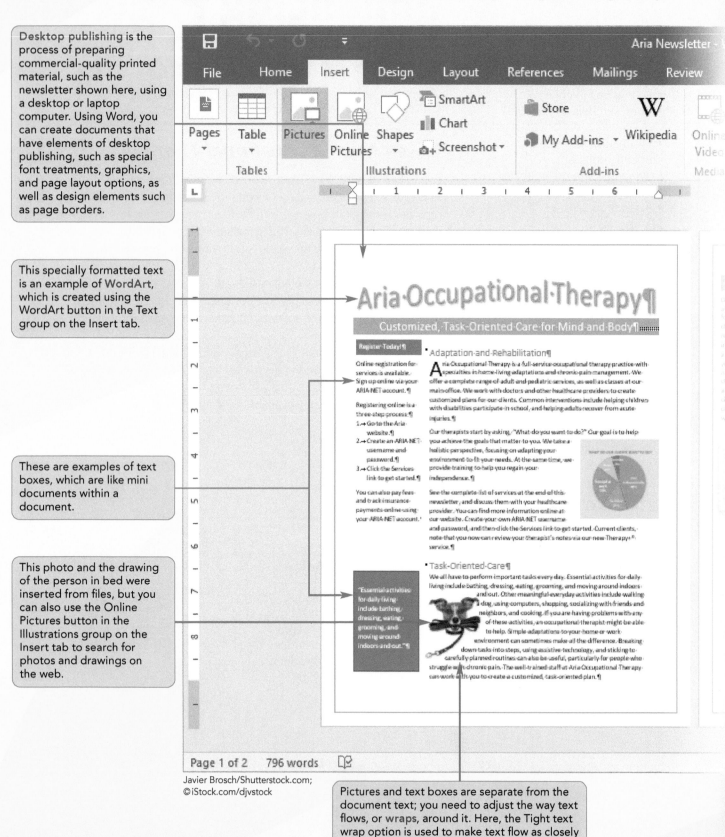

Javier Brosch/Shutterstock.com;
©iStock.com/djvstock

Pictures and text boxes are separate from the document text; you need to adjust the way text flows, or wraps, around it. Here, the Tight text wrap option is used to make text flow as closely as possible around the shape of the dog.

Elements of Desktop Publishing

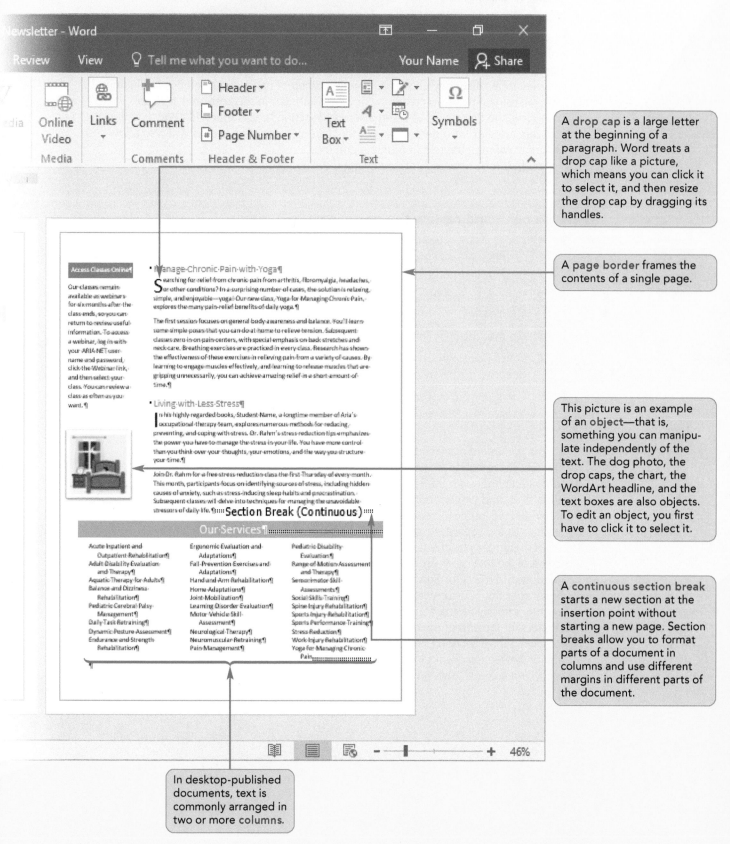

A drop cap is a large letter at the beginning of a paragraph. Word treats a drop cap like a picture, which means you can click it to select it, and then resize the drop cap by dragging its handles.

A page border frames the contents of a single page.

This picture is an example of an object—that is, something you can manipulate independently of the text. The dog photo, the drop caps, the chart, the WordArt headline, and the text boxes are also objects. To edit an object, you first have to click it to select it.

A continuous section break starts a new section at the insertion point without starting a new page. Section breaks allow you to format parts of a document in columns and use different margins in different parts of the document.

In desktop-published documents, text is commonly arranged in two or more columns.

Using Continuous Section Breaks to Enhance Page Layout

Newsletters and other desktop-published documents often incorporate multiple section breaks, with the various sections formatted with different margins, page orientations, column settings, and other page layout options. Continuous section breaks, which start a new section without starting a new page, are especially useful when creating a newsletter because they allow you to apply different page layout settings to different parts of a single page. To create the newsletter shown in the Session 4.1 Visual Overview, the first step is to insert a series of section breaks that will allow you to use different margins for different parts of the document. Section breaks will also allow you to format some of the text in multiple columns.

You'll start by opening and reviewing the document.

To open and review the document:

▶ **1.** Open the document **Aria** from the Word4 > Module folder included with your Data Files, and then save it as **Aria Newsletter** in the location specified by your instructor.

▶ **2.** Display nonprinting characters and the rulers, and switch to Print Layout view, if necessary.

▶ **3.** On the ribbon, click the **View** tab.

▶ **4.** In the Zoom group, click **Multiple Pages** so you can see both pages of the document side by side.

▶ **5.** Compare the document to the completed newsletter shown in the Session 4.1 Visual Overview.

The document is formatted with the Office theme, using the default margins. The first paragraph is formatted with the Title style, and the remaining headings are formatted either with the Heading 1 style or with orange paragraph shading, center alignment, and white font color. The document doesn't yet contain any text boxes or other desktop-publishing elements. The list of services at the end of the document appears as a standard, single column of text.

To make room for the text boxes, you need to change the left margin to 2.5 inches for all of the text between the "Customized, Task-Oriented Care for Mind and Body" heading and the "Our Services" heading. To accomplish this, you'll insert a section break after the "Customized, Task-Oriented Care for Mind and Body" heading and another one before the "Our Services" heading. You'll eventually format the list of services, at the end of the document, in three columns. To accomplish that, you need to insert a third section break after the "Our Services" heading. Because you don't want any of the section breaks to start new pages, you will use continuous sections breaks for all three. See Figure 4-1.

Figure 4-1   Aria Newsletter document before adding section breaks

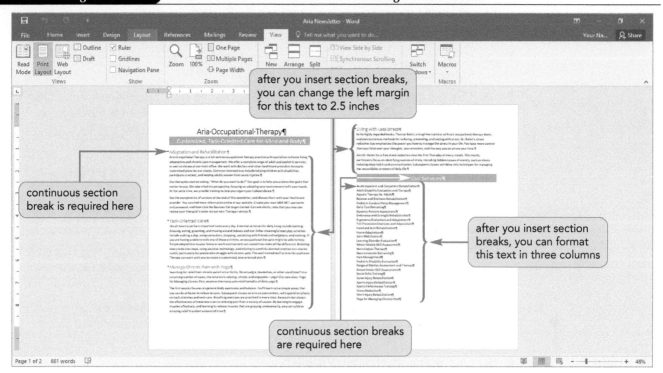

To insert continuous section breaks in the document:

▶ 1. Change the Zoom level to **120%**.

▶ 2. In the document, click at the beginning of the third paragraph, which contains the heading "Adaptation and Rehabilitation."

▶ 3. On the ribbon, click the **Layout** tab.

▶ 4. In the Page Setup group, click the **Breaks** button, and then click **Continuous**. A short dotted line, indicating a continuous section break, appears in the orange shading at the end of the preceding paragraph. If the paragraph text were shorter, you would see a longer line with the words "Section Break (Continuous)." You'll be able to see the section break text more clearly when you insert the next one.

▶ 5. Scroll down to page 2, click at the beginning of the shaded paragraph "Our Services," and then insert a continuous section break. A dotted line with the words "Section Break (Continuous)" appears at the end of the preceding paragraph.

▶ 6. Click at the beginning of the next paragraph, which contains the text "Acute Inpatient and Outpatient Rehabilitation," and then insert a continuous section break. A dotted line with the words "Section Break (Continuous)" appears in the orange shading at the end of the preceding paragraph.

Now that you have created sections within the Aria Newsletter document, you can format the individual sections as if they were separate documents. In the following steps, you'll format the first and third sections by changing their left and right margins to .75 inch. Then, you'll format the second section by changing its left margin to 2.5 inches.

To set custom margins for sections 1, 2, and 3:

▶ **1.** Press the **Ctrl+Home** keys to position the insertion point in section 1.

▶ **2.** In the Page Setup group, click the **Margins** button, and then click **Custom Margins** to open the Page Setup dialog box.

▶ **3.** Change the Left and Right margin settings to **.75** inch, and then click the **OK** button. The orange shading expands slightly on both sides of the paragraph.

▶ **4.** On page 1, click anywhere in the heading "Adaptation and Rehabilitation" to position the insertion point in section 2.

▶ **5.** In the Page Setup group, click the **Margins** button, and then click **Custom Margins** to open the Page Setup dialog box.

▶ **6.** Change the Left margin setting to **2.5** inches, and then click the **OK** button. The text in section 2 shifts to the right, and the document text flows to a third page.

   Throughout this module, as you add and resize various elements, the text will occasionally expand from two pages to three or four. But by the time you are finished, the newsletter will consist of only two pages.

▶ **7.** Scroll down to page 2, click in the shaded heading "**Our Services**" to position the insertion point in section 3, and then change the Left and Right margin settings to **.75** inch.

▶ **8.** On the ribbon, click the **View** tab.

▶ **9.** In the Zoom group, click **Multiple Pages** so you can see all three pages of the document side by side. See Figure 4-2.

Figure 4-2   **Sections 1, 2, and 3 with new margins**

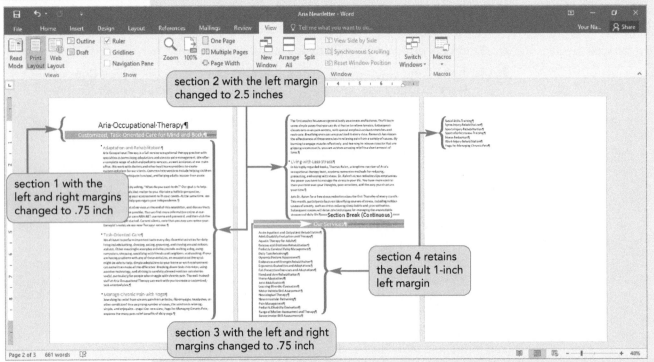

▶ **10.** Save the document.

In addition to allowing you to format parts of a document with different margins, section breaks allow you to format part of a document in columns. You'll add some columns to section 4 next.

Formatting Text in Columns

Text meant for quick reading is often laid out in columns, with text flowing down one column, continuing at the top of the next column, flowing down that column, and so forth. To get started, click the Columns button in the Page Setup group on the Layout tab, and then click the number of columns you want in the Columns gallery. For more advanced column options, you can use the More Columns command to open the Columns dialog box. In this dialog box, you can adjust the column widths and the space between columns and choose to format either the entire document in columns or just the section that contains the insertion point.

As shown in the Session 4.1 Visual Overview, Avanti wants section 4 of the newsletter document, which consists of the services list, to be formatted in three columns.

To format section 4 in three columns:

▶ **1.** Click anywhere in the list of services at the end of the document to position the insertion point in section 4.

▶ **2.** On the ribbon, click the **Layout** tab.

▶ **3.** In the Page Setup group, click the **Columns** button to display the Columns gallery. At this point, you could simply click Three to format section 4 in three columns of equal width. However, it's helpful to take a look at the columns dialog box so you can get familiar with some more advanced column options.

▶ **4.** Click **More Columns** to open the Columns dialog box, and then in the Presets section, click **Three**. See Figure 4-3.

Figure 4-3   **Columns dialog box**

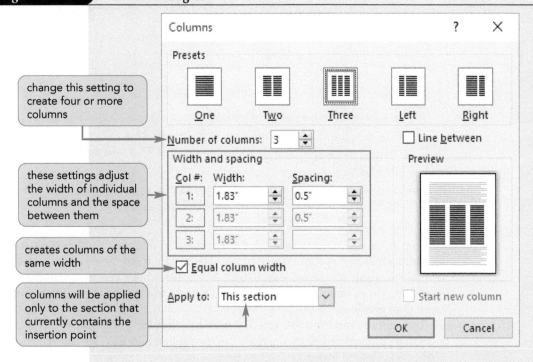

To format text in four or more columns, you can change the setting in the Number of columns box instead of selecting an option in the Presets section. By default, the Apply to box, in the lower-left corner, displays "This section," indicating that the three-column format will be applied only to the current section. To apply columns to the entire document, you could click the Apply to arrow and then click Whole document. To change the width of the individual columns or the spacing between the columns, you can use the settings in the Width and spacing section of the Columns dialog box.

5. Click the **OK** button. Section 4 is now formatted in three columns of the default width. See Figure 4-4.

Figure 4-4 | **Section 4 formatted in three columns**

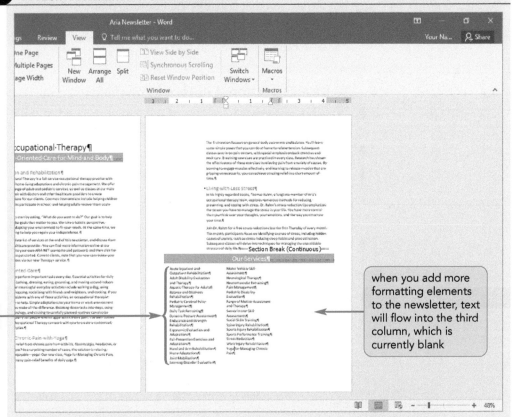

column format applied to only this section

when you add more formatting elements to the newsletter, text will flow into the third column, which is currently blank

Note that the third column is currently blank. This will change when you add more formatting elements to the newsletter. The newsletter text now fits on two pages.

6. Change the document Zoom level to **120%**, scroll down so you can see the entire list of services, and then save the document.

Keep in mind that you can restore a document or a section to its original format by formatting it as one column. You can also adjust paragraph indents within columns, just as you would in normal text. In fact, Avanti would like you to format the columns in section 4 with hanging indents so that it's easier to read the service titles that take up more than one line.

To indent the service titles, you first need to select the three columns of text. Selecting columns of text by dragging the mouse can be tricky. It's easier to use the Shift+click method instead.

To format the columns in section 4 with hanging indents:

1. Make sure the **Layout** tab is selected on the ribbon.

2. Click at the beginning of the first service title ("Acute Inpatient and Outpatient Rehabilitation"), press and hold the **Shift** key, and then click at the end of the last service title ("Yoga for Managing Chronic Pain"). The entire list of services is selected.

3. In the Paragraph group, click the **Dialog Box Launcher** to open the Paragraph dialog box with the Indents and Spacing tab displayed.

4. In the Indentation section, click the **Special** arrow, click **Hanging**, and then change the By setting to **0.2"**.

5. Click the **OK** button to close the Paragraph dialog box, and then click anywhere in the list to deselect it. The services list is now formatted with a hanging indent, so the second line of each paragraph is indented .2 inches. See Figure 4-5.

| Figure 4-5 | Text formatted in columns with hanging indent |

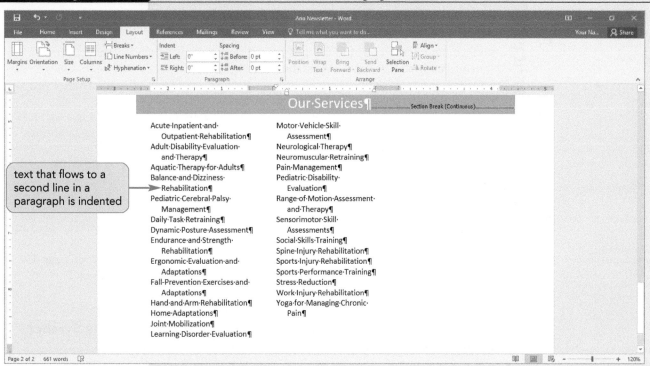

Inserting Symbols and Special Characters

When creating documents in Word, you can change some of the characters available on the standard keyboard into special characters or symbols called **typographic characters**. Word's AutoCorrect feature automatically converts some standard characters into typographic characters as you type. In some cases, you need to press the spacebar and type more characters before Word inserts the appropriate typographic character. If Word inserts a typographic character that you don't want, you can click the Undo button to revert to the characters you originally typed. See Figure 4-6.

Figure 4-6 Common typographic characters

To Insert This Symbol or Character	Type	Word Converts To
Em dash	word--word	word—word
Smiley face	:)	☺
Copyright symbol	(c)	©
Trademark symbol	(tm)	™
Registered trademark symbol	(r)	®
Fractions	1/2, 1/4	½, ¼
Arrows	<-- or -->	← or →

Most of the typographic characters in Figure 4-6 can also be inserted using the Symbol button on the Insert tab, which opens a gallery of commonly used symbols, and the More Symbols command, which opens the Symbol dialog box. The Symbol dialog box provides access to all the symbols and special characters you can insert into a Word document.

Inserting Symbols and Special Characters from the Symbol Dialog Box

- Move the insertion point to the location in the document where you want to insert a particular symbol or special character.
- On the ribbon, click the Insert tab.
- In the Symbols group, click the Symbol button.
- If you see the symbol or character you want in the Symbol gallery, click it to insert it in the document. For a more extensive set of choices, click More Symbols to open the Symbol dialog box.
- In the Symbol dialog box, locate the symbol or character you want on either the Symbols tab or the Special Characters tab.
- Click the symbol or special character you want, click the Insert button, and then click the Close button.

Avanti forgot to include a registered trademark symbol (®) after "Therapy+" on page 1. He asks you to add one now. After you do, you'll explore the Symbol dialog box.

To insert the registered trademark symbol and explore the Symbol dialog box:

1. Use the Navigation pane to find the term Therapy+ in the document, and then close the Navigation pane.

2. Click to the right of the plus sign to position the insertion point between the plus sign and the space that follows it.

3. Type **(r)**. AutoCorrect converts the "r" in parentheses into the superscript ® symbol.

   If you don't know which characters to type to insert a symbol or special character, you can review the AutoCorrect replacements in the AutoCorrect: English (United States) dialog box.

4. On the ribbon, click the **File** tab.

5. In the navigation bar, click **Options** to open the Word Options dialog box.

6. In the left pane, click **Proofing**, and then click the **AutoCorrect Options** button. The AutoCorrect: English (United States) dialog box opens, with the AutoCorrect tab displayed.

7. Review the table at the bottom of the AutoCorrect tab. The column on the left shows the characters you can type, and the column on the right shows what AutoCorrect inserts as a replacement. See Figure 4-7.

Figure 4-7	AutoCorrect: English (United States) dialog box

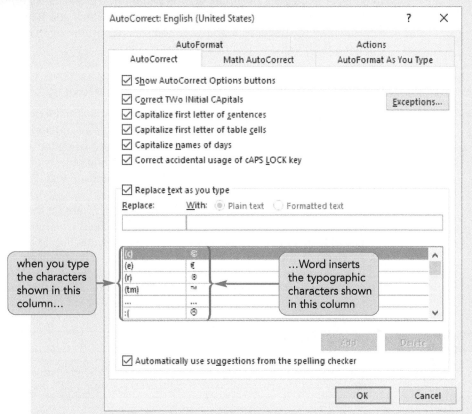

8. Scroll down to review the AutoCorrect replacements, click the **Cancel** button to close the AutoCorrect: English (United States) dialog box, and then click the **Cancel** button to close the Word Options dialog box.

Now you can explore the Symbol dialog box, which offers another way to insert symbols and special characters.

9. On the ribbon, click the **Insert** tab.

10. In the Symbols group, click the **Symbol** button, and then click **More Symbols**. The Symbol dialog box opens with the Symbols tab displayed.

11. Scroll down the gallery of symbols on the Symbols tab to review the many symbols you can insert into a document. To insert one, you would click it, and then click the Insert button.

12. Click the **Special Characters** tab. The characters available on this tab are often used in desktop publishing. Notice the shortcut keys that you can use to insert many of the special characters.

13. Click the **Cancel** button to close the Symbol dialog box.

Introduction to Working with Objects

An object is something that you can manipulate independently of the document text. In desktop publishing, you use objects to illustrate the document or to enhance the page layout. To complete the newsletter for Avanti, you'll need to add some text boxes, drop caps, and pictures. These are all examples of objects in Word.

Inserting Graphic Objects

Objects used for illustration purposes or to enhance the page layout are sometimes called **graphic objects**, or simply **graphics**. The Insert tab is the starting point for adding graphics to a document. After you insert a graphic object, you typically need to adjust its position on the page. Your ability to control the position of an object depends on whether it is an inline object or a floating object.

Distinguishing Between Inline and Floating Objects

An **inline object** behaves as if it were text. Like an individual letter, it has a specific location within a line of text, and its position changes as you add or delete text. You can align an inline object just as you would align text, using the alignment buttons in the Paragraph group on the Home tab. However, inline objects are difficult to work with because every time you add or remove paragraphs of text, the object moves to a new position.

In contrast, you can position a **floating object** anywhere on the page, with the text flowing, or wrapping, around it. Unlike an inline object, which has a specific position in a line of text, a floating object has a more fluid connection to the document text. It is attached, or **anchored**, to an entire paragraph—so if you delete that paragraph, you will also delete the object. However, you can also move the object independently of that paragraph. An anchor symbol next to an object tells you that the object is a floating object rather than an inline object, as illustrated in Figure 4-8.

Figure 4-8	**An inline object compared to a floating object**

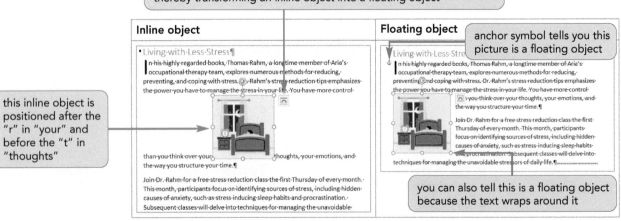

© iStock.com/djvstock

You'll typically want to transform all inline objects into floating objects because floating objects are far more flexible.

Wrapping Text Around an Object

To transform an inline object into a floating object, you apply a **text wrapping setting** to it. First, click the object to select it, click the Layout Options button next to the object, and then click an option in the Layout Options gallery. For example, you can select Square text wrapping to make the text follow a square outline as it flows around the object, or you can select Tight text wrapping to make the text follow the shape of the object more exactly. Figure 4-9 describes the different types of wrapping.

Figure 4-9   **Text wrapping options in the Layout Options gallery**

Menu Icon	Type of Wrapping	Description
	Square	Text flows in a square outline around the object, regardless of the shape of the object; by default, Square text wrapping is applied to preformatted text boxes inserted via the Text Box button on the Insert tab.
	Tight	Text follows the exact outline of the object; if you want the text to flow around an object, this is usually the best option.
	Through	Text flows through the object, filling up any open areas; this type is similar to Tight text wrapping.
	Top and Bottom	Text stops above the object and then starts again below the object.
	Behind Text	The object is layered behind the text, with the text flowing over it.
	In Front of Text	The object is layered in front of the text, with the text flowing behind it; if you want to position an object in white space next to the text, this option gives you the greatest control over its exact position. By default, In Front of Text wrapping is applied to any shapes inserted via the Shapes button in the Illustrations group on the Insert tab.

Most graphic objects, including photos and SmartArt, are inline by default. All text boxes and shapes are floating by default. Objects that are inserted as floating objects by default have a specific text wrapping setting assigned to them, but you can change the default setting to any text wrapping setting you want.

Displaying Gridlines

When formatting a complicated document like a newsletter, you'll often have to adjust the position of objects on the page until everything looks the way you want. To make it easier to see the relative position of objects, you can display the document's gridlines. These vertical and horizontal lines are not actually part of the document. They are simply guidelines you can use when positioning text and objects on the page. By default, when gridlines are displayed, objects align with, or **snap to**, the nearest intersection of a horizontal and vertical line. The figures in this module do not show gridlines because they would make the figures difficult to read. However, you will have a chance to experiment with gridlines in the Case Problems at the end of this module. To display gridlines, click the View tab on the ribbon, and then click the Gridlines check box to insert a check.

Inserting Text Boxes

You can choose to add a preformatted text box to a document, or you can create your own text box from scratch and adjust its appearance. To insert a preformatted text box, you use the Text Box button in the Text group on the Insert tab. Text boxes inserted this way include placeholder text that you can replace with your own text. Preformatted text boxes come with preset font and paragraph options that are designed to match the text box's overall look. However, you can change the appearance of the text in the text box by using the options on the Home tab, just as you would for ordinary text. The text box, as a whole, is designed to match the document's current theme. You could alter its appearance by using the Shape Styles options on the Drawing Tools Format tab, but there's typically no reason to do so.

Because the preformatted text boxes are so professional looking, they are usually a better choice than creating your own. However, if you want a very simple text box, you can use the Shapes button in the Illustrations group to draw a text box. After you draw the text box, you can adjust its appearance by using the Shape Styles options on the Drawing Tools Format tab. You can type any text you want inside the text box at the insertion point. When you are finished, you can format the text using the options on the Home tab.

REFERENCE

Inserting a Text Box

To insert a preformatted, rectangular text box, click in the document where you want to insert the text box.
- On the ribbon, click the Insert tab.
- In the Text group, click the Text Box button to open the Text Box gallery, and then click a text box style to select it.
- In the text box in the document, delete the placeholder text, type the text you want to include, and then format the text using the options on the Home tab.

or
- To insert and format your own rectangular text box, click the Insert tab on the ribbon.
- In the Illustrations group, click the Shapes button to open the Shapes gallery, and then click Text Box.
- In the document, position the pointer where you want to insert the text box, press and hold the mouse button, and then drag the pointer to draw the text box.
- In the text box, type the text you want to include, and then format the text using the options on the Home tab.
- Format the text box using the options in the Shape Styles group on the Drawing Tools Format tab.

Inserting a Preformatted Text Box

Avanti's newsletter requires three text boxes. You need to insert the first text box on page 1, to the left of the "Adaptation and Rehabilitation" heading. For this text box, you'll insert one that is preformatted to work as a sidebar. A **sidebar** is a text box designed to look good positioned to the side of the main document text. A sidebar is typically used to draw attention to important information.

To insert a preformatted text box in the document:

▶ **1.** Scroll up to the top of page 1, and then click anywhere in the "Adaptation and Rehabilitation" heading.

▶ **2.** Change the Zoom level to **Multiple Pages** so you can see both pages of the document.

▶ **3.** On the ribbon, click the **Insert** tab.

▶ **4.** In the Text group, click the **Text Box** button to display the Text Box gallery, and then use the scroll bar to scroll down the gallery to locate the Ion Sidebar 1 text box.

▶ **5.** Click **Ion Sidebar 1**. The text box is inserted in the left margin of page 1. See Figure 4-10.

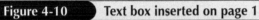

| Figure 4-10 | Text box inserted on page 1 |

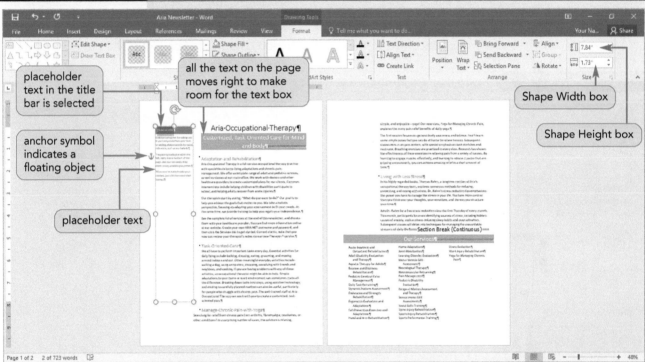

All the text on page 1 moves right to make room for the text box. Later, after you resize and move the text box, the first two paragraphs will resume their original positions, centered at the top of the page. The anchor symbol next to the text box tells you it is a floating object.

The text box consists of a blue title bar at the top that contains placeholder text, with additional placeholder text below the title bar. The dotted outline with handles indicates the borders of the text box. When you first insert a text box, the placeholder text in the title bar is selected, ready for you to type your own title. In this case, however, before you add any text, you'll resize and reposition the text box.

▶ **6.** On the ribbon, click the **Drawing Tools Format** tab, if necessary.

▶ **7.** In the Size group, click the **Shape Height** box, type **4.3**, click the **Shape Width** box, type **1.5**, and then press the **Enter** key. The text box is now shorter and narrower.

▶ **8.** Change the Zoom level to **120%**.

Next, you need to drag the text box down below the first two paragraphs. Currently, only the placeholder text in the text box title bar is selected. Before you can move it, you need to select the entire text box.

▶ **9.** Position the pointer somewhere over the text box border until the pointer changes to ⬚⬚.

▶ **10.** Click the **text box border** to select the entire text box. The text box border changes from dotted to solid, and the Layout Options button ⬚ appears to the right of the text box.

▶ **11.** Position the ⬚ pointer over the text box's title bar, press and hold the **mouse button**, and then drag the text box down so that the top of the text box aligns with the first line of text below the "Adaptation and Rehabilitation" heading. The left edge of the text box should align with the left edge of the orange shaded heading "Customized, Task-Oriented Care for Mind and Body," as indicated by the green alignment guide that appears when you have the text box aligned along the margin. The anchor symbol remains in its original position, next to the orange shaded paragraph. See Figure 4-11.

Figure 4-11 **Resized and repositioned text box**

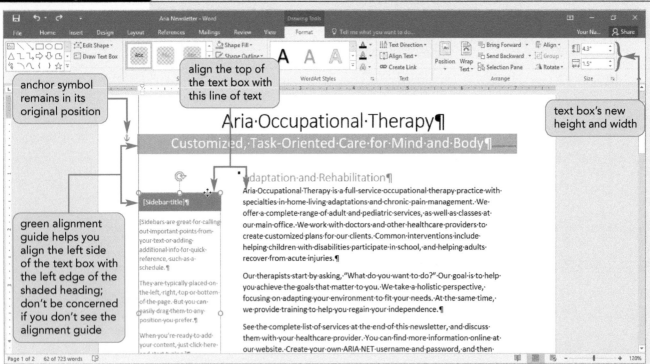

Trouble? If you don't see the green alignment guide, position the text box as described as carefully as you can.

▶ **12.** When you are sure the text box is positioned as shown in Figure 4-11, release the mouse button.

After you insert a text box or other object, you usually need to adjust its relationship to the surrounding text; that is, you need to adjust its text wrapping setting.

Changing the Text Wrapping Setting for the Text Box

A preformatted text box inserted via the Text box button on the Insert tab is, by default, a floating object formatted with Square text wrapping. You will verify this when you open the Layout Options gallery in the following steps. Then you'll select the In Front of Text option instead to gain more control over the exact position of the text box on the page.

To open the Layout Options gallery and change the wrapping option:

1. Change the Zoom level to **70%** so you can see the text box's position relative to the text on page 1.

2. Click the **Layout Options** button. The Layout Options gallery opens with the Square option selected. See Figure 4-12.

Figure 4-12   **Square text wrapping currently applied to text box**

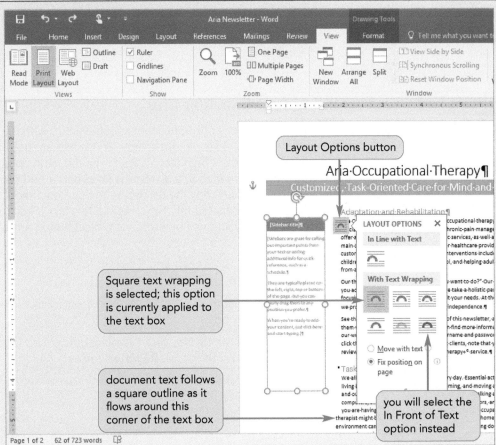

Square text wrapping is currently applied to the text box. You can see evidence of Square text wrapping where the document text flows around the lower-right corner of the text box. You'll have a chance to see some more dramatic examples of text wrapping later in this module, but it's important to be able to identify subtle examples of it.

3. Click any of the other options in the Layout Options gallery, and observe how the document text and the text box shift position. Continue exploring the Layout Options gallery, trying out several of the options.

▶ **4.** Click the **In Front of Text** option ▣, and then click the **Close** button ☒ in the upper-right corner of the Layout Options gallery to close the gallery. The document text shifts so that it now flows directly down the left margin, without wrapping around the text box.

Your next formatting task is to make sure the text box is assigned a fixed position on the page. You could check this setting using the Layout Options button, but you'll use the Wrap Text button in the Arrange group instead.

▶ **5.** On the ribbon, click the **Drawing Tools Format** tab.

▶ **6.** In the Arrange group, click the **Wrap Text** button. The Wrap Text menu gives you access to all the options in the Layout Options gallery, plus some more advanced settings.

▶ **7.** Verify that **Fix Position on Page** has a checkmark next to it. To avoid having graphic objects move around unexpectedly on the page as you add or delete other elements, it's a good idea to check this setting either in the Wrap Text menu or in the Layout Options menu for every graphic object.

▶ **8.** Click anywhere in the document to close the gallery, and then save the document.

Adding Text to a Text Box

Now that the text box is positioned where you want it, with the correct text wrapping, you can add text to it. In some documents, text boxes are used to present new information, while others highlight a quote from the main document. A direct quote from a document formatted in a text box is known as a **pull quote**. To create a pull quote text box, you can copy the text from the main document, and then paste it into the text box. You can also simply type text in a text box. Finally, you can insert text from another Word document by using the Object button arrow on the Insert tab.

To insert text in the text box:

▶ **1.** Change the Zoom level to **120%**, and then scroll as necessary so you can see the entire text box.

▶ **2.** In the text box's title bar, click the placeholder text **[Sidebar title]** to select it, if necessary, and then type **Register Today!**

▶ **3.** Click the placeholder text below the title bar to select it. See Figure 4-13.

Figure 4-13   Text box with placeholder text selected

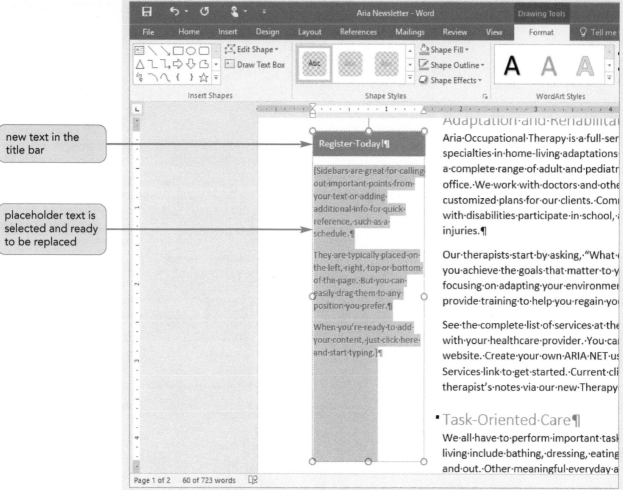

new text in the title bar

placeholder text is selected and ready to be replaced

▶ **4.** Press the **Delete** key to delete the placeholder text. Now you can insert new text from another Word document.

▶ **5.** On the ribbon, click the **Insert** tab.

▶ **6.** In the Text group, click the **Object** button arrow to open the Object menu, and then click **Text from File**. The Insert File dialog box opens. Selecting a Word document to insert is just like selecting a document in the Open dialog box.

▶ **7.** Navigate to the **Word4 > Module** folder included with your Data Files, click **Online** to select the file, and then click the **Insert** button. The registration information contained in the Online document is inserted directly into the text box. The inserted text was formatted in 9-point Calibri in the Online document, and it retains that formatting when you paste it into the Aria Newsletter document. To make the text easier to read, you'll increase the font size to 11 points.

▶ **8.** With the insertion point located in the last paragraph in the text box (which is blank), press the **Backspace** key to delete the blank paragraph, and then click and drag the mouse pointer to select all the text in the text box, including the title in the shaded title box.

▶ **9.** On the ribbon, click the **Home** tab.

▶ **10.** In the Font group, click the **Font Size** arrow, and then click **11**. The size of the text in the text box increases to 11 points. See Figure 4-14.

Figure 4-14   **Registration information inserted in text box**

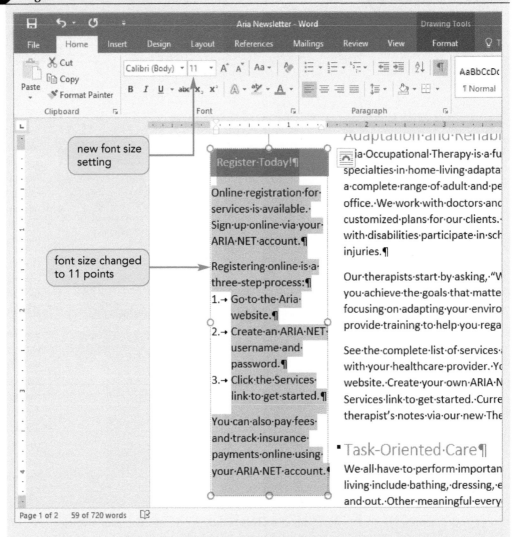

Trouble? Don't be concerned if the text in your text box wraps slightly differently from the text shown in Figure 4-14. The same fonts can vary slightly from one computer to another, causing slight differences in the way text wraps within and around text boxes.

▶ **11.** Click anywhere outside the text box to deselect it, and then save the document.

The first text box is complete. Now you need to add one more on page 1 and another on page 2. Avanti wants the second text box on page 1 to have a different look from the first one, so he asks you to use the Shapes button to draw a text box.

Drawing and Formatting a Text Box Using the Shapes Menu

A text box is considered a shape, just like the other shapes you can insert via the Shapes button on the Insert tab. This is true whether you insert a text box via the Text Box button or via the Shapes button. While text boxes are typically rectangular, you can actually turn any shape into a text box. Start by using the Shapes button to draw a shape of your choice, and then, with the shape selected, type any text you want. You won't see an insertion point inside the shape, but you can still type text inside it and then format it. You can format the shape itself by using the Shape Styles options on the Drawing Tools Format tab.

To draw and format a text box:

▶ **1.** Scroll down to display the bottom half of page 1.

▶ **2.** On the ribbon, click the **Insert** tab.

▶ **3.** In the Illustrations group, click the **Shapes** button to display the Shapes gallery. See Figure 4-15.

Figure 4-15 **Shapes gallery**

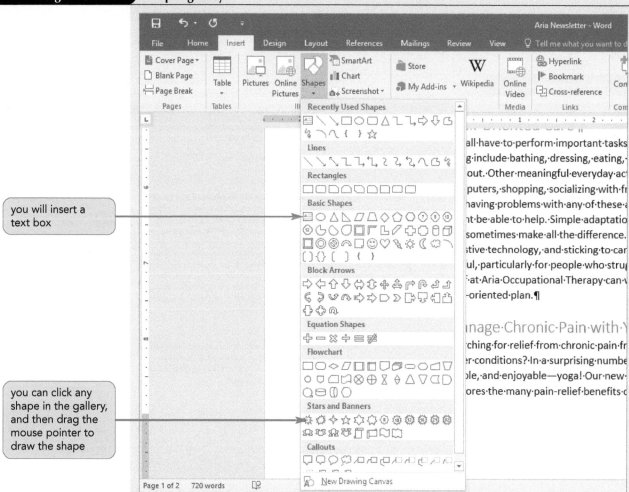

you will insert a
text box

you can click any
shape in the gallery,
and then drag the
mouse pointer to
draw the shape

At this point, you could click any shape in the gallery, and then drag the
pointer in the document to draw that shape. Then, after you finish drawing
the shape, you could start typing in the selected shape to insert text.

▶ **4.** In the Basic Shapes section of the Shapes gallery, click the **Text Box** icon ⊞.
The gallery closes, and the mouse pointer turns into a black cross ✛.

▶ **5.** Position the pointer in the blank area in the left margin at about the 6-inch
mark (according to the vertical ruler), and then click and drag down and to
the right to draw a text box approximately 1.5 inches wide and 2.5 inches
tall. When you are satisfied with the text box, release the mouse button.

Don't be concerned about the text box's exact dimensions or position on the
page. For now, just make sure it fits in the blank space to the left of the last
two paragraphs on the page.

TIP

On computers with a
touch screen, the Review
tab contains the Start
Inking button, which you
can click to begin drawing
on the screen by dragging
the pointer.

The new text box is selected, with handles on its border and the insertion point blinking inside. The Layout Options button is visible, and the text box's anchor symbol is positioned to the left of the paragraph below the heading "Task-Oriented Care." By default, a shape is always anchored to the nearest paragraph that begins above the shape's top border. It doesn't matter where the insertion point is located.

▶ **6.** Use the Shape Height and Shape Width boxes on the Drawing Tools Format tab to set the height to **2.2** inches and the width to **1.5** inches.

▶ **7.** Drag the text box as necessary to align its bottom border with the last line of text on the page and its left border with the left edge of the text box above. See Figure 4-16.

Figure 4-16 Text box created using the Shapes button

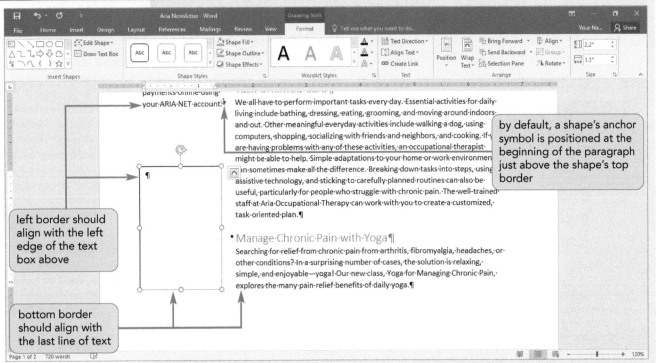

Now you need to add some text to the blank text box. Instead of inserting text from another Word document, you will copy a sentence from the newsletter and paste it into the text box to create a pull quote. After you add the text, you'll format the text box to make it match the one shown earlier in the Session 4.1 Visual Overview.

To copy text from the newsletter and paste it into the text box:

▶ **1.** Select the second sentence after the heading "Task-Oriented Care" (which begins "Essential activities for daily living. . ."), and then press the **Ctrl+C** keys to copy it to the Office Clipboard.

▶ **2.** Click in the blank text box, and then press the **Ctrl+V** keys to paste the copied sentence into the text box. The newly inserted sentence is formatted in 11-point Calibri, just as it was in the main document.

3. Add quotation marks at the beginning and end of the sentence, so it's clear the text box is a pull quote. Your next task is to center the sentence between the top and bottom borders of the text box. Then you'll add some color.

4. On the ribbon, click the **Drawing Tools Format** tab, if necessary.

TIP

You can use the Text Direction button in the Text group to rotate text within a text box.

5. In the Text group, click the **Align Text** button to display the Align text menu, and then click **Middle**. The text is now centered between the top and bottom borders of the text box. Next, you'll change the text's font color and add a background color.

6. In the Shape Styles group, click the **More** button to display the Shape Styles gallery. Like the text styles you have used to format text, shape styles allow you to apply a collection of formatting options, including font color and shading, with one click.

7. Move the mouse pointer over the various options in the Shape Styles gallery, and observe the Live Previews in the document. When you are finished, position the mouse pointer over the **Colored Fill - Blue, Accent 5** style, which is a dark blue box, the second from the right in the second row. See Figure 4-17.

Figure 4-17 **Shape Styles gallery**

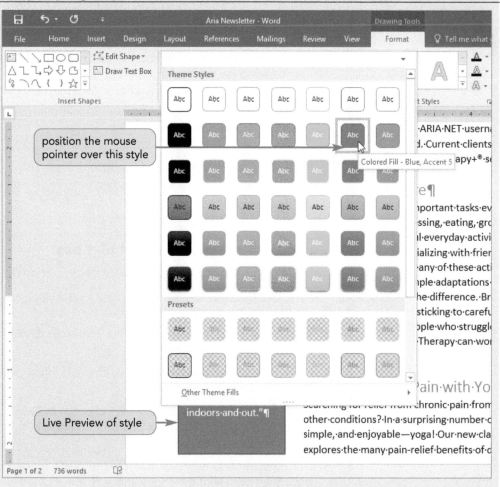

8. In the Shape Styles gallery, click the **Colored Fill - Blue, Accent 5** style. The style is applied to the text box, and the Shape Styles gallery closes.

Now, you need to make sure the text box is located in a fixed position on the page. In the following steps, you'll also experiment with making some changes involving the text box's anchor symbol. It's important to understand the role the anchor symbol plays in the document's overall layout.

To fix the text box's position on the page and experiment with the anchor symbol:

▶ **1.** Verify that the text box is still selected, with the Drawing Tools Format tab displayed on the ribbon.

▶ **2.** In the Arrange group, click the **Wrap Text** button. A checkmark appears next to Move with Text because that is the default setting for shapes.

▶ **3.** Click **Fix Position on Page** to add a checkmark and close the Wrap Text menu. This setting helps ensure that the text box will remain in its position on page 1, even if you add text above the paragraph it is anchored to. However, if you add so much text that the paragraph moves to page 2, then the text box will also move to page 2, but it will be positioned in the same location on the page that it occupied on page 1.

If you select the entire paragraph to which the text box is anchored, you will also select the text box, as you'll see in the next step.

▶ **4.** Triple-click the paragraph below the "Task-Oriented Care" heading. The entire paragraph and the text box are selected. If you pressed the Delete key at this point, you would delete the paragraph of text and the text box. If you ever need to delete a paragraph but not the graphic object that is anchored to it, you should first drag the anchor to a different paragraph.

▶ **5.** Click anywhere in the document to deselect the text and the text box, and then save the document.

You've finished creating the second text box on page 1. Avanti wants you to add a third text box at the top of page 2. For this text box, you'll again use the preformatted Ion Side Bar 1 text box.

To insert another preformatted text box:

▶ **1.** Scroll down to display the top half of page 2, and then click in the first line on page 2.

▶ **2.** On the ribbon, click the **Insert** tab.

▶ **3.** In the Text group, click the **Text Box** button to display the menu, scroll down, and then click **Ion Sidebar 1**.

▶ **4.** Click the **text box border** to select the entire text box and display the Layout Options button.

▶ **5.** Click the **Layout Options** button 📷, click the **In Front of Text** option 📷, if necessary, verify that the **Fix position on page** button is selected, and then close the Layout Options gallery.

▶ **6.** Drag the text box left to center it in the blank space to the left of the document text, with the top of the text box aligned with the first line of text on page 2. Note that a green alignment guide might appear if you try to position the right border of the text box too close to the document text.

▶ **7.** Change the text box's height to **3.5** inches and the width to **1.5** inches.

8. In the title bar, replace the placeholder text with **Access Classes Online**.

9. In the main text box, click the **placeholder text** to select it, and then press the **Delete** key.

10. On the ribbon, click the **Insert** tab.

11. In the Text group, click the **Object button arrow**, and then click **Text from File**.

12. Navigate to the **Word4 > Module** folder, if necessary, and then insert the document named **Webinar**.

13. Delete the extra paragraph at the end of the text box, increase the font size for the text to **11** points, click anywhere inside the text box to deselect the text, and then make sure your text box is positioned like the one shown in Figure 4-18.

Figure 4-18	Completed text box on page 2

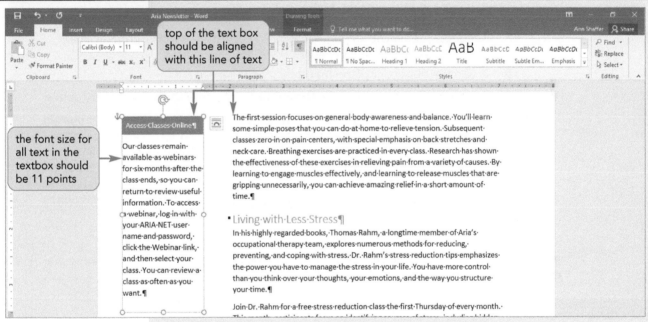

14. Click anywhere in the document to deselect the text box, and then save the document.

Linking Text Boxes

If you have a large amount of text that you want to place in different locations in a document, with the text continuing from one text box to another, you can use linked text boxes. For example, in a newsletter, you might have an article that starts in a text box on page 3 of the newsletter and continues in a text box on page 4. To flow the text automatically from one text box to a second, blank text box, click the first text box to select it (this text box should already contain some text). Next, on the ribbon, click the Drawing Tools Format tab, click the Create Link button in the Text group, and then click the empty text box. The text boxes are now linked. You can resize the first text box without worrying about how much text fits in the box. The text that no longer fits in the first text box is moved to the second text box. Note that you'll find it easier to link text boxes if you use simple text boxes without title bars.

To make the main document text look more polished, you will add some drop caps.

Inserting Drop Caps

As you saw in the Session 4.1 Visual Overview, a drop cap is a graphic that replaces the first letter of a paragraph. Drop caps are commonly used in newspapers, magazines, and newsletters to draw the reader's attention to the beginning of an article. You can place a drop cap in the margin or next to the paragraph, or you can have the text of the paragraph wrap around the drop cap. By default, a drop cap extends down three lines, but you can change that setting in the Drop Cap dialog box.

Avanti asks you to create a drop cap for some of the paragraphs that follow the headings. He wants the drop cap to extend two lines into the paragraph, with the text wrapping around it.

To insert drop caps in the newsletter:

▶ **1.** Scroll up to page 1, and then click anywhere in the paragraph below the "Adaptation and Rehabilitation" heading.

▶ **2.** On the ribbon, click the **Insert** tab.

▶ **3.** In the Text group, click the **Drop Cap** button. The Drop Cap gallery opens.

▶ **4.** Move the mouse pointer over the **Dropped** option and then the **In margin** option, and observe the Live Preview of the two types of drop caps in the document. The default settings applied by these two options are fine for most documents. Clicking Drop Cap Options, at the bottom of the menu, allows you to select more detailed settings. In this case, Avanti wants to make the drop cap smaller than the default. Instead of extending down through three lines of text, he wants the drop cap to extend only two lines.

▶ **5.** Click **Drop Cap Options**. The Drop Cap dialog box opens.

▶ **6.** Click the **Dropped** icon, click the **Lines to drop** box, and then change the setting to **2**. See Figure 4-19.

Figure 4-19 Drop Cap dialog box

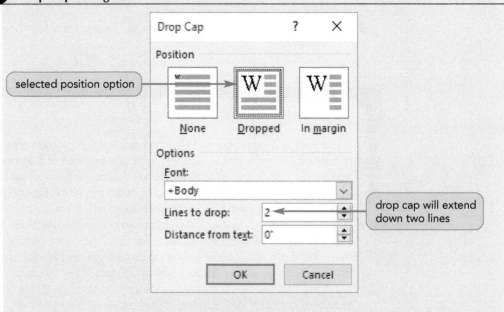

TIP

To delete a drop cap, click the paragraph that contains it, open the Drop Cap dialog box, and then click None.

7. Click the **OK** button. Word formats the first character of the paragraph as a drop cap "A," as shown in the Session 4.1 Visual Overview. The dotted box with selection handles around the drop cap indicates it is selected.

8. Near the bottom of page 1, insert a similar drop cap in the paragraph following the "Manage Chronic Pain with Yoga" heading. You skipped the paragraph following the "Task-Oriented Care" heading because you'll eventually insert a graphic there. Including a drop cap there would make the paragraph look too cluttered.

9. On page 2, insert a similar drop cap in the paragraph following the "Living with Less Stress" heading.

10. Click anywhere in the text to deselect the drop cap, and then save your work.

PROSKILLS

Written Communication: Writing for a Newsletter

Pictures, WordArt, and other design elements can make a newsletter very appealing to readers. They can also be a lot of fun to create and edit. But don't let the design elements in your desktop-published documents distract you from the most important aspect of any document—clear, effective writing. Because the newsletter format feels less formal than a report or letter, some writers are tempted to use a casual, familiar tone. If you are creating a newsletter for friends or family, that's fine. But in most other settings—especially in a business or academic setting—you should strive for a professional tone, similar to what you find in a typical newspaper. Avoid jokes; you can never be certain that what amuses you will also amuse all your readers. Worse, you risk unintentionally offending your readers. Also, space is typically at a premium in any printed document, so you don't want to waste space on anything unessential. Finally, keep in mind that the best writing in the world will be wasted in a newsletter that is overburdened with too many design elements. You don't have to use every element covered in this module in a single document. Instead, use just enough to attract the reader's attention to the page, and then let the text speak for itself.

REVIEW

Session 4.1 Quick Check

1. Explain how to format a document in three columns of the default width.

2. What should you do if you don't know which characters to type to insert a symbol or special character?

3. What does the anchor symbol indicate?

4. How do you convert an inline object into a floating object?

5. What is a pull quote?

6. How many lines does a drop cap extend by default?

Session 4.2 Visual Overview:

You can use the Remove Background button for photos and some drawings. For all other pictures, you need to crop instead.

You can click the Crop button arrow to access more advanced cropping options, including cropping to a shape such as an oval or an arrow.

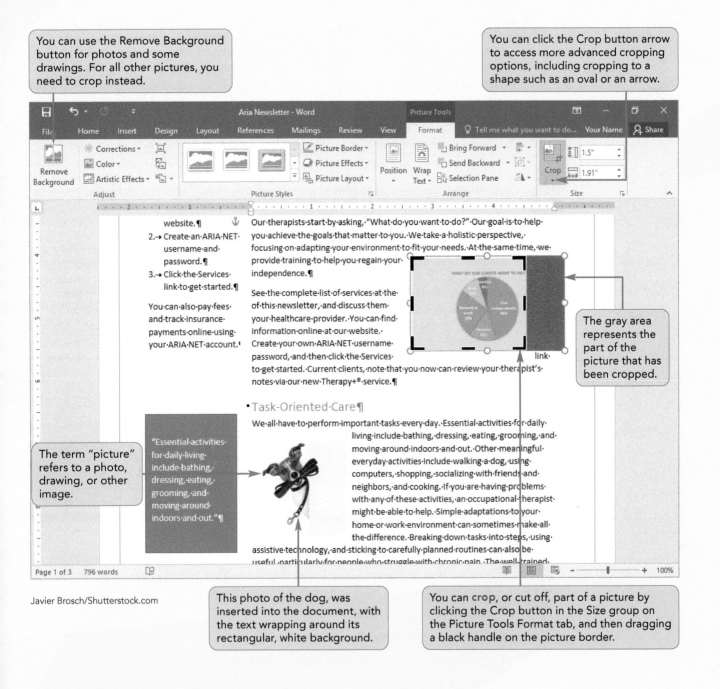

The gray area represents the part of the picture that has been cropped.

The term "picture" refers to a photo, drawing, or other image.

Javier Brosch/Shutterstock.com

This photo of the dog, was inserted into the document, with the text wrapping around its rectangular, white background.

You can crop, or cut off, part of a picture by clicking the Crop button in the Size group on the Picture Tools Format tab, and then dragging a black handle on the picture border.

Editing Pictures

Clicking the Remove Background button in the Adjust group on the Picture Tools Format tab displays the Background Removal tab, with tools for removing a photo's background.

The photo of the dog is displayed here with its background removed, which allows the text to wrap around the shape of the dog itself.

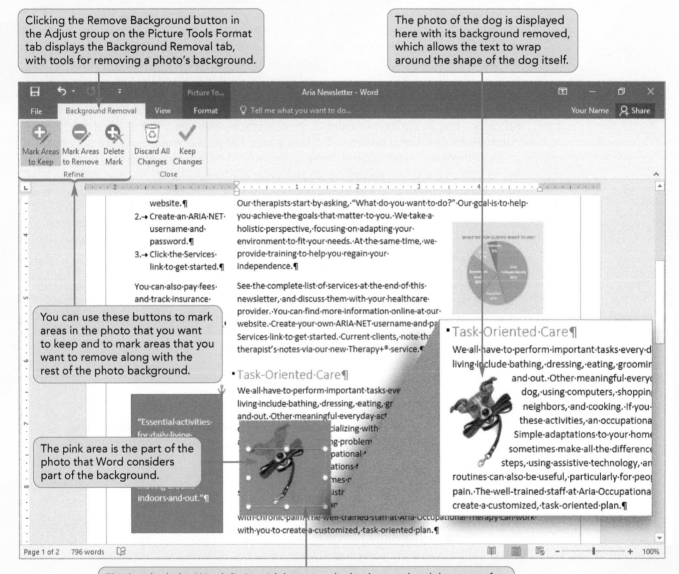

You can use these buttons to mark areas in the photo that you want to keep and to mark areas that you want to remove along with the rest of the photo background.

The pink area is the part of the photo that Word considers part of the background.

This border helps Word distinguish between the background and the parts of the image you want to keep. Any area of the image outside the border will be automatically excluded. In this case, part of the dog's head lies outside the border, so Word considers that area part of the background. To fix this problem, you can drag one of the border handles to expand the border until the dog's entire head is inside the border.

Formatting Text with WordArt

To create special text elements such as a newspaper headline, you can use decorative text known as WordArt. Essentially, WordArt is text in a text box that is formatted with a text effect. Before you move on to learning about WordArt, it's helpful to review the formatting options available with text effects.

To begin applying a text effect, you select the text you want to format. Then you can choose from several preformatted text effects via the Text Effects and Typography button in the Font group on the Home tab. You can also modify a text effect by choosing from the options on the Text Effects and Typography menu. For example, you can add a shadow or a glow effect. You can also change the **outline color** of the characters—that is, the exterior color of the characters—and you can change the style of the outline by making it thicker or breaking it into dashes, for example. To change the character's **fill color**—that is, the interior color of the characters—you just select a different font color via the Font Color button in the Font group, just as you would with ordinary text.

All of these text effect options are available with WordArt. However, the fact that WordArt is in a text box allows you to add some additional effects. You can add rounded, or **beveled**, edges to the letters in WordArt, format the text in 3-D, and transform the text into waves, circles, and other shapes. You can also rotate WordArt text so it stretches vertically on the page. In addition, because WordArt is in a text box, you can use page layout and text wrap settings to place it anywhere you want on a page, with text wrapped around it.

To start creating WordArt, you can select text you want to transform into WordArt, and then click the WordArt button in the Text group on the Insert tab. Alternatively, you can start by clicking the WordArt button without selecting text first. In that case, Word inserts a text box with placeholder WordArt text, which you can then replace with something new. In the following steps, you'll select the first paragraph and format it as WordArt to create the newsletter title that Avanti wants.

To create the title of the newsletter using WordArt:

▶ **1.** If you took a break after the last session, make sure the **Aria Newsletter** is open and zoomed to **120%**, with the rulers and nonprinting characters displayed.

▶ **2.** On page 1, select the entire paragraph containing the "Aria Occupational Therapy" heading, including the paragraph mark.

To avoid unexpected results, you should start by clearing any formatting from the text you want to format as WordArt, so you'll do that next.

▶ **3.** On the ribbon, click the **Home** tab, if necessary.

▶ **4.** In the Font group, click the **Clear All Formatting** button 🔥. The paragraph reverts to the Normal style. Now you can convert the text into WordArt.

▶ **5.** On the ribbon, click the **Insert** tab.

▶ **6.** In the Text group, click the **WordArt** button. The WordArt gallery opens.

▶ **7.** Position the mouse pointer over the WordArt style that is second from the left in the top row. A ScreenTip describes some elements of this WordArt style—"Fill - Blue, Accent 1, Shadow." See Figure 4-20.

Be sure to select the paragraph mark so the page layout in your newsletter matches the figures.

Figure 4-20   WordArt gallery

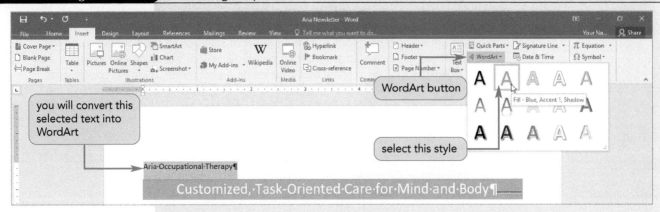

8. Click the WordArt style **Fill - Blue, Accent 1, Shadow**. The gallery closes, and a text box containing the formatted text is displayed in the document. See Figure 4-21.

Figure 4-21   WordArt text box inserted in document

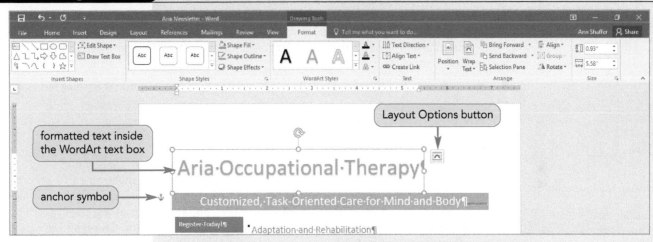

The Drawing Tools Format tab appears as the active tab on the ribbon, displaying a variety of tools that you can use to edit the WordArt. Before you change the look of the WordArt, you need to fix its position on the page and change its text wrap setting.

9. Make sure the **Drawing Tools Format** tab is selected on the ribbon.

10. In the Arrange group, click the **Wrap Text** button to open the Wrap Text menu, click **Top and Bottom**.

11. Save the document.

Next, you will modify the WordArt in several ways.

Modifying WordArt

Your first task is to resize the WordArt. When resizing WordArt, you need to consider both the font size of the text and the size of the text box that contains the WordArt. You change the font size for WordArt text just as you would for ordinary text—by selecting it and then choosing a new font size using the Font size box in the Font group on the Home tab. If you choose a large font for a headline, you might also need to resize the text box to ensure that the resized text appears on a single line. Avanti is happy with the font size of the new WordArt headline, so you only need to adjust the size of the text box so it spans the width of the page. The larger text box will then make it possible for you to add some more effects.

To resize the WordArt text box and add some effects:

▶ **1.** Make sure the **Drawing Tools Format** tab is selected on the ribbon.

▶ **2.** Change the width of the text box to **7** inches. The text box height should remain at the default .93 inches.

By default, the text is centered within the text box, which is what Avanti wants. Note, however, that you could use the alignment buttons on the Home tab to align the text any way you wanted within the text box borders. You could also increase the text's font size so that it expands to span the full width of the text box. Instead, you will take advantage of the larger text box to apply a transform effect, which will expand and change the overall shape of the WordArt text. Then you'll make some additional modifications.

▶ **3.** Make sure the **WordArt** text box is a solid line, indicating that it is selected.

▶ **4.** In the WordArt Styles group, click the **Text Effects** button A▾ to display the Text Effects gallery, and then point to **Transform**. The Transform gallery displays options for changing the WordArt's shape.

▶ **5.** Move the mouse pointer over the options in the Transform gallery and observe the Live Previews in the WordArt text box. Note that you can always remove a transform effect that has been previously applied by clicking the option in the No Transform section, at the top of the gallery. When you are finished, position the mouse pointer over the **Chevron Up** effect. See Figure 4-22.

Figure 4-22   Applying a Transform text effect

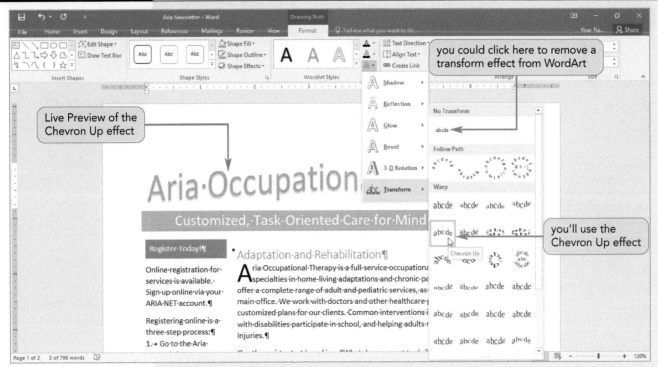

Trouble? If you don't see the Live Preview, press the Esc key twice to close the Transform and Text Effects galleries. Then, click outside the WordArt text box to deselect it, click the blue WordArt text to display the text box border, click the text box border to select it, and then begin again with Step 4.

6. Click the **Chevron Up** effect. The Transform menu closes, and the effect is applied to the WordArt. Now you will make some additional changes using the options in the WordArt Styles group. You'll start by changing the fill color.

7. In the WordArt Styles group, click the **Text Fill button arrow** to display the Text Fill color gallery.

8. In the Theme Colors section of the gallery, click the square that is fifth from the right in the top row to select the **Orange, Accent 2** color. The Text Fill gallery closes, and the WordArt is formatted in a shade of orange that matches the shading in the paragraph below. Next, you'll add a shadow to make the headline more dramatic.

9. In the WordArt Styles group, click the **Text Effects** button to display the Text Effects gallery, and then point to **Shadow** to display the Shadow gallery, which is divided into several sections.

10. In the Outer section, point to the top-left option to display a ScreenTip that reads "Offset Diagonal Bottom Right."

11. Click the **Offset Diagonal Bottom Right** shadow style. A shadow is added to the WordArt text. See Figure 4-23.

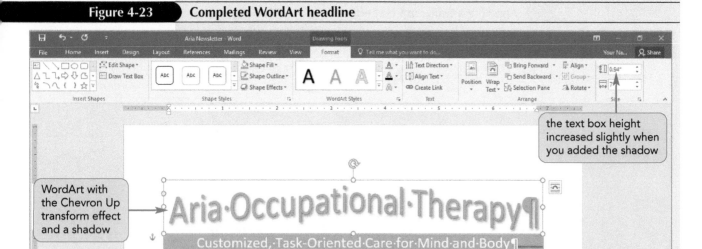

Figure 4-23 Completed WordArt headline

the text box height increased slightly when you added the shadow

WordArt with the Chevron Up transform effect and a shadow

Aria·Occupational·Therapy¶

Customized,·Task-Oriented·Care·for·Mind·and·Body¶

Note that the height of the text box that contains the WordArt increased slightly, to 0.94 inches.

▶ **12.** Click a blank area of the document to deselect the WordArt, and then save the document.

The WordArt headline is complete. Your next job is to add some pictures to the newsletter.

Working with Pictures

In Word, a picture is a photo, drawing, or other image. Although you can copy and paste pictures into a document from other documents, you'll typically insert pictures via either the Pictures button or the Online Pictures button, both of which are located in the Illustrations group on the Insert tab. You use the Pictures button to insert a picture from a file stored on your computer. You use the Online Pictures button to insert images that you find online using Bing Image Search or that you have stored on OneDrive. As you saw in the Session 4.1 Visual Overview, the final version of the Aria Newsletter document will contain a photograph of a dog and a drawing of someone in bed. The newsletter will also contain a picture of a chart, which Avanti's coworker created earlier and saved as a separate file.

After you insert a picture into a document, it functions as an object that you can move, resize, wrap text around, and edit in other ways using the appropriate contextual tab on the ribbon. In general, the skills you used when modifying text boxes apply to pictures as well.

Written Communication: Understanding Copyright Laws

The ownership of all forms of media, including text, drawings, photographs, and video, is governed by copyright laws. You should assume that anything you find on the web is owned by someone who has a right to control its use. It's your responsibility to make sure you understand copyright laws and to abide by them. The U.S. Copyright Office maintains a Frequently Asked Questions page that should answer any questions you might have: www.copyright.gov/help/faq.

Generally, copyright laws allow a student to reuse a photo, drawing, or other item for educational purposes, on a one-time basis, without getting permission from the owner. However, to avoid charges of plagiarism, you need to acknowledge the source of the item in your work. You don't ever want to be accused of presenting someone else's work as your own. Businesses face much more stringent copyright restrictions. To reuse any material, you must request permission from the owner, and you will often need to pay a fee.

When you use Bing Image Search in the Insert Pictures window, all of the images that initially appear as a result of your search will be licensed under a Creative Commons license. There are several types of Creative Commons licenses. One type allows you to use an image for any reason, including commercial use, and to modify the image, as long as the photographer is credited or attributed (similar to the credits under the photos in some figures in this book). Another type of license allows you to use an image with an attribution as long as it is not for commercial purposes and as long as you do not modify the image. Even if an image has a Creative Commons license, you must still review the exact license on the website on which the image is stored. When you point to an image in the search results in the Insert Pictures window, its website appears as a link at the bottom of the window.

Inserting and Cropping a Picture

You can use the Chart button in the Illustrations group on the Insert tab to enter data into a data sheet and then create a chart that illustrates the data. However, the chart Avanti wants to insert in the newsletter was created by a coworker using a different program and then saved as a PNG file named Chart.png. That means you can insert the chart as a picture using the Pictures button in the Illustrations group.

Avanti asks you to insert the chart picture on page 1.

To insert the chart picture on page 1:

▶ **1.** On page 1, click at the end of the first paragraph below the "Adaptation and Rehabilitation" heading to position the insertion point between "…acute injuries." and the paragraph mark. Normally, there's no need to be so precise about where you click before inserting a picture, but doing so here will ensure that your results match the results described in these steps exactly.

▶ **2.** On the ribbon, click the **Insert** tab.

▶ **3.** In the Illustrations group, click the **Pictures** button to open the Insert Picture dialog box.

▶ **4.** Navigate to the **Word4 > Module** folder included with your Data Files, and then insert the picture file named **Chart.png**. The chart picture is inserted in the document as an inline object. It is selected, and the Picture Tools Format tab is displayed on the ribbon.

▶ **5.** Scroll down if necessary so you can see the entire chart.

The chart is wider than it needs to be and would look better as a square. So you'll need to cut off, or crop, part of it. In addition to the ability to crop part of a picture, Word offers several more advanced cropping options. One option is to crop to a shape, which means trimming the edges of a picture so it fits into a star, an oval, an arrow, or another shape. You can also crop to a specific ratio of height to width.

Whatever method you use, once you crop a picture, the part you cropped is hidden from view. However, it remains a part of the picture in case you change your mind and want to restore the cropped picture to its original form.

Before you crop off the sides of the chart, you'll try cropping it to a specific shape.

To crop the chart picture:

▶ **1.** In the Size group, click the **Crop button arrow** to display the Crop menu, and then point to **Crop to Shape**. A gallery of shapes is displayed, similar to the gallery you saw in Figure 4-15.

▶ **2.** In the Basic Shapes section of the gallery, click the **Lightning Bolt** shape ⬩ (third row down, sixth from the right). The chart picture takes on the shape of a lightning bolt, with everything outside the lightning bolt shape cropped off.

   Obviously, this isn't a useful option for the chart, but cropping to shapes can be very effective with photos in informal documents such as party invitations or posters, especially if you then use the Behind Text wrapping option, so that the document text flows over the photo.

▶ **3.** Press the **Ctrl+Z** keys to undo the cropping.

▶ **4.** In the Size group, click the **Crop** button (not the Crop button arrow). Dark black sizing handles appear around the picture borders.

▶ **5.** Position the pointer directly over the middle sizing handle on the right border. The pointer changes to ⊢.

▶ **6.** Press and hold down the mouse button, and drag the pointer slightly left. The pointer changes to ✛.

▶ **7.** Drag the pointer toward the left until the chart border aligns with the 4-inch mark on the horizontal ruler, as shown in Figure 4-24.

| Figure 4-24 | Cropping a picture |

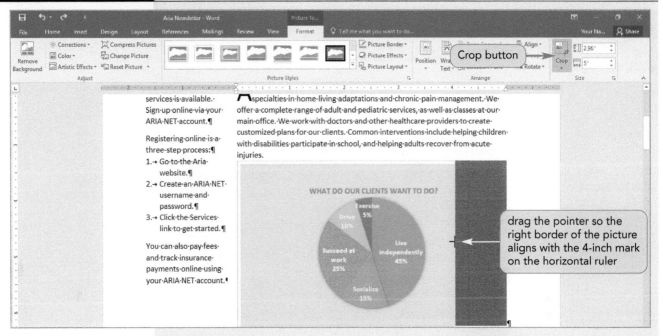

8. When the chart looks like the one shown in Figure 4-24, release the mouse button. The right portion of the chart picture is no longer visible. The chart shifts position slightly. Because the chart is an inline object, the text also shifts slightly. You can ignore the text wrapping for now. The original border remains, indicating that the cropped portion is still saved as part of the picture in case you want to undo the cropping.

9. Drag the middle handle on the left border to the right until the left border aligns with the 1.5-inch mark on the horizontal ruler.

The chart now takes up much less space, but it's not exactly a square. To ensure a specific ratio, you can crop the picture by changing its **aspect ratio**—that is, the ratio of width to height. You'll try that next. But first, you'll restore the picture to its original state.

10. In the Adjust group, click the **Reset Picture button arrow** to display the Reset Picture menu, and then click **Reset Picture & Size**. The chart picture returns to its original state.

11. In the Size group, click the **Crop button arrow**, and then point to **Aspect Ratio** to display the Aspect Ratio menu, which lists various ratios of width to height. A square has a 1-to-1 ratio of width to height.

12. Under "Square," click **1:1**. The chart is cropped to a square shape. See Figure 4-25.

Figure 4-25   Chart cropped to a 1:1 aspect ratio

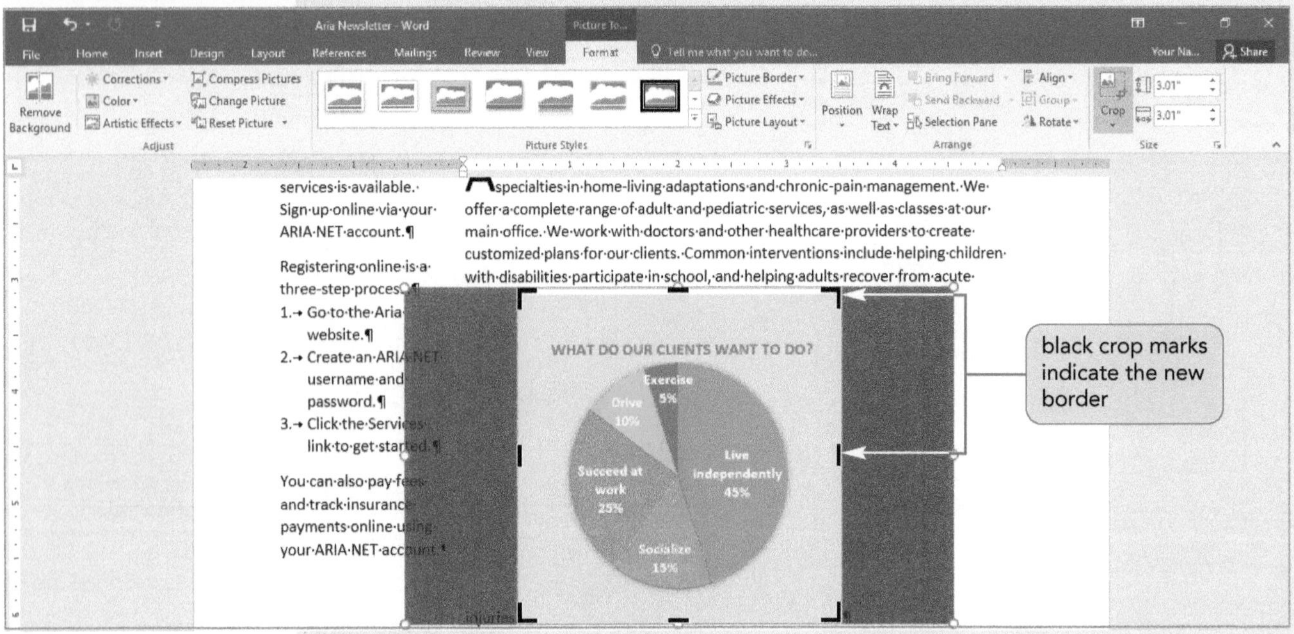

black crop marks indicate the new border

> **13.** Click anywhere outside the chart to deselect it and complete the cropping procedure.

Next, you need to change the chart from an inline object to a floating object by wrapping text around it. You also need to position it on the page. You can complete both of these tasks at the same time by using the Position button in the Arrange group.

To change the chart's position and wrapping:

> **1.** Change the Zoom level to **One Page**, and then click the **chart** to select it.

> **2.** On the ribbon, click the **Picture Tools Format** tab.

> **3.** In the Arrange group, click the **Position** button to display the Position gallery. You can click an icon in the "With Text Wrapping" section to move the selected picture to one of nine preset positions on the page. As with any gallery, you can see a Live Preview of the options before you actually select one.

> **4.** Move the mouse pointer over the various icons, and observe the changing Live Preview in the document, with the chart picture moving to different locations on the page and the text wrapping around it.

> **5.** Point to the icon in the middle row on the far right side to display a ScreenTip that reads "Position in Middle Right with Square Text Wrapping," and then click the **Position in Middle Right with Square Text Wrapping** icon ▣. The chart picture moves to the middle of the page along the right margin. By default, it is formatted with Tight text wrapping, so the text wraps to its left, following its square outline.

Your final step is to resize the chart picture to make it a bit smaller.

TIP

When you select an option in the Position gallery, Fix Position on Page is also selected on the Wrap Text menu by default.

6. In the Size group, click the **Shape Height** box, type **1.8**, and then press the **Enter** key. The settings in both the Shape Height and Shape Width boxes change to 1.8 inches. For most types of graphics, the aspect ratio is locked, meaning that when you change one dimension, the other changes to match. In this case, because the aspect ratio of the chart is 1:1, when you changed the height to 1.8 inches, the width also changed to 1.8 inches, ensuring that the chart retained its square shape.

7. Click anywhere outside the chart picture to deselect it, and then save the document.

INSIGHT

Aligning Graphic Objects and Using the Selection Task Pane

The steps in this module provide precise directions about where to position graphic objects in the document. However, when you are creating a document on your own, you might find it helpful to use the Align button in the Arrange group on the Picture Tools Format tab to align objects relative to the margin or the edge of the page. Aligning a graphic relative to the margin, rather than the edge of the page, is usually the best choice because it ensures that you don't accidentally position a graphic outside the page margins, causing the graphic to get cut off when the page is printed.

After you choose whether to align to the page or margin, you can open the Align menu again and choose an alignment option. For example, you can align the top of an object at the top of the page or align the bottom of an object at the bottom of the page. You can also choose to have Word distribute multiple objects evenly on the page. To do this, it's helpful to open the Selection task pane first by clicking the Layout tab and then clicking Selection Pane in the Arrange group. Press and hold the Ctrl key, and then in the Selection task pane, click the objects you want to select. After the objects are selected, there's no need to switch back to the Picture Tools Format tab. Instead, you can take advantage of the Align button in the Arrange group on the Layout tab to open the Align menu, where you can then click Distribute Horizontally or Distribute Vertically.

The chart picture is finished. Next, Avanti asks you to insert the dog photo near the bottom of page 1.

Searching for and Inserting Online Pictures

The first step in using online pictures is finding the picture you want. Most image websites include a search box where you can type some descriptive keywords to help you narrow the selection down to a smaller range. To search for images from within Word, click the Online Pictures button in the Illustrations group on the Insert tab. This opens the Insert Pictures window, shown in Figure 4-26, where you can use Bing Image Search to look for images.

Figure 4-26   **Inserting an online picture**

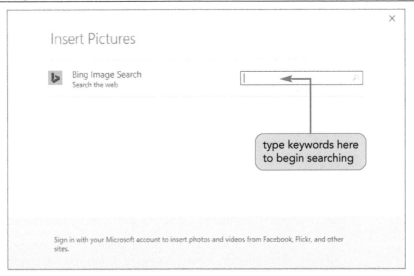

To start a search, you would type keywords, such as "walking a dog," in the Bing Image Search box and then click the Search button. Images from all over the web that have the keywords "walking a dog" and that are licensed under Creative Commons would appear below the Search box. Typically, these images are premade drawings known as **clip art**, which can be used to illustrate a wide variety of publications. To insert one of those images, you would click it, and then click the Insert button. To widen your search to all the images on the web (the vast majority of which are subject to strict copyright restrictions), you could click the Show all web results button at the bottom of the Insert Pictures window. At that point, the search results would expand to include photos in addition to clip art.

Because results from an online search are unpredictable, in the following steps you will insert an image included with your Data Files.

To insert a photo in the Aria Newsletter document:

▶ **1.** Zoom in so you can read the document text at the bottom of page 1, and then click at the end of the paragraph below the "Task-Oriented Care" heading to position the insertion point between "task-oriented plan." and the paragraph mark.

▶ **2.** Change the Zoom level to **Multiple Pages** so you can see the entire document.

▶ **3.** On the ribbon, click the **Insert** tab.

▶ **4.** In the Illustrations group, click the **Pictures** button to display the Insert Picture dialog box, and then navigate to the **Word4 > Module** folder included with your Data Files.

▶ **5.** Click the image **Terrier.jpg**, and then click the **Insert** button. The dialog box closes, and the photo of a dog is inserted as an inline object at the current location of the insertion point. See Figure 4-27.

Figure 4-27 | **Photo inserted as inline object**

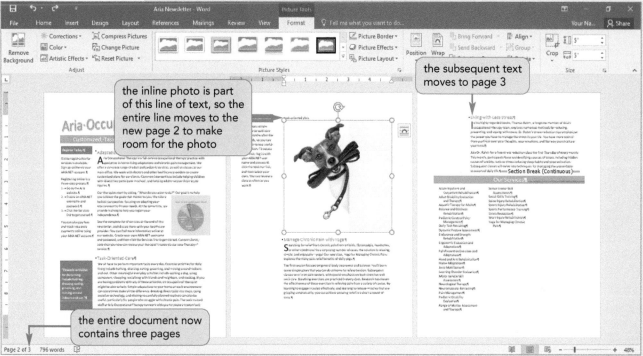

the inline photo is part of this line of text, so the entire line moves to the new page 2 to make room for the photo

the subsequent text moves to page 3

the entire document now contains three pages

Javier Brosch/Shutterstock.com

Because the photo is too large to fit on page 1, the line that contains the insertion point jumps to page 2, with the photo displayed below the text. The rest of the document text starts below the photo on page 2 and flows to page 3. The photo is selected, as indicated by its border with handles. The Picture Tools Format tab is displayed on the ribbon. Now you can reduce the photo's size, wrap text around it, and position it on the page.

6. In the Size group, click the **Shape Height** box, type **2**, and then press the **Enter** key. To maintain the photo's preset 1:1 aspect ratio, Word also changes the photo's width to 2 inches. Some of the text from page 3 moves up to fill the space below the smaller photo on page 2.

7. In the Arrange group, click the **Wrap Text** button, and then click **Tight**. The photo is now a floating object.

8. Drag the photo to page 1, and position it so the first two lines line of the paragraph under "Task-Oriented Care" wraps above it. See Figure 4-28. The anchor symbol for the photo is no longer visible because it's covered by the blue text box.

| Figure 4-28 | **Resized photo as a floating object** |

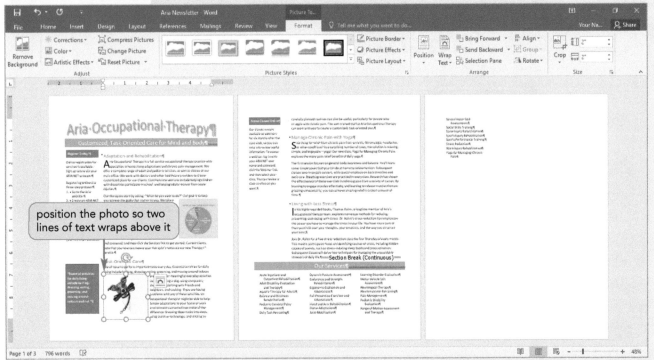

position the photo so two lines of text wraps above it

Javier Brosch/Shutterstock.com

Trouble? Don't be concerned if you can't get the text to wrap around the dog photo exactly as shown in Figure 4-28.

▶ 9. Click the **Layout Options** button , click **Fix position on page**, and then close the Layout Options gallery.

Avanti likes the photo, but he asks you to make a few changes. First, he wants you to rotate the dog to the right to position it vertically on the page. Also, Avanti wants the text to wrap around the curved shape of the dog, instead of around the photo's rectangular outline. To accomplish that, you need to remove the photo's background.

Rotating a Picture

You can quickly rotate a picture by dragging the Rotation handle that appears on the photo's border when the photo is selected. To access some preset rotation options, you can click the Rotate button in the Arrange group to open the Rotate menu. To quickly rotate a picture 90 degrees, click Rotate Right 90° or Rotate Left 90° in the Rotate menu. You can also flip a picture, as if the picture were printed on both sides of a card and you wanted to turn the card over. To do this, click Flip Vertical or Flip Horizontal in the Rotate menu.

Avanti only wants to rotate the picture slightly so the dog is upright. You can do that by dragging the Rotation handle.

To rotate the photo:

▶ **1.** Change the document Zoom level to **120%**, and then scroll down so you can see the bottom half of page 1.

▶ **2.** Click the **dog picture**, if necessary, to select it, and then position the mouse pointer over the circular rotation handle above the middle of the photo's top border. The mouse pointer changes to ⊕.

▶ **3.** Drag the mouse pointer down and to the right, until the dog rotates to a vertical position. The surrounding text wraps awkwardly around the picture's angled borders. See Figure 4-29.

Figure 4-29	Dragging the Rotation handle

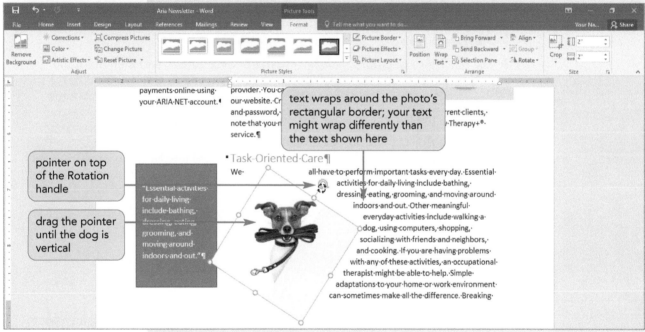

Javier Brosch/Shutterstock.com

Trouble? Don't be concerned if the text wrapping around your rotated picture looks different from the text wrapping in Figure 4-29. You'll adjust the picture's position soon.

▶ **4.** Release the mouse button. The dog is displayed in the new, rotated position.

▶ **5.** Save the document.

You're almost finished editing the dog photo. Your last task is to remove its background so the text wraps around the shape of the dog. But before you remove the background from the dog photo, you'll explore the options in the Adjust group.

Adjusting a Picture

The Adjust group on the Picture Tools Format tab provides several tools for adjusting a picture's overall look. Some, such as the Remove Background button, work only for photos. Others, such as the Color button, provide some options that work only for photos and some that work for both photos and line drawings. You'll explore some of these options in the following steps.

To try out some options in the Adjust group:

▶ 1. Make sure that the **dog photo** is still selected, and that the **Picture Tools Format** tab is selected on the ribbon.

▶ 2. In the Adjust group, click the **Corrections** button, and then move the mouse pointer over the various options in the Corrections gallery and observe the Live Preview in the document. You can use the Corrections gallery to sharpen or soften a photo's focus or to adjust the brightness of a photo or line drawing.

▶ 3. Press the **Esc** key to close the Corrections gallery.

▶ 4. In the Adjust group, click the **Color** button, and then move the mouse pointer over the options in the Color gallery, and observe the Live Preview in the document. For photos, you can adjust the color saturation and tone. For photos and line drawings, you can use the Recolor options to completely change the picture's colors.

▶ 5. Press the **Esc** key to close the Color gallery.

▶ 6. In the Adjust group, click the **Artistic Effects** button, and then move the mouse pointer over the options in the Artistic Effects gallery, and observe the Live Preview in the document. Artistic Effects can be used only on photos.

▶ 7. Press the **Esc** key to close the Artistic Effects gallery.

▶ 8. In the Adjust group, click the **Compress Pictures** button to open the Compress Pictures dialog box. In the Target output portion of the dialog box, you can select the option that reflects the purpose of your document. Compressing pictures reduces the file size of the Word document but can result in some loss of detail.

▶ 9. Click the **Cancel** button to close the Compress Pictures dialog box.

Now you are ready to remove the white background from the dog photo.

Removing a Photo's Background

Removing a photo's background can be tricky, especially if you are working on a photo with a background that is not clearly differentiated from the foreground image. For example, you might find it difficult to remove a white, snowy background from a photo of an equally white snowman. You start by clicking the Remove Background button in the Adjust group, and then making changes to help Word distinguish between the background that you want to exclude and the image you want to keep.

REFERENCE

Removing a Photo's Background

- Select the photo, and then on the Picture Tools Format tab, in the Adjust group, click the Remove Background button.
- Drag the handles on the border as necessary to include any parts of the photo that have been incorrectly marked for removal.
- To mark areas to keep, click the Mark Areas to Keep button in the Refine group on the Background Removal tab, and then use the drawing pointer to select areas of the photo to keep.
- To mark areas to remove, click the Mark Areas to Remove button in the Refine group on the Background Removal tab, and then use the drawing pointer to select areas of the photo to remove.
- Click the Keep Changes button in the Close group.

You'll start by zooming in so you can clearly see the photo as you edit it.

To remove the white background from the dog photo:

▶ **1.** On the Zoom slider, drag the slider button to change the Zoom level to **180%**, and then scroll as necessary to display the selected dog photo.

▶ **2.** In the Adjust group, click the **Remove Background** button. See Figure 4-30.

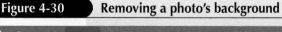

Figure 4-30 | **Removing a photo's background**

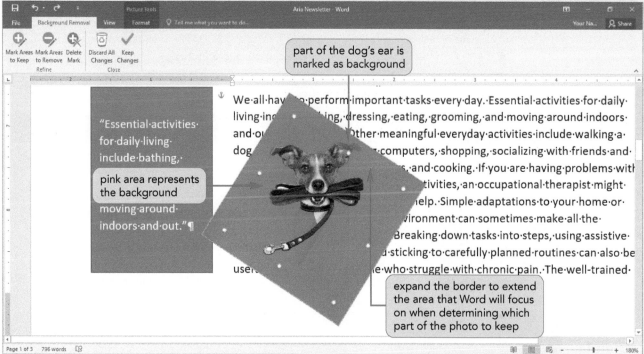

Javier Brosch/Shutterstock.com

The part of the photo that Word considers to be the background turns pink, and the Background Removal tab appears on the ribbon. A border with white handles surrounds the dog. The border helps Word narrow the area of focus as it tries to distinguish between the background and the parts of the image you want to keep. Word will automatically remove any part of the image outside the border when you click the Keep Changes button.

Trouble? If you don't see the border with the white handles, click the Mark Areas to Remove button in the Refine group on the Background Removal tab, and then click in the pink background, in the top corner of the picture. This will insert a small white circle with a negative sign inside it, which you can ignore. The border with the white handles should now be displayed.

Notice that the top of the dog's ears are pink, indicating that Word considers them to be part of the background. The same is probably true of the dog's chest, below his collar, although this can vary from one computer to another. To ensure that Word keeps the parts of the photo you want, you need to expand the border with the white handles. Then you can make additional adjustments using the tools on the Background Removal tab. In the following steps, your goal is to retain the dog's head above the collar and all of the leash.

3. If necessary, drag the handle in the top corner of the border up slightly until the border encloses the dog's entire head. The dog's ears should now be visible in their original colors, with no pink shading, indicating that Word no longer considers any part of the dog's ears to be part of the background. Depending on how far up you dragged the border handle, the border might have disappeared, or it might still be visible. At this point, most of the dog's chest is pink, which is what you want. If a few white spots are still visible, you can fix the problem by marking these white spots as areas to remove.

4. On the Background Removal tab, click the **Mark Areas to Remove** button in the Refine group to select it, if necessary, and then move the drawing pointer ⌀ over the dog. You can use this pointer to click any areas you want to remove.

5. Move the pointer over a white area on the dog's chest. See Figure 4-31.

Figure 4-31	**Marking an area to remove**

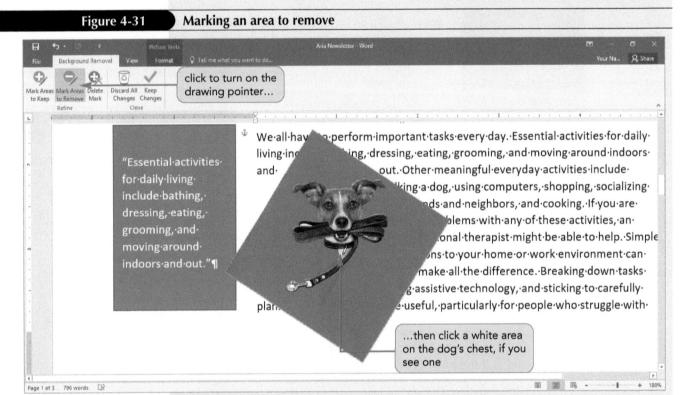

Javier Brosch/Shutterstock.com

6. Click the mouse button. A small circle with a negative sign appears where you clicked, and the white area turns pink, indicating that Word now considers it part of the background.

7. Click any other remaining white spots on the dog's chest. You can ignore any white spots in the folds of the leash or around the dog's ears, because they will be invisible when the photo is displayed on the document's white background.

   Note that you could click the Mark Areas to Keep button and then use the mouse pointer in a similar way to mark parts of the photo that you want to retain, rather than remove. You can also click and drag the Mark Areas to Remove pointer or the Mark Areas to Keep pointer to select a larger area of the photo for deletion or retention.

Now you will accept the changes you made to the photo.

8. In the Close group, click the **Keep Changes** button. The background is removed from the photo, leaving only the image of the dog with the leash. Now the text wrapping follows the curved shape of the dog, just as Avanti requested. Depending on exactly where you positioned the dog, some of the text might now wrap to the left of the leash.

9. Change the Zoom level to **100%** so that you can see the entire dog, as well as the top of page 2, and then drag the dog as necessary so the text wraps similar to the text shown in Figure 4-32.

Figure 4-32	Dog photo with background removed

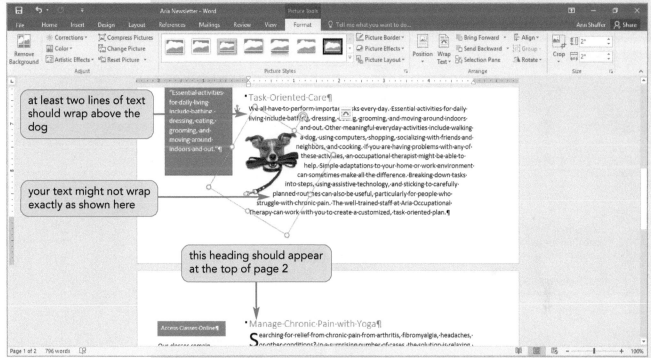

Javier Brosch/Shutterstock.com

Don't be concerned if you can't get the text wrapping to match exactly. The most important thing is that when you are finished, the "Manage Chronic Pain with Yoga" heading should be positioned at the top of page 2. Also, at least two lines of text should wrap above the dog.

10. Click outside the picture to deselect it, and then save the document.

You're finished with your work on the dog photo. Now Avanti asks you to add a drawing of someone in bed, on page 3.

Inserting and Editing a Drawing

You could search for a drawing by clicking the Online Pictures button in the Illustrations group on the Insert tab and then typing some keywords. In the following steps, however, you will insert a drawing from a file. Then, you'll add a picture style to it from the Picture Styles gallery.

To insert a drawing and add a style to it:

▶ **1.** Change the Zoom level to **120%**, and then scroll to display the middle of page 2. You'll insert the drawing in the blank space below the text box.

▶ **2.** Click at the end of the paragraph below the "Living with Less Stress" heading to position the insertion point between "…your time." and the paragraph mark.

▶ **3.** On the ribbon, click the **Insert** tab.

▶ **4.** In the Illustrations group, click the **Pictures** button, navigate to the **Word4 > Module** folder included with your Data Files, click the image **Sleep**, and then click the **Insert** button. The drawing of the person in bed is inserted as an inline object on page 3, because there is not enough room for it on page 2. See Figure 4-33.

Figure 4-33	Drawing inserted in document

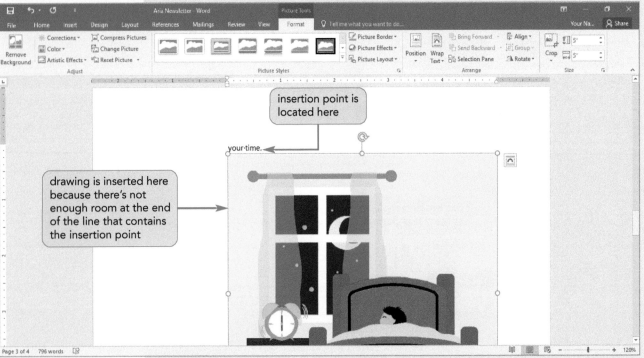

©iStock.com/djvstock

Next, you need to resize the drawing, apply a picture style, wrap text around it, and then position it on the page.

▶ **5.** In the Size group, click the **Shape Height** box, type **1.4**, and then press the **Enter** key. To maintain the picture's preset aspect ratio, the width automatically adjusts to 1.4 inches. The picture moves up to page 2 because it's now small enough to fit.

▶ **6.** Scroll up to page 2 so you can see the picture, if necessary.

▶ **7.** In the Arrange group, click the **Wrap Text** button to open the Wrap Text menu. The In Line with Text option is selected. Because the picture is still an inline picture, the Move with Text and Fix Position on Page options are grayed out, indicating that they are not available.

▶ **8.** Click **In Front of Text** to select it and close the Wrap Text menu.

9. Click the **Wrap Text** button again, and then click **Fix Position on Page**. The picture appears layered on top of the document text. Keep in mind that even though you selected Fix Position on Page, the picture is not stuck in one place. You can drag it anywhere you want. The point of the Fix Position on Page setting is that it prevents the picture from moving unexpectedly as you make changes to other parts of the document.

10. In the Picture Styles group, click the **Simple Frame, White** style, which is the first style in the visible row of the Picture Styles gallery. A frame and a shadow are applied to the drawing.

11. Drag the picture to center it in the white space below the text box in the margin, deselect it, and then save the document. See Figure 4-34.

Figure 4-34   **Resized picture with picture style**

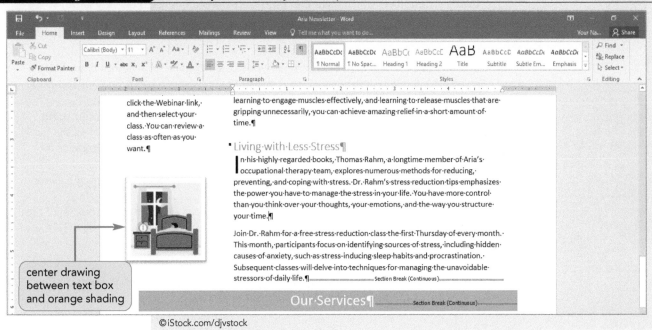

©iStock.com/djvstock

INSIGHT

Working with Digital Picture Files

Digital picture files come in two main types—vector graphics and raster graphics. A vector graphics file stores an image as a mathematical formula, which means you can increase or decrease the size of the image as much as you want without affecting its overall quality. Vector graphics are often used for line drawings and, because they tend to be small, are widely used on the web. File types for vector graphics are often proprietary, which means they work only in specific graphics programs. In Word, you will sometimes encounter files with the .wmf file extension, which is short for Windows Metafiles. A WMF file is a type of vector graphics file created specifically for Windows. In most cases, though, you'll work with raster graphics, also known as bitmap graphics. A **bitmap** is a grid of square colored dots, called **pixels**, that form a picture. A bitmap graphic, then, is essentially a collection of pixels. The most common types of bitmap files are:

- **BMP**—These files, which have the .bmp file extension, tend to be very large, so it's best to resave them in a different format before using them in a Word document.
- **EPS**—These files, which have the .eps file extension, are created by Adobe Illustrator and can contain text as graphics.
- **GIF**—These files are suitable for most types of simple line art, without complicated colors. A GIF file is compressed, so it doesn't take up much room on your computer. A GIF file has the file extension .gif.
- **JPEG**—These files are suitable for photographs and drawings. Files stored using the JPEG format are even more compressed than GIF files. A JPEG file has the file extension .jpg. If conserving file storage space is a priority, use JPEG graphics for your document.
- **PNG**—These files are similar to GIF files but are suitable for art containing a wider array of colors. A PNG file has the file extension .png.
- **TIFF**—These files are commonly used for photographs or scanned images. TIFF files are usually much larger than GIF or JPEG files but smaller than BMP files. A TIFF file has the file extension .tif.

Now that you are finished arranging the graphics in the newsletter, you need to make sure the columns are more or less the same length.

Balancing Columns

To **balance** columns on a page—that is, to make them equal length—you insert a continuous section break at the end of the last column. Word then adjusts the flow of content between the columns so they are of equal or near-equal length. The columns remain balanced no matter how much material you remove from any of the columns later. The columns also remain balanced if you add material that causes the columns to flow to a new page; the overflow will also be formatted in balanced columns.

To balance the columns:

▶ **1.** Press the **Ctrl+End** keys to move the insertion point to the end of the document, if necessary.

▶ **2.** Insert a continuous section break. See Figure 4-35.

Figure 4-35 | **Newsletter with balanced columns**

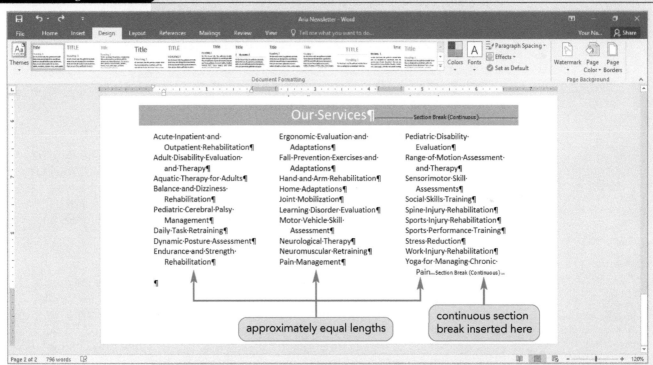

Word balances the text between the three columns, moving some text from the bottom of the left column to the middle column, and from the middle column to the right column, so the three columns are approximately the same length.

Note that you can also adjust the length of a column by inserting a column break using the Breaks button in the Page Setup group on the Layout tab. A column break moves all the text and graphics following it to the next column. Column breaks are useful when you have a multipage document formatted in three or more columns, with only enough text on the last page to fill some of the columns. In that case, balancing columns on the last page won't work. Instead, you can use a column break to distribute an equal amount of text over all the columns on the page. However, as with page breaks, you need to be careful with column breaks because it's easy to forget that you inserted them. Then, if you add or remove text from the document, or change it in some other significant way, you might end up with a page layout you didn't expect.

Inserting a Border Around a Page

The newsletter is almost finished. Your last task is to add a border around both pages. The default style for a page border is a simple black line that forms a box around each page in the document. However, you can choose more elaborate options, including a dotted line, double lines, and, for informal documents, a border of graphical elements such as stars or trees. In this case, Avanti prefers the default line style, but he wants it to be orange.

To insert a border around both pages of the newsletter:

▶ **1.** Change the Zoom level to **Multiple Pages**.

▶ **2.** On the ribbon, click the **Design** tab.

▶ **3.** In the Page Background group, click the **Page Borders** button. The Borders and Shading dialog box opens with the Page Border tab displayed. You can use the Setting options on the left side of this tab to specify the type of border you want. Because a document does not normally have a page border, the default setting is None. The Box setting is the most professional and least distracting choice, so you'll select that next.

▶ **4.** In the Setting section, click the **Box** setting.

At this point, you could scroll the Style box and select a line style for the border, such as a dotted line, but Avanti prefers the default style—a simple line. He's also happy with the default width of 1/2 pt. For very informal documents, you could click the Art arrow and select a predesigned border consisting of stars or other graphical elements. However, the only change Avanti wants to make is to change the border color to orange.

▶ **5.** Click the **Color** arrow to open the Color gallery, and then click the **Orange, Accent 2** square, which is the fifth square from the right in the top row of the Theme Colors section. The Color gallery closes and the Orange, Accent 2 color is displayed in the Color box. See Figure 4-36.

Be sure to select the Box setting before you select other options for the border. Otherwise, when you click the OK button, your document won't have a page border, and you'll have to start over.

| Figure 4-36 | Adding a border to the newsletter |

use the default line style

use a simple Box border

select the Orange, Accent 2 color

use the default width for the line style

apply to the whole document

6. In the lower-right corner of the Borders and Shading dialog box, click the **Options** button. The Border and Shading Options dialog box opens.

By default, the border is positioned 24 points from the edges of the page. If you plan to print your document on an older printer, it is sometimes necessary to change the Measure from setting to Text, so that the border is positioned relative to the outside edge of the text rather than the edge of the page. Alternatively, you can increase the settings in the Top, Bottom, Left, and Right boxes to move the border closer to the text. For most modern printers, however, the default settings are fine.

7. In the Border and Shading Options dialog box, click the **Cancel** button, and then click the **OK** button in the Borders and Shading dialog box. The newsletter now has a simple, orange border, as shown earlier in the Session 4.1 Visual Overview.

8. Save the document. Finally, to get a better sense of how the document will look when printed, it's a good idea to review it with nonprinting characters turned off.

9. On the ribbon, click the **Home** tab.

10. In the Paragraph group, click the **Show/Hide** button to turn off nonprinting characters. Notice that the WordArt headline increases slightly in size to take up the space formerly occupied by the nonprinting paragraph mark.

11. Change the Zoom level to **120%**, and then scroll to display page 2.

12. On page 2, in the first line below the heading, "Living with Less Stress," replace "Thomas Rahm" with your first and last names, and then save the document.

Avanti plans to have the newsletter printed by a local printing company. Sophia, his contact at the printing company, has asked him to email her the newsletter as a PDF.

Saving a Document as a PDF

A **PDF**, or **Portable Document Format file**, contains an image showing exactly how a document will look when printed. Because a PDF can be opened on any computer, saving a document as a PDF is a good way to ensure that it can be read by anyone. This is especially useful when you need to email a document to people who might not have Word installed on their computers. All PDFs have a file extension of .pdf. By default, PDFs open in Adobe Acrobat Reader, a free program installed on most computers for reading PDFs, or in Adobe Acrobat, a PDF-editing program available for purchase from Adobe.

To save the Aria Newsletter document as a PDF:

1. On the ribbon, click the **File** tab to display Backstage view.

2. In the navigation bar, click **Export** to display the Export screen with Create PDF/XPS Document selected.

3. Click the **Create PDF/XPS** button. The Publish as PDF or XPS dialog box opens.

4. If necessary, navigate to the location specified by your instructor for saving your files, and then verify that "Aria Newsletter" appears in the File name box. Below the Save as type box, the "Open file after publishing" check box is selected. By default, the "Standard (publishing online and printing)" button is selected. This generates a PDF suitable for printing. If you plan to distribute a PDF only via email or over the web, you should select the "Minimum size (publishing online)" button instead. See Figure 4-37.

> **TIP**
>
> To save a document as a PDF and attach it to an email message in Outlook, click the File tab, click Share in the navigation bar, click Email, and then click Send as PDF.

Figure 4-37 **Publish as PDF or XPS dialog box**

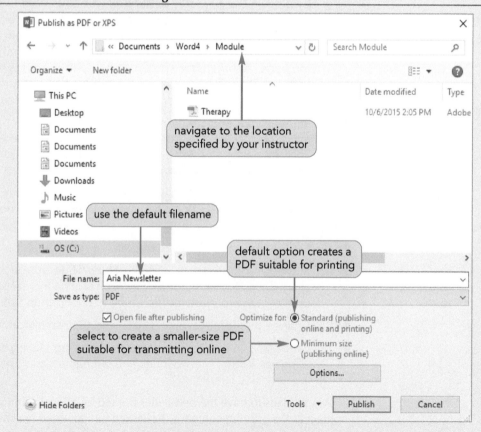

5. Click the **Publish** button. The Publish as PDF or XPS dialog box closes, and, after a pause, either Adobe Acrobat Reader or Adobe Acrobat opens with the Aria Newsletter.pdf file displayed.

Trouble? If the Aria Newsletter PDF does not open, your computer might not have Acrobat Reader or Acrobat installed. In that case, skip Step 6.

6. Scroll down and review the PDF, and then close Adobe Acrobat Reader or Adobe Acrobat.

7. In Word, close the Aria Newsletter document, saving changes if necessary, but keep Word running.

In addition to saving a Word document as a PDF, you can convert a PDF to a Word document.

Converting a PDF to a Word Document

You may sometimes need to use text from a PDF in your own Word documents. Before you can do this, of course, you need to make sure you have permission to do so. Assuming you do, you can open the PDF in Acrobat or Acrobat Reader, drag the mouse pointer to select the text you want to copy, press the Ctrl+C keys, return to your Word document, and then press the Ctrl+V keys to paste the text into your document. If you need to reuse or edit the entire contents of a PDF, it's easier to convert it to a Word document. This is a very useful option with PDFs that consist mostly of text. For more complicated PDFs, such as the Aria Newsletter.pdf file you just created, the results are less predictable.

Avanti has a PDF containing some text about the Therapy+ service. He asks you to open it in Word and make some minor edits before converting it back to a PDF.

To open the PDF in Word:

1. On the ribbon, click the **File** tab to display Backstage view.

2. In the navigation bar, click **Open**, if necessary, to display the Open screen, and then navigate to the **Word4 > Module** folder included with your Data Files.

3. If necessary, click the **arrow** to the right of the File name box, and then click **All Word Documents**.

4. In the file list, click **Therapy**, click the **Open** button, and then, if you see a dialog box explaining that Word is about to convert a PDF to a Word document, click the **OK** button. The PDF opens in Word, with the name "Therapy.pdf" in the title bar. Now you can save it as a Word document.

> **5.** Click the **File** tab, click **Save As**, and then navigate to the location specified by your instructor.

> **6.** Verify that "Word Document (*.docx)" appears in the Save as type box, and then save the document as **Therapy Revised**.

> **7.** Turn on nonprinting characters, set the Zoom level to **120%**, and then review the document, which consists of a WordArt headline and a paragraph of text formatted in the Normal style. If you see some extra spaces at the end of the paragraph of text, they were added during the conversion from a PDF to a Word document. In a more complicated document, you might see graphics overlaid on top of text, or columns broken across multiple pages.

> **8.** Close the **Therapy Revised** document.

Session 4.2 Quick Check

REVIEW

1. What term refers to the interior color of the characters in WordArt?

2. Name six types of bitmap files.

3. What kind of laws govern the use of media, including text, line drawings, photographs, and video?

4. When cropping a picture, how can you maintain a specific ratio of width to height?

5. What is the most professional and least distracting style of page border?

6. What should you do if you need to ensure that your document can be read on any computer?

Review Assignments

Data Files needed for the Review Assignments: Books.jpg, Festival.docx, Genres.png, Hours.docx, Library.docx, Party.jpg

Avanti has been hired to create a newsletter for another organization, the Singleton Valley Library. This newsletter provides the latest information about the library, with articles about an upcoming celebration and a retirement. He has already written the text, and he asks you to transform it into a professional-looking newsletter. He also asks you to save the newsletter as a PDF so he can email it to the printer and to edit some text currently available only as a PDF. The finished newsletter should match the one shown in Figure 4-38.

Figure 4-38 **Completed Library Newsletter document**

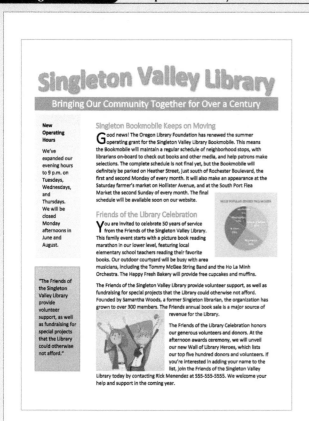
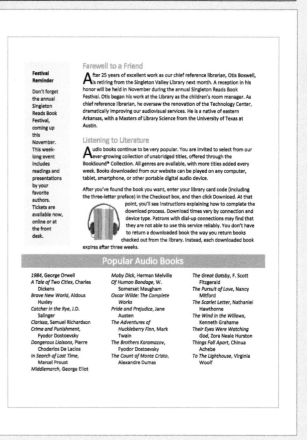

Happy_Inside/Shutterstock.com; photo.ua/Shutterstock.com

Complete the following steps:

1. Open the file **Library** from the Word4 > Review folder included with your Data Files, and then save the document as **Library Newsletter** in the location specified by your instructor.

2. Insert continuous section breaks in the following locations:

   a. On page 1, at the beginning of the "Singleton Bookmobile Keeps on Moving" heading, to the left of the "S" in "Singleton"

   b. On page 2, at the beginning of the shaded heading "Popular Audio Books," to the left of the "P" in "Popular"

   c. On page 2, at the beginning of the first book title, to the left of the "1" in "1984"

3. In sections 1 and 3, change the left and right margins to .75 inches. In section 2, change the left margin to 2.5 inches.

4. Format section 4 in three columns of equal width, and then format the entire list of book titles and authors with a 0.2-inch hanging indent.

5. Search for the term **BookSound** in the newsletter, and then add the ® symbol to the right of the final "d."

6. On page 1, click anywhere in the "Singleton Bookmobile Keeps on Moving" heading, and then insert a preformatted text box using the Grid Sidebar option.

7. Change the text wrapping setting for the text box to In Front of Text. Change the height of the text box to 4 inches and its width to 1.3 inches, and then drag it left to position it in the white space in the left margin, with its top edge aligned with the first line of text below the "Singleton Book Mobile Keeps on Moving" heading. The left border of the text box should align with the left edge of the shaded paragraph above. Verify that the text box's position is fixed on the page, but note that its placement will shift slightly relative to other elements in the newsletter as you make changes. Eventually, it will be positioned as it is in the Figure 4-38.

8. Delete all the placeholder text in the text box, and then insert the text of the Word document **Hours**, which is located in the Word4 > Review folder included with your Data Files. Delete any extra paragraph marks at the end of the text, if necessary.

9. On the Insert tab, use the Shapes button to draw a rectangular text box that roughly fills the blank space in the lower-left margin of page 1. When you are finished, adjust the height and width as necessary to make the text box 2.9 inches tall and 1.3 inches wide.

10. Make sure the text wrap setting for the text box is set to In Front of Text and that the text box has a fixed position on the page. Drag the text box's anchor up to slightly above or below the "Friends of the Library Celebration" heading to keep the text box from moving to page 2 later, when you add a graphic to page 1.

11. On page 1, in the second paragraph below the "Friends of the Library Celebration" heading, select the first sentence (which begins "The Friends of the Singleton..."), and then copy it to the Office Clipboard.

12. Paste the copied sentence into the text box at the bottom of page 1, and then add quotation marks at the beginning and end.

13. Use the Align Text button to align the text in the middle of the text box, and then apply the Subtle Effect - Blue, Accent 1 shape style (the light blue style option in the fourth row of the Shape Styles gallery).

14. On page 2, click in the heading "Listening to Literature," and then insert a preformatted text box using the Grid Sidebar option.

15. Change the text wrapping setting for the text box to In Front of Text. Change the height of the text box to 5.1 inches and its width to 1.3 inches, and then drag it left to position it in the white space in the left margin, with its top edge aligned with the first line of text. Verify that its position is fixed on the page. Don't be concerned that it overlaps the shaded paragraph below. This will change as you add more elements to the newsletter.

16. Delete all the placeholder text in the text box, and then insert the text of the Word document **Festival**, which is located in the Word4 > Review folder included with your Data Files. Delete any extra paragraph marks at the end of the text, if necessary.

17. In the first line of text after each of the four headings formatted with orange font, insert a drop cap that drops two lines.

18. On page 1, select the entire first paragraph, "Singleton Valley Library," including the paragraph mark. Clear the formatting from the paragraph, and then format the text as WordArt, using the Fill - Orange, Accent 2, Outline - Accent 2 style.

19. Use the Position button to place the WordArt in the top center of the document, with square text wrapping, and make sure the WordArt has a fixed position on the page.

20. Change the WordArt text box width to 7 inches, and retain the default height of .87 inches.

21. Apply the Chevron Up transform text effect, change the text fill to Orange, Accent 2 (the orange square in the top row of the Theme Colors section), and then add a shadow using the Offset Diagonal Bottom Right style (the first option in the top row of the Outer section).

22. Click at the end of the paragraph below the "Singleton Bookmobile Keeps on Moving" heading, and then insert the picture file named **Genres.png** from the Word4 > Review folder included with your Data Files.

23. Practice cropping the chart to a shape, and then try cropping it by dragging the cropping handles. Use the Reset Picture button as necessary to restore the picture to its original appearance. When you are finished, crop the picture using a square aspect ratio, and then change its height and width to 1.8 inches. Use the Position button to place the chart picture in the middle of the right side of page 1 with square text wrapping.

24. On page 1, click at the end of the second paragraph below the "Friends of the Library Celebration" heading, and then insert the drawing **Party.jpg** from the Word4 > Review folder included with your Data Files.

25. Apply Square text wrapping, change the picture's height to 1.7 inches, and position the picture as shown in Figure 4-38. When the picture is properly positioned, the heading "Farewell to a Friend" should be positioned at the top of page 2, as shown in Figure 4-38.

26. On page 2, click at the end of the first paragraph below the "Listening to Literature" heading, and then insert the photo **Books.jpg** from the Word4 > Review folder included with your Data Files.

27. Rotate the photo so the books are positioned vertically, with the earphones on top, change the photo's height to 1.2 inches, and retain the default width of 1.42 inches. Apply Tight text wrapping, fix its position on the page, and then remove the photo's background.

28. Drag the photo to position it as shown in Figure 4-38.

29. Balance the columns at the bottom of page 2.

30. Insert a simple box outline of the default style and width for the entire document. For the border color, use Blue, Accent 1 (the fifth square from the left in the top row of the Theme Colors). Make any additional adjustments necessary to ensure that your newsletter matches the one shown in Figure 4-38.

31. In the second line on page 2, replace "Otis Boswell" with your first and last names.

32. Save the document, and then save it again as a PDF named **Library Newsletter.pdf** in the location specified by your instructor. Wait for the PDF to open, review it, and then close the program in which it opened. Close the **Library Newsletter.docx** document, but leave Word open.

33. In Word, open the **Library Newsletter.pdf** file, save it as a Word document named **Library Newsletter from PDF.docx**, review its appearance, note the problems with the formatting that you would have to correct if you actually wanted to use this new DOCX file, and then close it.

Case Problem 1

Data Files needed for this Case Problem: Bike.png, Biking.docx, Pump.png, Sidebar.docx

Dallas Riders Bicycle Club   Philip Schuster is president of the Dallas Riders Bicycle Club, a recreational cycling organization in Dallas, Texas. He has written the text of the club's monthly newsletter. Now he needs your help to finish it. The newsletter must fit on one page so the route for this month's ride can be printed on the other side. The finished newsletter should match the one shown in Figure 4-39.

Figure 4-39   Completed Biking Newsletter document

Dallas Riders Bicycle Club
News From the Road

Lake View Passes

Don't forget to buy your annual pass for the Lake View Bike Path, available now on our website, or at any local bike shop. The $35 fee goes to support trail maintenance and youth programs. Daily passes are also available for out-of-town guests. Note that you can now purchase daily passes online, or at the Lake View Overlook trailhead.

See this month's ride route on the other side of this newsletter.

Dallas Riders Receive $3000 Grant

We're extremely happy to announce that the Dallas Riders Bicycle Club has been awarded a $3000 Ride the Roads grant from the Texas Department of Tourism. The money will pay for the publication of the club's "Top 100 Dallas Rides" pamphlet, which will be distributed at tourist sites throughout the Dallas-Fort Worth area.

Many thanks go to Clarice Orleans, who spent many hours completing the grant application, and to Peter Suarez and Leah Chang who compiled the information about the rides, based on a club survey. The pamphlet will be published by the end of the summer. It's packed with helpful information about biking in the Dallas-Fort Worth area.

Annual Big Southwest Ride

The Big Southwest Ride, October 15-20, is our most exciting event of the year. We encourage all participants to register before the September 15 deadline to ensure that we can accommodate everyone who wants to take part. The registration fee is $250. Online registration opens August 15.

Each rider is allowed one medium-sized backpack and one sleeping bag on the baggage truck. This year we will be staying in high school gyms along the route, so tents are not necessary. Charlie Yellow Feather, our generous volunteer chef, will once again oversee all meals. The registration fee entitles you to breakfast, lunch, and dinner. Note that this year the mid-day meal will take the form of a bagged lunch. Surveys from last year's ride suggested that most people prefer the flexibility of being able to eat lunch when and where they want.

Yellow Jersey Service Award Winners

Sasha Ann Ramirez-Beech	Carole Laydra	Seamus Brennan	Maria Morelo-Jimenez
Paul Michael Bernault	Thomas Butler	Jacqueline Fey-Esperanza	Elizabeth Juarez
Avi Cai	Lisa Erbe	Haiyan Jiang	Mario Mondre
Emma Gotlieb	Henry Douglas	Louis Jeschke	Heidi Roys
Markus Carnala	Carlos Caruccio	Jaques Lambeau	Student Name
	Cecilia Carrucio		
	Dennis McKay		

Complete the following steps:

1. Open the file **Biking** located in the Word4 > Case1 folder included with your Data Files, and then save it as **Biking Newsletter** in the location specified by your instructor.

2. Change the document margins to Narrow, and then, where indicated in the document, insert continuous section breaks. Remember to delete each instance of the highlighted text "[Insert SECTION BREAK]" before you insert a section break.

3. In section 2, change the left margin to 3 inches, and then format section 4 in four columns.

4. Format the second paragraph in the document ("News From the Road") as WordArt, using the Gradient Fill - Dark Green, Accent 1, Reflection style (second from the left in the middle row of the WordArt gallery). Change the text box height to 0.7 inches and the width to 7 inches.

5. Insert drop caps that drop two lines in the first paragraph after the "Dallas Riders Receive $3000 Grant" heading and in the first paragraph after the "Annual Big Southwest Ride" heading.

6. Click in the fourth paragraph in the document (the one with the drop cap "W"), and then insert a preformatted text box using the Ion Sidebar 1 option. Change the text wrapping setting for the text box to In Front of Text, and then change its height to 3 inches and its width to 2.3 inches.

7. Drag the text box down, and then align its top border with the "Dallas Riders Receive $3000 Grant" heading.

8. Delete the title placeholder text in the text box, and type **Lake View Passes**. In the main text box, delete the placeholder text, and insert the text of the Word document **Sidebar** from the Word4 > Case1 folder included with your Data Files. Delete any extra blank paragraphs, and change the font size for all the text in the text box, including the title, to 11 points.

9. In the blank space below the "Lake View Passes" text box, draw a rectangular text box. When you are finished, adjust the height and width to make the text box 1.3 inches tall and 2 inches wide. Apply the Moderate Effect - Blue, Accent 2 shape style (third from the left in the second row from the bottom), and then position the text box as shown in Figure 4-39, leaving room for the graphic you will add later.

10. In the text box, type **See this month's ride route on the other side of this newsletter.** Align the text in the middle of the text box, and then use the Center button to center the text between the text box's left and right borders.

11. At the end of the fifth paragraph (which begins "Many thanks go to…"), insert the drawing **Pump.png** from the Word4 > Case1 folder included with your Data Files. Crop the picture to an oval shape, apply Tight text wrapping, fix its position on the page, and then change its height to 1 inch. Drag the picture to position it so the first two lines of the fifth paragraph wrap above it, as shown in Figure 4-39.

12. At the end of the first paragraph below the "Annual Big Southwest Ride" heading, insert the drawing **Bike.png** from the Word4 > Case1 folder included with your Data Files. Change the picture's height to 1.3 inches, apply In Front of Text text wrapping, add the Center Shadow Rectangle picture style (second from right in the second row of the Picture Styles gallery), and then position the picture in the left margin, centered between the two text boxes, with a fixed position on the page, as shown in Figure 4-39.

13. Add a box page border using a line style with a thick exterior line and a thinner interior line in the default width and in the same color as the font for the "Dallas Riders Receive $3000 Grant" heading.

14. In the last paragraph, replace "Pete Del Rio" with your first and last names.

15. Make any adjustments necessary so that your newsletter matches the one shown in Figure 4-39, and then save the document.

16. Save the document as a PDF named **Biking Newsletter** in the location specified by your instructor. Review the PDF, and then close the program in which it opened.

17. In Word, open the PDF named **Biking Newsletter.pdf**, save it as **Biking Newsletter from PDF. docx**, review its contents, note the corrections you would have to make if you actually wanted to use this document, and then close it, as well as the Biking Newsletter document.

APPLY

Case Problem 2

Data Files needed for this Case Problem: Ben.jpg, Franklin.docx, Treaty.docx

Benjamin Franklin Association Anne Rawson is a member of the Benjamin Franklin Association in Philadelphia, Pennsylvania, an organization of professional and amateur historians that works to promote Franklin's legacy. Anne has decided to create a series of handouts about important historical documents related to Franklin. Each handout will contain the document text, with red accent colors, along with a picture of Franklin and a text box with essential facts about Franklin and the document. Anne has asked you to help her complete her first handout, which is about the Treaty of Paris. You will create the handout shown in Figure 4-40.

Figure 4-40 | **Completed Treaty of Paris handout**

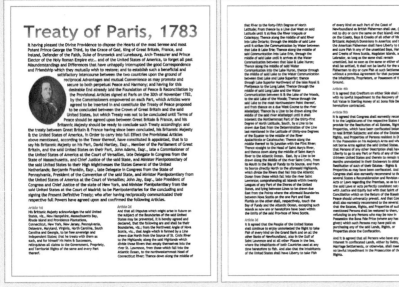

Everett Historical/Shutterstock.com

Complete the following steps:

1. Open the file **Treaty** located in the Word4 > Case2 folder included with your Data Files, and then save it as **Treaty of Paris** in the location specified by your instructor.

2. Display the document gridlines.

3. Change the theme to Facet, and format all the heading text using the Red, Accent 5 font color in the first row of the Theme Colors section of the Font Color gallery.

4. At the top of the document, add the text **Treaty of Paris, 1783** as a new paragraph, and then format it as WordArt, using the Gradient Fill - Red, Accent 1, Reflection style (the second from the left in the middle row). Add Top and Bottom text wrapping. If the position of the WordArt shifts, drag it back up to the top of the page. Change its height to .7 inches and its width to 7 inches. Apply the Square transform text effect (the first effect in the top row of the Warp section). Remove the reflection effect. Drag the WordArt as necessary to center it at the top of the page. The top edge of the text box should align with the top gridline. Don't be concerned if it extends beyond the left and right edges of the gridlines.

5. At the end of the paragraph below the WordArt, insert the picture **Ben.jpg** from the Word4 > Case2 folder included with your Data Files.

6. Apply Tight text wrapping to the photo, change the height to 2 inches, remove the portrait's gray background, leaving only the oval portrait, and then position it along the left margin, so the first six lines of regular text wrap above it, as shown in Figure 4-40.

7. Format the paragraphs containing the list of articles in two columns. (Note that the last three lines of the document are not part of the list of articles.) Use a column break to format the articles as shown in Figure 4-40, with Article 8 at the top of the second column on page 3.

8. At the end of the last paragraph on page 3, insert a preformatted text box using the Grid Sidebar style. Apply In Front of Text text wrapping, and then change the height to 3.3 inches and the width to 6.3 inches. Position the text box at the bottom of page 3, centered in the white space, with a fixed position on the page. Don't be concerned that the text box extends into the space without gridlines, at the bottom of the page.

9. Delete the placeholder text in the text box, and then insert the text of the Word document named **Franklin** from the Word4 > Case2 folder included with your Data Files. If necessary, delete any extra paragraph marks.

10. Add a box page border, using the default style in the default width and in the same color as the headings with the article numbers.

11. Make any adjustments necessary so that your newsletter matches the one shown in Figure 4-40, and then hide the gridlines.

12. At the end of the text box on page 3, insert a new, bulleted paragraph, and then insert the text **Prepared by Student Name**, with your first and last names replacing the text "Student Name." Save the document.

13. Save the document as a PDF named **Treaty of Paris.pdf** in the location specified by your instructor. Review the PDF in Acrobat or Acrobat Reader.

14. From within Acrobat or Acrobat Reader, use the appropriate keyboard shortcut to copy the text in the text box, open a new, blank Word document, and then paste the copied text into it. In a new bulleted list at the end of the document, list three differences between the formatting of the text in the current document and in the Treaty of Paris.pdf file. Format the new paragraphs in red so they are easy to spot.

15. Save the Word document as **Facts from PDF** in the location specified by your instructor, and then close it, as well as the Treaty of Paris document. Close Acrobat or Acrobat Reader.

TROUBLESHOOT

Case Problem 3

Data Files needed for this Case Problem: Porter.docx, Raffle.pdf

Porter and Mills Accounting   You are the publications manager at Porter and Mills Accounting, in Cincinnati, Ohio. Your supervisor explains that while working on the company's monthly newsletter, he left his laptop briefly unattended. His young child took advantage of the opportunity to make some unwelcome changes to his Word document. You've offered to troubleshoot the document and format the newsletter to look like the one shown in Figure 4-41. Your second task is to open a PDF containing a document announcing a charity raffle and edit the text to remove any irregularities that occurred in the conversion from a PDF to a Word document.

Figure 4-41   Completed Porter and Mills newsletter

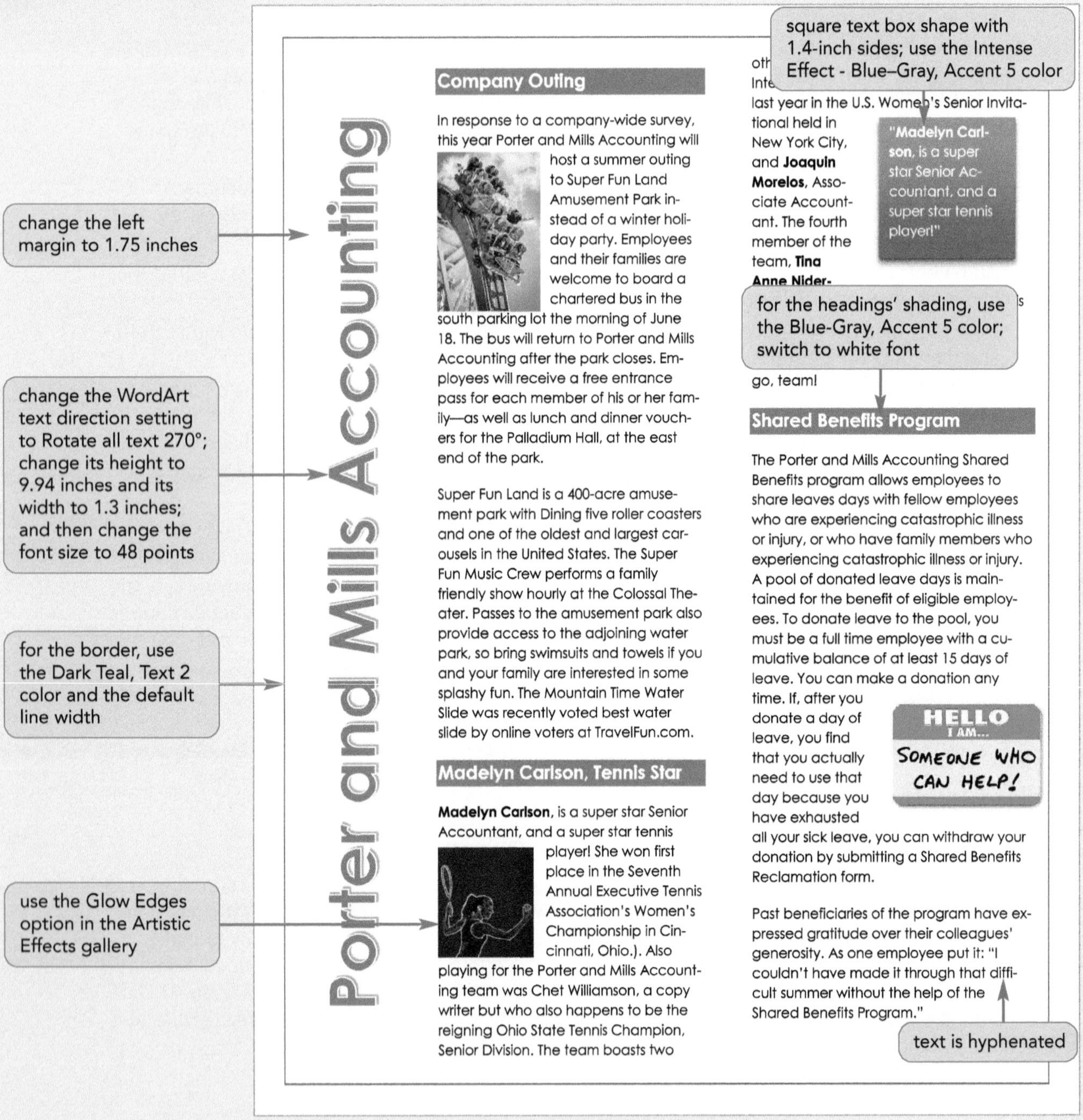

change the left margin to 1.75 inches

change the WordArt text direction setting to Rotate all text 270°; change its height to 9.94 inches and its width to 1.3 inches; and then change the font size to 48 points

for the border, use the Dark Teal, Text 2 color and the default line width

use the Glow Edges option in the Artistic Effects gallery

square text box shape with 1.4-inch sides; use the Intense Effect - Blue–Gray, Accent 5 color

for the headings' shading, use the Blue-Gray, Accent 5 color; switch to white font

text is hyphenated

Porter and Mills Accounting

Company Outing

In response to a company-wide survey, this year Porter and Mills Accounting will host a summer outing to Super Fun Land Amusement Park instead of a winter holiday party. Employees and their families are welcome to board a chartered bus in the south parking lot the morning of June 18. The bus will return to Porter and Mills Accounting after the park closes. Employees will receive a free entrance pass for each member of his or her family—as well as lunch and dinner vouchers for the Palladium Hall, at the east end of the park.

Super Fun Land is a 400-acre amusement park with Dining five roller coasters and one of the oldest and largest carousels in the United States. The Super Fun Music Crew performs a family friendly show hourly at the Colossal Theater. Passes to the amusement park also provide access to the adjoining water park, so bring swimsuits and towels if you and your family are interested in some splashy fun. The Mountain Time Water Slide was recently voted best water slide by online voters at TravelFun.com.

Madelyn Carlson, Tennis Star

Madelyn Carlson, is a super star Senior Accountant, and a super star tennis player! She won first place in the Seventh Annual Executive Tennis Association's Women's Championship in Cincinnati, Ohio.). Also playing for the Porter and Mills Accounting team was Chet Williamson, a copy writer but who also happens to be the reigning Ohio State Tennis Champion, Senior Division. The team boasts two

oth
Inte
last year in the U.S. Women's Senior Invitational held in New York City, and **Joaquin Morelos**, Associate Accountant. The fourth member of the team, **Tina Anne Nider-**

"Madelyn Carlson, is a super star Senior Accountant, and a super star tennis player!"

go, team!

Shared Benefits Program

The Porter and Mills Accounting Shared Benefits program allows employees to share leaves days with fellow employees who are experiencing catastrophic illness or injury, or who have family members who experiencing catastrophic illness or injury. A pool of donated leave days is maintained for the benefit of eligible employees. To donate leave to the pool, you must be a full time employee with a cumulative balance of at least 15 days of leave. You can make a donation any time. If, after you donate a day of leave, you find that you actually need to use that day because you have exhausted all your sick leave, you can withdraw your donation by submitting a Shared Benefits Reclamation form.

HELLO I AM... SOMEONE WHO CAN HELP!

Past beneficiaries of the program have expressed gratitude over their colleagues' generosity. As one employee put it: "I couldn't have made it through that difficult summer without the help of the Shared Benefits Program."

Allen.G/Shutterstock.com; Elnur/Shutterstock.com; iQoncept/Shutterstock.com

Complete the following steps:

1. Open the file **Porter** located in the Word4 > Case3 folder included with your Data Files, and then save it as **Porter and Mills** in the location specified by your instructor.

☼ **Troubleshoot** 2. Change the border and the left margin as described in Figure 4-41.

☼ **Troubleshoot** 3. Fix the WordArt as described in Figure 4-41, and apply column formatting as necessary.

☼ **Troubleshoot** 4. Reset the pictures and then format, resize, and crop them to match the pictures shown in Figure 4-41. Keep in mind that you can use the Selection Task Pane to select a picture. Also, you'll need to flip one picture horizontally. You should be able to size the pictures appropriately by looking at their sizes relative to the text in Figure 4-41. You will position the pictures in the next step.

☼ **Troubleshoot** 5. Position the pictures as shown in Figure 4-41. In the Arrange group, use the Selection Pane button and the Align Objects button to align the photo of the roller coaster and the tennis player with the left margin. Also, align the name tag image with the right margin.

6. Replace the double hyphens with an em dash.

7. In the middle of the second column, replace "Joaquin Morelos" with your first and last names.

☼ **Troubleshoot** 8. Make any adjustments necessary so that your newsletter matches the one shown in Figure 4-41. You might need to drag the WordArt text box left slightly to keep all the text on one page. Save the document.

9. Save the document as a PDF named **Porter and Mills.pdf** in the location specified by your instructor. Review the PDF in Acrobat or Acrobat Reader, and then close Acrobat or Acrobat Reader. Close the Porter and Mills document in Word.

10. Open the PDF **Raffle.pdf** located in the Word4 > Case3 folder included with your Data Files, and then save it as a Word document named **Raffle Reminder** in the location specified by your instructor.

☼ **Troubleshoot** 11. Edit the text to remove the WordArt and the text box, including the green textbox title. Format the remaining text as one column, and then remove any extra spaces and paragraph breaks. Keep the last two paragraphs formatted as a bulleted list. Add the default amount of paragraph spacing after each paragraph to make the text easier to read. Make any other edits necessary so that the text is formatted with consistent paragraph and line spacing throughout.

12. Save and close the document.

CREATE

Case Problem 4

There are no Data Files needed for this Case Problem.

Delicious Restaurant Design Associates You are an intern at Delicious Restaurant Design Associates, a firm that specializes in designing restaurant interiors. As part of your training, your supervisor asks you to review examples of menu designs on the web and then re-create the first page of one of those menus in a Word document. Instead of writing the complete text of the menu, you can use placeholder text. Complete the following steps:

1. Open a new, blank document, and then save it as **Menu Design** in the location specified by your instructor.

2. Open your browser and search online for images of sample menus by searching for the keywords **restaurant menu image**. Review at least a dozen images of menus before picking a style that you want to re-create in a Word document. The style you choose should contain at least two pictures. Keep the image of the menu visible in your browser so you can return to it for reference as you work.

3. In your Word document, create the first page of the menu. To generate text that you can use to fill the page, type **=lorem()** and then press the Enter key. Change the document theme, if necessary, to a theme that provides colors and fonts that will allow you to more closely match the menu you are trying to copy. Don't worry about the menu's background color; white is fine.

4. Add at least two pictures to the menu, using pictures that you find online. Rotate or flip pictures, and remove their backgrounds as necessary to make them work in the menu layout.

5. Make any other changes necessary so that the layout and style of your document match the menu example that you found online.

6. Somewhere in the document, attach a comment that reads **I used the following webpage as a model for this menu design:**, and then include the URL for the menu image you used as a model. To copy a URL from a browser window, click the URL in the browser's Address box, and then press the Ctrl+C keys.

7. Save the document, close it, and then close your browser.

INDEX